"Who I Am", is a question that so many of us have been wondering about, but yet we NEVER seek the answer to that question as to WHO I AM! I will try to shed a light on that question concerning "WHO I AM"

So to you my readers I only ask for you to sit back and take it easy. Have a cup of coffee or a cup of tea, Hell take off your shoes, and for those of you who wish to ride this train with me and met those who played a role in my life, maybe it will be good or maybe it will be bad, check it out for yourself.

Who knows you just might find some answers that you yourself have been seeking, so I say to you "WELCOME" now come help me to find out

"WHO I AM",

Who I Am

The Four Blocks of My Life

HORACE ARMOUR

authorHOUSE®

AuthorHouse™
1663 Liberty Drive
Bloomington, IN 47403
www.authorhouse.com
Phone: 1 (800) 839-8640

Published by AuthorHouse 05/21/2019

ISBN: 978-1-5462-5357-0 (sc)
ISBN: 978-1-5462-5356-3 (e)

Print information available on the last page.

This book is printed on acid-free paper.

ACKNOWLEDGMENTS

I'm sure that some of you have heard those words before because they have been spoken throughout history. Even today those very words roll out of my mouth, "That things happen for a reason." First of all I'd like to thank the all Mighty Creator, for when I was running wild and acting crazy and those nights when I was in my darkest hour, you offered me light and showed me the right road that I should travel down. You also gave me a second chance in life, when I was suffering with "Stage Three Lung Cancer, without you looking after me, I might not be here today writing" this book and those others that I have written before. "Thank you Lord."

At this time I wish to thank some amazing women who not only came into my life, but were there for a reason.

MOM: You brought me into this world and cared for me and you thought me something that only a loving mother could do and that thing was "RESPECT.

Grandmother: From you I understood what those words mean "That you have to learn how to "CRAWL" before one can WALK, also those words of wisdom" Son if that's not your cup of tea, don't put any sugar in it."

Red: The woman that I could not forget, you were that flame that could not go out. Even today I still remember those words that you spoke! The ones that came from the heart. Those words were "Honey love is not love until someone loves you back."

Donna Jean Armour: You always had the time for me, even when you were tired from work; you went that extra mile for me. You rolled out that "Red Carpet" for me when I came back to Detroit to see how everyone was doing. Those special Friday nights that you and I had together laughing and having fun at the Race Track not worrying about anything because this was OUR night.

Lucia Manelse Armour" My wife, you gave me so much, yet I only gave you a little in return. Your love was strong when I was running around acting crazy. You were there from the very start of things. When we had nothing you gave more. When I became sick with Lung Cancer, even through you were sick yourself, that love became stronger for All of US.

Yes, Darling even today that LOVE is still here. Our water began to flow on February 14th 1959

That day that you became my wife. On November 27, of 2006 that's the day that my WELL ran dry.

Jennifer C. Armour. You always had my back and were there to guide me through my very first novel "How Strong is Your Love" and my second novel "Coming Home." I can still see that day? That's the day those Dark Clouds came rolling into my Life and covered "My Sunshine."

Your wedding day, as you lay there in my arms in the cold streets of San Francisco, California, shot by a-drive-by, in a pool of your own blood from a gaping wound, baby feeling your warm blood on my fingers, as you gurgled out those words!" Daddy hole me, hold me tight Daddy.

Before I could say a word your eyes rolled back in your head and you exhaled a strained breath. Then you were gone from me, but you are here in my Heart always my darling.

"I love you."

CAST

Like in any books, may it be Non-Fiction or Fiction. The inputs of those who have actually experienced the events therein are essential. The name of those persons who actually experienced those events throughout my life can be found in blocks numbers 1 – 4 of this novel.

Block # 1 Horace D. Armour, Sr.
Block # 2 Horace D. Armour, Sr.
Block # 3 Lucia Armour (my wife) you were there
Block # 3 Donna J. Armour (my Road Dog) If Not for You
Block # 4 Horace D. Armour, Sr.

All other names that you might read about are made up names, not the TRUE names of those who actually played a part in Who I Am from 1935 until now.

MAIN CAST

Horace Armour, a man at one time who had Wonder the vast Wilderness of life trying to find his-self, and looking for something! Now Armour is on a mission knowing that he has many roads blocks and pit falls that he has to overcome, yet he is not letting anything keeping him from that one important task that he must do.

Armour, a twenty year military Veteran, a Vietnam Vet. WHO overcame that special "GIFT" that the military gave to him, that GIFT which he shall never forget? This was "CANCER" all Armour really wants to do is too find out who he is.

Lucia Manelse Armour: A special breed of women, a devoted military wife of a service man who gave his life to the U.S. Military for twenty years. Lucia, you also gave your life to that very same military service. The mother of his children. You're Wonderful Love for Forty-Seven years still burns deep down inside of him; even on that very special day that OUR LORD sent his Special Angle down to guide you safely home. It hurt him but he knew that NO one else could ever take your place in his Heart and Soul.

Donna J. Armour: His road-dog. You were always there for him only a phone call away, never to tire to spend time with him or take him out about town or where ever he wanted to-go-to. Those Friday nights (your night) just the two of you. Family and all others had to take a back seat on this very special night, and all other Friday nights. This was Race Track Night.

Donna, always remember those Race Track Rules, that he told you about, the very same RULES that he has been going by for the last thirty-nine years.

1. Never take a Credit Card with you to the Race Track.
2. ONLY take the amount of money with you, which you can AFFORD to spend without worrying about that money if you had suffered a loss.
3. Have FUN and ENJOY yourself.

PREFACE

This may not be the story you're expecting to read about the story of my life, because it's just might be interesting to some and not to others, but whatever the case may be, what it all boils down to is that for many years I have always asked myself "Who I Am." Some of us at one time or another have gone down this very same road and have asked that very same question." Who I Am!

I will try to shed some light on Who I Am, so you my readers as you follow me down this road and as you read this novel, I do hope that you'll hear my voice speaking from these pages. Who knows you just might find yourself reflecting on your very own life, with that very same question that I am seeking myself.

This book is neither a Fairy Tale nor a Sea Story it's far from that... It's written because so many of us are pondering over that same question that I am seeking an answer too. Which is "Who I Am"; knowing that I'm just another one of Gods amazing creatures who wakes up in the morning to face another day and wonder the face of this earth.

Now, I must deal with those Four Blocks of my Life.

1. 1935 - 1955
2. 1955 - 1976
3. 1976 -2010
4. 2010 - until the present

Now these four blocks will answer that question that I have been looking for. I just don't want to be that last "FOUR" numbers in my Social Security number (you know the ones that everyone is always you for) I just want to know "Who I Am"

WHO I AM

In order for me to answer this question, I must turn back the clock of time. Yes, turn back the clock to February 11 1935 when I first came into this world, not knowing what I'll get into nor know what awaits me in the years to come. You see a very special event took place on this date at eleven a.m. in the morning. I Horace Daniel Armour was born in Detroit, Michigan.

One might say that I was what they call the "7th Son." Well I'm sure that some of you might have heard stories about the 7th son. The overview of the legend and mythology of the seventh son by Global Psychics, the seventh son's importance stems from scarcity of the number 7. One ultimately roots in the seven islands of Atlantis and the seven sea of Humanity.

The legend, although mentioned in special detail through many books of the King James Version of the Bible, predates to the dawn of time in all philosophies and cultures of the world. "That's a part of Who I Am." I wish to invite you into my world, but before we start down this road about my life, let me back up and explain that there's plenty of things that I would like to say, but sometimes I am lost for words to express myself or find the correct words to fit into the overview of my life on paper.

As we wonder down the road of life, we never stop to smell the roses, just doing our thing day after day. Then one day we STOP and look around and wonder how others are doing, but there is an old saying "you never understand what someone else has gone through until you have walk in their shoes.

So, I invite you to come and walk in my shoes so that you might hear my Cry of please help me find that answer which I am seeking. Yet in my life time I have been there and done that, you see I have ran the Rice fields of Korea, walk the back streets of Japan and slept on the roof tops in Hong Kong. Wipe the dust from my shoes in Mexico and drank in those dark rooms. Ran with the Flower Children in San Francisco and lay in the grass in Peoples' Park in Berkeley California on a hot sunny day and still have not found that answer to what I am looking for.

Now you can see why I have ask you to walk in my shoes, not just to feel my pain or to stop the Rain of Pain that has been eating away at my soul for so many years. I need to know "Who I Am" So hang in there with me just a little bit longer. Did you know that some of us would like to write a book or tell a story; yet like me we don't know where to start it from or how to go about it, in writing a book. Maybe we don't do it because we are afraid to do so, knowing that we might be judge by others or looked down on by those who don't even know us, because we don't use the correct words, or play by the rules of Society. Knowing from the get-go there will be those who will be saying, "Man" you are a damn fool for putting your life on paper for all to see and judge you.

I think that some of you are asking yourself, could I put my life out there like he's doing? Would I want the world to judge me! Some of those very same people just might think that I'm crazy. Yet my question to you, does one have to be "CRAZY" when they are asking for help! This is my life knowing that it might be interesting to some and not to others. There are others out there just like me, who have been down this very same road before, standing at the cross road wondering should I step out there and ask that question, "Who I Am." Yet in the very end I'm just a ripple on a pound, but most of all I thank God for being a live to see another day with the warmth of the Sun upon my face.

OTHER WRITTINGS

CONTENTS

PART ONE

Block One 1

Block Two 12

Block Three 45

Block Four 52

Could I 53

Who You Were 57

Blew My Mind 64

What Am I Looking For 69

The Devil 73

What You Did 77

Gone From Me 82

Make A Choice 85

Lady In The Red Dress 94

Good News/ Bad News 97

The Question 106

Feeling Ashame 111

Sacrificeing Your Soul 119

Thanksgiving Weekend 124

When I'm Old 127

What's Eating At Me 132

Black History 140

PART TWO

Super Bowl Weekend 144

Hate Comes Alive 148

What's Next 152

If Not Foryou...158

Moving On.. 161

Today Is Our Day 164

It's All Good..168

Notes 170

To Young To Love 173

Letters To My Family..178

Close That Door...201

I Wish That..204

What You Will Learn... 226

In Closing...228

Persons Of Interst..232

This Is My Story, What's Yours... 234

Thank You...237

About The Author...243

Who I Am..245

BLOCK ONE

GROWING UP

1935 – 1955

GROWING UP

Wow! Even before I took to the pen in writing this book, I sat down and had a talk with some of my close friends about this book. In a way of speaking all EIGHT of them came up with the very same thing about this book! Armour, man, make sure that you talk about your family! Where your mother and father came from and also about your childhood days back then.

Sure I could tell you that my mother was born in Newborn, Georgia, and that she was a house-wife. My father was born in Rutledge, Georgia and he was a truck driver. I don't even know if Rutledge or Newborn is in the Northern or Southern part of Georgia. My family moved from Georgia to Detroit, Michigan in 1923.

Now about my family! Well my sister used to write for the Detroit Free Press Paper there in Detroit, at one time or another. Some of my brothers join the military around or close to World War 11. We didn't have a car, like so many others in my area, the only car that we all had was the Street Car. Our main ride.

Let me tell you this, I would walk to school in the dead of winter, knee deep in snow, put news papers in my shoes to keep my feet warm and dry. I don't mean any disrespect to my other family members by not really talking about them in this book. I had to ask myself why I am writing this book and just what I am looking for.

Then it came to me just why I was writing this book, it's because I am on a mission! What do I wish to discover? Well there is only ONE answer that I'm seeking and that's "Who I am."

I hope that you want mind if I use some of my words from my last two books. "How Strong is Your Love and Coming Home." You see those two books are a part of "Who I am." This story might not be interesting to some, but then again it might be interesting to others. What it all boils down to is that I am trying to find myself and that one important answer of them all is "Who I am."

You the readers who will judge me as you ride with me down this road. The mistakes that I have made and the Ultimate betrayed that I have done to those that I was in love with. Yet, I have been confused about Love, and I did lock my feelings behind lock doors, never shearing those true feelings with anyone; at times I thought that the storm was over, because I was to wild and crazy to stop and hear the wind, knowing that this wind was trying to tell me something.

My enter feelings had me trying to understand myself, my life and the wind that kept on howling at me calling out my name. So here goes my story about me and my life. Some of it was Good and some of it was Bad. You see I was born in 1935, there in Detroit, Michigan. We lived in a small house at 8781 Cardonia on the North Inn.

The last child from a family of thirteen. The last boy at that. Yet my birth records only speak of ten living. I have asked some of my family members about this? It appears that three of the children passed away before I was born. Now I wonder just who they were.

As for my father? He passed away when I was just eight years old. I don't remember too much about him. I do remember that his name was Caunerl Nelson Armour, and I don't remember to much more about the man who was my father, only that he did register for the draft in 1917.

Even today I can still remember that old house a very small place. The Pot-Belly stove that kept the house nice and warm at nights. It's funny that I still remember that I would go down to the Smoke Shop as a small boy and watch Pops (my step-father) and Uncle Lonnie play checkers. They would let me play checkers with them sometimes, but these old men had that game down pat, and there was NO way in HELL that I could beat them (the old men) at this game.

Now, there was that little Church down the street from us. Those old folks, man those folks would be getting down in there. One could stand outside and get down along with them. I do remember that one of my brothers Bobbie would go down there. I was just a small boy then, but sure as shit man, they were having a Hell of a good time in there.

I didn't understand just what was going on at that time, being a small boy; all I thought about was playing with the other kids on the block. Man, life was SWEET back then. The fun and games "NO" bull-shit and no worries what so ever.

I was brought up on the North side of Detroit, but mostly on the other side of Russell. I attuned Moore School. I was a good student and not getting into any trouble, because in those days fighting in school was like stealing a Chicken in Georgia if you were Black. You understood that you were going to get it. The teachers would Jack you up in school for acting out. Today the teachers can't do no such thing.

For you folks who lived back then you knew what was waiting for you when you got home from school. Yes! An ass-beat down from your mother, not from your dad, because mom was the Sheriff in town, (in my family that's how it went down) Now please don't get into a fight with another boy and he beats your ass. Well friend you just got some more ass-whipping FOUR in all. One from that boy, one from the teacher, one from mom, and your Big brother would kick your ass because you lost that fight to that other kid.

Maybe you want to ask me "Armour", did you ever get your ass beat FOUR times while you were in school? I want lie about it. Yes I did receive FOUR of those ass-kicking. Man, you see that the first time that I got an ass-kicking I told my family a "LIE" about that fight and who had beat my ass. You see I was ashamed to tell my brothers that a "GIRL" had kicked my ass. Yes, a girl, you see back then there were some girls in school who could and would go toe to toe with the best of them and would come out on top... Shirley was her name. It's funny after over sixty years I can still remember about that time as a child that someone had beat my ass and it came from a girl; who turned out to become my girlfriend. Shit, now that's funny as hell. I have just kind of told you a little about mf First Block of 1935

But you see there was more to it. Man I could not wait to got out of school and got home to play with my dog Shady. That was my dog which I got from Doctor Joe our family doctor. You see back then we had a family doctor who came to the house and checked on you. I never went to his office, (I don't recall doing so) anyway my dog Shady was born on the very same day and time and year that I was. That's what my doctor had said when he gave Shady to us

Why do I remember this dog so well? It's because I had her name put on my arm when I first join the Air Force. I'm what one might call "The Seventh Son." For those of you who might not have read the legend and the mythology of the Seventh Son by the Global Psychics. The Seventh Son's importance stems from the Scarcity of the number 7. One ultimately roots in the Seven Island of Atlantis and the Seven Seas of Humanity. The Legend although mentioned in special detail through many books of the Old and New Testaments of the King James Version of the Bible, predates to the dawn of time in all philosophies and cultures of the world. That's a part of "Who I am

Like I have said before I came from a large family. We didn't have much money, but I would always find something to do and make me some money. Like going out cleaning snow from people's homes to make myself some money. Man, you knew that was one hell of-a job going out there in that cold ass winters there in Detroit. We lived on East Euclid I would walk from my house down to Boston Blvd. For those of you who knew where Euclid was to where Boston Blvd. was, that's one long ass walk just to clean snow off at the rich people's home.

Man, back in the day, Black and White people who had some money, they lived in those big ass homes there on Boston Blvd. That money that you received from cleaning snow was all good. I can recall when I rode the bus for only five cents and the movies were just ten cents. As I got older and went off to another school. That's when life took on a new meaning for me. I no longer got my ass whipped in school by the teachers for acting out and being a fool. Now thinking back I remember the very first time that I got a kiss from my girlfriend. Shirley, a cute little thing (the very same one who had kicked my ass when we were in Moore School) Shit, her kiss burn my lips. I didn't know what a kiss was supposed to feel like. Sheared was this new school which wasn't a very long walk from my house. Man, when those winters got to be a bitch, you did everything to keep warm.

It's funny how some of us can still re-call those days, brown bag lunch with Peanut Butter and Jelly sandwich in them. Now don't you forget those Syrup sandwiches and the Sugar ones also? Hell some of you do remember those? You aren't that old that you forgot about them. I remember shop class and home-eco where I learn to sew, and some girls had shop classes; after spending sometime there off to high school, half way on becoming a young man and a new life.

The road to man hood. I didn't give it much thought to lots of things like kick the can and stealing Christmas trees from someone's back yard and selling them back to others and stealing fruit from

People's trees in their back yards. I was in high school. Those were some good old days. The young girls with the White-Bobbie socks, the long skirts to hide their legs. I wasn't one of those jocks, but someone who believed that one should keep his head in the books. Now I did play sports. I was on the

Swim Team, played Football and also on the Track Team now the track team was something else. You see all of the Armour boys had attended Northern High School and we were all into sports, some of my brothers were into baseball.

Now each Armour before me generation after generation all ran track. Man you had to keep that name going (the Armour name) and you had to be better than those Armour's before you. It was all most like that old crazy saying "that all Black people could dance." What it was saying that ALL of the Armour boys could run, because the ones before you had cast that stone for you. If one would fail to get a letter in track and kept the "Armour" name going, it was like removing that stone and casting it into the sea of the unknown, never to be found or thought of. I ran the 880 (the half-mile) and also the one mile. I was not a big dude or ladies man, but I did have my eyes on this one young lady. She was a cheer leader. A beautiful Brown skin young lady. Even as I sit here, I can still remember her name which was Barbara, her last name I will not get into.

Let's move away from her (Barbara) but I shall return back to her later on. First we need to deal with the high school stage of my life. You see high school was the gate-way into life for me and also for so many others. Still thinking about high school there was that one teacher that lots of students didn't even like him. His name was (let's say Mr. X) those who were in grade twelve and man if you had him, you had better had all of your SHIT in one bag, if not, a repeat was do for you in summer school.

Now high school had its good parts and its bad parts. When it came to the cheer leader team? Even back then the early part of the fifties there was that COLOR thing!

If you were Bright and damn near White, you were all right. If you were Brown stick around, man, if you were Black get back. The first two were that type of women who made the cheer team. Now check this out, I had this friend that they wanted her on the team (she had light skin) in place of this dark skin person, even though this other lady (the light skin lady) was not a good dancer.

You see even in a school that was eighty-five per cent Black there was bull-shit like this going on concerning COLOR. One would think that in a school like this COLOR would not be a "Big Thing" now man if you believe that, you had to be crazy and running around with your head up your ass, because the color of one's skin can be a bitch in some schools. Yet lots of us turn our backs on things like this. Walk the halls of an ALL BLACK school today, and you come back and tell me what you saw, and who was with whom? Now let's move away from COLOR for now, but color will always play a role in our life and in society.

In order for me to have some money I worked for the Detroit Free Press delivering news papers. My route was on one of the streets (lets call it W5th Ave) from Woodward back to Oakland. While working my paper route that's when I met Pat. A light skin sister with light brown hair, yet there was something about Pat. I began to have feelings for her and I would stop back to her house after I finished my paper route. Trying to get off into her panties. Damn, Pats sister always came in at the wrong time, like she knew what I was up to. Damn this girl was a "CB" (cock blocker) I don't know how she knew, but it looked like when the hands began to move up and the panties started to move down her sorry as would always show up or call Pat into the house.

Shit this went on for a while and I gave up on trying to get into her panties. (Yet in the end I feel that this move and that she just might have saved my life. That's another story for another time. I had to worry about school and keep my head into those books, so let's move away from Pat, for now but I shall return back to her later on. I also had a part time job working for Joe at his market, cleaning up and keep the reef. Full of Beer and Soda-Pops (that's what they were called back in the day) When I wasn't doing anything I would go sit on top of beer cases and do my home work and also watch the store to keep kids from stealing things.

Man, for some reason this store was left alone, maybe it's because the other kids on the block knew that I worked there.

If you stole something from there (the store) you had to deal with me and my side-kick. I was kind of a low key person, but I would not run away from a good fight. This family was good to me. I used to baby sit for them. (Lance was his name) Joe's son turned me onto Jazz and the beauty of it. Helping me to understand all types of music. I never told Johnnie that I wanted to be like him, he had this ear for music. Whenever I came over to his house he would put some music on and tell me to close my eyes and then ask me what I felt or saw? I was there with them as they played. I felt what they felt, we became as one body and one mind. You know when you are young and didn't understand that saving your money was the key to it all.

Mary-Ann Joes' daughter-in-law help me to open my first bank account and the very first thing that she said to me was "Save your money for that day when the clouds cover the sun. Shit, to tell the truth about this it took me many years to understand this. It wasn't until something happen in my very own family that really made me understand about "Save your money." I don't want to go into this right now, because it's getting close to 1955, but on April 11, 1989 34 years later I understood what she really meant by "Save your money." As we move on there was my step-father. We never call him by his first name; we just call him "POPS." Some of us have had step-fathers in our lives, and we can re-call many stories about them, some was good and then there were those that made one want to run away from home and on the other hand many young boys and young girls life was F----ked up because of a step-father or step-mother.

My life with my step-father was very good; in fact I wanted to be like him. A man who stood tall and took care of the family. Pops never put a hand on me, which was mom's job. As I sit here writing this book, I can re-call many things that I went through as a kid, like being in the house when the street lights came on Belonging to the Clean Plate Club! Mom didn't care how much food that you put on your plate, but man you had better ate everything that was on your plate; after dinner we would clean up the kitchen and then the KITCEN went into Lock Down?

In my house when what LOCK DOWN means was your ass could not go into the kitchen and get some food to eat and make a mess. Whenever I or Anyone else broke moms rules we knew that we was going to get an ass beat down, but the ass kicker was that my mom made us go outside and get our own switch for that ass whipping.

Now I was in high school at this time, but there were things that were still set in place back then. My ass was in the house by 10:00 on a school night. Do your home work, it was never spoken of, but your ass knew that you had better had it done. My mom, didn't play when it came to home work or school. For you young people, I just had to give you a little insight how it was back then; even if you're crazy ass was in high school, and even if you thought that you were a young man or a young woman, the rules still stood (in my house that is) if for some reason you think that I'm blowing smoke up your ass, then talk with your great-grand mother. (now you notice that I didn't say to speak to your grandmother, because some of you just might have a grandmother just a few years older than you are) she will tell you how it was and she just might even tell you about the "VILLAGE" that we lived in.

I am sure that some of you are thinking that I have left something out about my life! Yes I have. Remembering about my step-father! There was this special bond between him and me. We would go out on those Saturday night runs to the Gin House. (That's where people would make that CORN Gin in the bath tub. Pops would drive over there to this one place and get out of the car in the middle of the street, and tell me Fella to park it. I didn't know shit about a stick, but I got that boy parked.

Now, growing up I wasn't always a saint, just another kid getting into things, me and my side kick. We were tight, when you saw one you saw the other. We drank together and we would fight together, I'm sure that some of you did the very same thing. Like going to church on Sunday Morning and say hello to the mothers and then slip out the side door going to the alley to shoot some dice. It wasn't until I wrote my first book "How Strong is Your Love" that I spoke of my early childhood, and even then I did leave one thing out of that book and also my second book Coming Home." I never spoke of that one fight that I had as a kid when I got my ass kicked by a girl. I never spoke of that because I was ashamed, because here I was the kid giving out the ass kicking, but to get your ass kick from a girl, man that shit didn't fly.

I was eleven years old then, this was the very first time that I have spoken of this in Seventy-One year's it's not like it is today, because it's a jungle out there, and you just might not live to see another day.

I'm sure that as you read this book someone might be saying "Wow' this guy must have had a hard childhood growing up in those days; Let me clear up something about my childhood, it was ALL GOOD. We might not have had the bull by the tail but back then WE had some things that I feel is missing in a lot of American Family today! You see "WE" had LOVE, a BOND and thank GOD we had "TOGETHERNESS"

To ALL of those Fathers, Mothers, Grandmothers and Great-grandmothers who were born back in the day, you know just what LOVE, BONDING and TOGETHERNESS MEANT TO A family.

"Thank you for being there for US."

Here I was ready to leave high school going out into the world, not sure what could be out there for me. 1955 the year that would prove to be something else and would change my life forever. There she was, warm and with fire in her touch. Red hair, it was like looking into fire without getting burned. Eyes the color of Jade that pulled you into her soul. Shit! I was in love, she was only just sixteen years old at that time, like B.B. said "Sweet Sixteen" the sweetest thing that I had ever seen.

Now, she is like a fine bottle of wine aged with grace. I love her even more today. Upon graduation from Northern High School my step-father got me a job at the Ford Motor Company in the tank department where it was kind of hot in there. My girlfriend and I would go to Edge Water Park and other places there in Detroit on Saturday nights, because I need to rest up on Sunday to return back to work on Monday. There was something about "Red" that's the name that I gave to her because of her Red Hair. I would spend some time at her house; but for some reason I didn't try to get into her panties right away, like I had done with Pat. She (Red) was special, the one that I was in love with, and the one that I wanted to marry and she would become the mother of my child.

Back then things were a lot different than they are today. Her mother and like many other mothers was from the Old School and man they would tell you about their daughters from the get-go. F------ing with my daughter and your sorry ass is F-------king with me. That was the rule back then and along with other rules that the mothers had set down for their daughters; like the "Five blocks of life." Which I can't get into those five blocks right now, but I shall return back to them at a later time. Right now I think that we should kick back and have a cup of tea or whatever you would like to have. Why not take off your shoes and stay a while.

I can remember my very first pay check that I received from Ford Motor Company. I gave it (the pay check) to my step-father so that he could buy some new tires for his car. I didn't have a car but I drove his car, and we had this deal, when you got the car and if it had a full tank of gas, that's the amount of gas that should be in there when the next person got the car. Now, I had my shit half-way together. I had a job, a nice looking girlfriend, now all I had to do next was to get myself some rags and get my head fried. I would go down on Oakland and get my kicks done (a shoe shine place) at the boot black parlor next to the record shop and night club.

Now those were the days when the city of Detroit really had it going on.

That B.B.Q. place and fish fry place; one could smell that food even before you got there it would be nice and hot.

The record shop where you got your jams (music) from and they would punch your record card for your next buy, to get a free record when you fill your card up, after buying 12 records. Now man, the Jazz would be kicking. I'm talking about Davis, Smith, Peterson, Jackson and even Coltrane and then on the other side of the street, man those Blues would be kicking your ass also.

I do mean those down home Blues and you could feel it working down to the bone. Hell I got some of those down home Blues on 78's and some 45, oh hell even on some LP records those 33 1/3.

BLOCK TWO
U.S. MILITARY

1955 – 1976

U. S. MILITARY

Right next door to the record shop was this night club, where those folks in there would be having a hella good time; that club was not like some of the clubs that we have today in some places. The music was live and there were NO one playing records but there was the juke box, when the band took five. That was the Detroit that I knew and grew up in.

Now on the other side of the tracks, there was Woodward Ave. they had a place up there which was also live. The "Paradise" where the Big guns rolled into town to play at this wonderful place. For those of you that weren't around at this time, ask your great-grand daddy or your great-grandmother about this place; some of them just might get tears into their eyes, because they too miss that old place and old times. I had stopped seeing Pat around this time, because I had the love of my life with me. I would go over to her house a few nights a week, but I wouldn't stay to long, because I had to get up early for work and she had to get up early for school

She was only sixteen and here I was twenty years old. I'm sure that her mom had her eyes on this twenty year old man, who was checking out her daughter. Back then bring four years older than your girlfriend wasn't like it is today. In some places that's Jail Bait. Right about that time something began to happen to me? I start to get tired of that factory life. Coming home every day tired, dirty, and beat from working in the Tank Engine Department. Hell when I got home from work, I would take a bath, eat and off to bed. I watched Pops and also my brother who was also a factory worker. He was only two years older than I, yet he looked about five or six years older than I was.

Man, I couldn't take this shit any more. I had to get away from that factory life. It was killing me, each day it was sucking my life away from me. Where could I go to or turn to and explain what I was feeling and what was going through my head. The only person that I knew who would understand me and what I was feeling and going through my head, the things that I would say to her, those things would remain there with her.

That one person was my Aunt Francis (who I named my daughter after her) after pouring my gut and feelings out to Aunt Francis all she said to me, was what do I want to do with my life? That was it and nothing more. I gave it some thought and after thinking about this for some time. The next day when I return back to work I told Mack my foreman that at the end of the month I was going to quit working here in the factory. Mack, ask me why? I told him that this factory life wasn't for me and that this factory work was sucking the life out of me. What was I going to do now? I didn't tell my mother about this; One day while downtown I saw this bill board about joining the U.S. Air Force.

On April the 25th I stab myself? You see I left Detroit on that day to go into the Air Force. I didn't tell my mother nor my girlfriend until the last minute; It was like I was really stabbing her, but what I didn't understand at that time I was stabbing myself also, because her pain became my pain. It's been inside of me for over fifty years. I loss the will to feel anything. Even today it's hard for me too feel something for someone who is close to me. My shield will not allow anyone to get close to me. It's like this shield is keeping me from loving anyone but her; even today I have not told her the reason that I left home.

You see when I was young, wild and acting crazy, I had a habit of doing things and I didn't care who I hurt or got hurt. That day, when she met me at the train station along with my mother and pops my stepfather to see me off. I was going to boot camp at Lackland Air Force Base in Texas. I saw the hurt in her eyes (saying why do you have to go and why didn't you talk to me about this, after all I'm your girlfriend) When I return back home on leave in July of 1955, I ask her mother if I could marry her daughter!

All she said was "the girl can't cook" You do remember that I told you that I would return back to the Five Blocks of Life? I did tell you about them didn't I? Well if not, I feel that this would be a very good time to tell you about those blocks, because I have just ask this lady could I marry her daughter. You see back in the day a young lady had to complete the Five Blocks of Life before she moved out and got married.

Lord, if she could not Complete those blocks, SHAME on the mother's part sending her out into society (the world) not ready to deal with it. People would look down on the mother, because her child did not know the responsibilities of a wife and a mother-to-be. Those of you that have gone on and gotten married and have not gained any knowledge of the FIVE BLOCKS, maybe your marriage has failed?

Little did I know there was so much more to learn about Sex and how to please a woman? I must say that Luna would not be my only teacher on sex, because there would be many more teachers out there to show me what to do and just how it must be done. I was saddened when I had to leave Luna, going to another duty station; after leaving Amarillo, Texas. I received orders going overseas to Korea. Damn, here I thought that I had learned lots from Luna, but now LEE, she was a master at having sex. Now here it was something else, there were other factors in play. One that I did not think that I would ever encounter in the military. I'm talking about "RACISM" and what was said about you, when you are "BLACK"!

Even sixty years after leaving Korea, I can still hear those words that a Korean woman ask me one night when I was sitting in a bar drinking a beer,

just outside of the base in Osoan? This lady ask me where was my "TAIL" was. Shit, I couldn't believe what she had said to me! I ask this lady what you are talking about, asking me where my tail was. All she said that Ice Cream G.I. said the CHOCOLATE G.I. had a tail and it came out at midnight. I didn't know what she was talking about, until I looked around the club. I was the only Black person in there. When I return back to the base and I was talking with other Black Airman and I told them what went down. One of the guys let out a laugh and ask me what club was I in and what part of the town was I in. I said just outside of the main gate?

He said, Armour that I was in the WHITE section of town, now F----K me dead, damn there was a White section and there was a Black section in town. A Black section just for us! When I did come to my right mind, I knew just where I should be; because even the women in different parts of that area were not the same. I remember that night when I was in that so called White club, I was paying more for those drinks because I was Black.

Well when I did get my shit into one bag, I understood things, in a way that part of the town, it was just like being in the Deep South. N----, you don't belong here, so take your Black-Ass where you belong and stay there.

After that event I found my section of town. It's funny when you are Black and even in the service looking for a good time, man all one has to do is follow the sound of the music and then you'll know just where you are and belong. Those blues would let you know that you were at home and in the right place. Well anyway back to my part of town. That's where I met LEE! There was something about her and I said to myself, "man" I got to get me some of that. Little did I know I would be returning back to school, when it came to understanding women and sex?

We hit it off after a number of times of me going there to see her night after night. I found out where she lived and went to visit her. Over time we became very close, in fact I started shacking up with her. Man, this was like being in the OUTER LIMITS. We didn't have a bed to sleep in, so we slept on the floor. You see back then the "FIRE" was built under the house, so you slept on the floor to keep warm. I remember that very first night that I got me some and after it was over I rolled off of that mat onto the floor, and burned my ass. It was funny to Lee, because I guess that she had never seen a Black man move as fast as I did, to get off of that floor the way that I did.

After that I learn to keep my ass on that mat. The treatment was something that I had never received in my whole life. Wow! The hot baths and treating you like you was someone. When I would get off of work, I found myself rushing home to her. One night we had this talk, "she" said to me Armour, I don't want to work in the club anymore. I said to her Lee why do you want to leave the club? All she said was "I just want to stay home and take care of you..." Like all things, there was a catch to all of that. The only way that she could get out of that club was to pay off her debt with the owner. Lee owed the owner of the club some money (she said to me) and the only way that she could get out of the club was that I would have to pay her debt off with the owner who she owe mama-son $ 50.00 dollars.

What it really came down to it that I was buying her... She was mine, free from debt with mama-son. Shit even here History was showing its dark face, just as it did back in the South in the old days. The master would sell off his slaves. Damn, by the rules of the Old South I had just become a slave owner! Only to set her free to live her own life as she pleased and not to answer to anyone.

This lady began to treat me like I have never been treated before, love me and made love to me until I had lost my rabbit-ass-mind, Yes that was what happen to me for twelve wonderful months. Shit, I thought that I had learn something from Luna about sex, but with Lee she taught me more, not only about sex, but about "Love" what it was like to care for someone and have that person to care for you in return. With Luna it was a sex thing. I'll teach this young boy how to please me the way that I wanted to be pleased. Hell man I was Luna sex slave, her boy-toy just following orders, even though I did learn something about sex, and those parts of a woman's body that would please and bring much needed joy to them. I sold my soul just to learn about sex and not about LOVE.

You see there was a difference between Luna and Lee? Luna was all about sex and being pleased the way that she wanted it, because she was the teacher, and I was the student only doing what the teacher told me and showed me what to do, too her body, in order to make her feel good.

Lee she gave me a warm kind of love, only wanting you to love her back in return. Yes, I did learn some new moves, but they were fun when loving someone who only wanted you to love them back. That was twelve months of joy. Yet there were other things going on in my life at that time. You see at that time the Air Force did not have a test system. It had what we called the ass-kissing promotion system. Let me give you a true event that happen to me while I was station there in Korea. I was a cook, man I could burn. When the time came around for promotion there was this White cook who was a drinking buddy with the First Sergeant.

I had more time in the service then he had, and a much better cook then he was, but when promotion time came around my name wasn't on the list; later on I found out from the shit-house hotline why my name was not on that list. I didn't kiss ass, besides I was Black. Once again "RACISM" shows its Ugly face and the color of your skin, or the shape of your eyes plays a part in your life.

Now please don't think that just because you are in the military shit like this don't happen, if you believe this, man you are a damn fool or out of your rabbit-ass-mind, because back in the day from the Civil War, until now the color of one's skin does matter; and plays a part in your life. I'm not bitter about what happen to me while I was in the Air Force. To tell the truth I believe that it made me stronger, because other events took place, that I want go into right now, but somewhere down the line I shall reveal those events that took place, not only in the service but in other places in the good old U.S.A.

Lee and I had many good times together and I didn't want to leave this place and return back to the states; about four months before I was to be shipped out, Lee came down with this fever, her body was burning like she was on fire. I didn't know what to do, because this was the very first time that something had happen to me like this. I was worried about her, because I had gown on her, but more so I had falling in love with her. Lee had become a part of my life and my soul.

Someone had called this old lady and told her what was going on with Lee. She (this lady) spoke with some of the people there, but I could not understand everything, because I had just learned a few words in Korean. I watch her as she placed Lee into the bed (the one that I had brought because I was tired of getting my ass burn on that damn floor) taking all of her clothes off, she was nude to the bone. She came to me and began to take my things off pointing to the bed where Lee lay. That I should get into the bed without any cloths on. I did what she showed me to do. I held Lee close to me. I could feel the heat from her body burning into me. The old lady pushes me closer to Lee and then place some covers over us. Shit, I wanted to let go of her and get out of that hot ass bed, because her body had set me on fire.

I did what that old lady told me to do, and then she gave me something to drink, at first I thought it was water, but it wasn't water, because it had a funny taste to it; after that I don't remember too much. All I did remember was waking up in a bed that was met, and still holding onto Lee, whose body was very cold. I got out of the bed putting on something's and covered her beautiful body from others, keeping them from looking at this wonderful woman whom I had falling in love with. This old lady was still there at the side of the bed, not looking at me, when I got out of the bed naked.

It's like she didn't even see me. When Lee came around the old lady gave her something to drink and explain to her what had happen to her. Then she just got up and left the room without saying a word to me, all she had on her face was just a smile...

I ask Lee what had happen to her and was she all right, and why had that old lady had me to take off all of my things and lay next to you and also what was that she gave me to drink? In broken English she explain that my body was used to pull the fire from her body and that drink was to keep my body cool while my body pulled the fire from my body and not let that fire eat into my soul.

Once again I learn something from the old people. I can recall when my grandmother use to do some things and at that time I thought that she was crazy, but now I see so much wisdom in the old people, that I could learn something from them. Never again when I see some old people doing something that I thought was crazy I want say a word about it. I tried to have my tour extended, but it was turn down, maybe someone had thought that I wanted to marry her and bring her back to the states. I felt at that time, the military wasn't ready for shit like that. A Black man marrying a Korean woman! Hell man, the Korean War had only been over for a few years, and there was that nasty taste in some people's mouth about the Korean War and its people.

Just as they had felt about W.W. 11 and the people from Japan. The very same people who were taken from their homes and placed in Cattle Cars and shipped away to "CAMPS" because of the war with Japan. Shit, know other group of people was treated this way. Man, America has lots of reasons to be ashamed of it when it came to treating people this way. I'm on my way back to the states, going to Randolph Air Force in Texas. Not taking any leave I just went straight to my new duty station. I was still in the South and the only two races of people that was look down on was Blacks and Mexicans, and even is some cases they (Blacks and Mexicans) were at odds with each other.

After getting set up on the base and meeting new people. I spent most of my time with other cooks and Airman from supply. We would go out to this club that set away from town. This place was called "The Barn," it was a mix club, because it was away from the Good Old Boys part of town; but still one had to watch his/her back, because when people start to drinking, your ass had better know who you were talking too or dancing with. After being there at Randolph AFB, "Mother Nature" came out of her bag, and Lake Charles, LA got hit. I can't recall just what year it was, but I'm sure that some of the old timers can remember that time and Lake Charles, LA.

Airman from the Air Base was sent to Lake Charles Louisiana, by me being a cook I too was sent there to help out by setting up a field kitchen to feed the people who were hit by "Mother Nature. On our way to Lake Charles we made a pit stop at this little Old Road side Bar. There was about fifteen of us... Ten White and five Black Airmen in the group. Damn, as soon as we hit the door, shit hit the fan. It was like walking up to a road block. We were told that the White Airman could stay and have their drinks but the N-------ers had to go out back and get their drinks.

We all look at each other, and turn around and walked right out of that Red Neck Bar. Damn, we were sent there to help them (the people of Lake Charles) but the color of ONE's skin stood out. It was okay to come here and feed and help the people out after "Mother Nature" had come alone and kick some ass and left Lake Charles on the bad foot. I couldn't believe this shit, you could take my help, but I could not come into your bar for a drink.

I saw people in the food lines, and the sight of these people you felt sorry for them, because some of them look like they had been sleeping in those cloths for days at a time.

After being there for about one month we had to pack up and return back to the base. Shit, I was glad that we were going back to Texas. Seeing this place was one thing, but being treated like shit just because you were Black. The ass-kicker you were sent by the military to help out to feed these people, and you had to deal with some off-of-the-wall bull shit. Life sucks at times and then on the other hand it could be a bitch.

I was glad to be away from those Red Necks mothers who didn't appreciate you being there to help them in time of need. That week-end some of the guys went to this litter border town of Mexico. I was glad for this because I could kick back and do my thing. I met this young Mexican lady in this bar that we were hanging out in. I end up going to bed with her, let's face it, that was one of the reasons that I went to this small town was to get myself a woman and have sex with her.

This was the very first time that I had sex with a Mexican lady, and it would not be my last time, because every other week-end I found myself back in that little bar looking for that very same woman who I had sex with before. I only wanted her when I went there. It was like I was the teacher and this lady was my student when it came to sex.; After all I had two very good teachers who had taught me things about sex that I had never dream of. I put my lesson to work, and I did enjoy having sex with this lady. I knew where the weak spots of her body were, and there was no need for her to tell me what I must be doing in order for me to make her feel good and enjoy it.

Like all good things must come to an end. I received orders going to the Philippines, where my life made a 180 turn about! When I arrived I was to report to the 6200 Food Service Squadron. One day while in town looking for something to buy for my mother, there she was! There was something about her; words just can't explain what I felt. Standing there and looking at HER long Black hair, her hair was as black as coal and fine brown skin. I had to know this lady. I found myself just going by there just to see her where she worked just to buy myself a cold beer. A strong woman, beautiful and down to earth and warm. She was more than one in a million.

I can't explain or understood just what I was looking for? I was like a sheep lost in an uninhabited region of love. She was like a Fire that you can't Extinguish inside of your soul, richly moving, offering a fresh perspective on love and a ray of hope. After sometime there, and seeing this lady, I ask her to marry me. One had to get permission from the military when you married a person from another country. There was that race thing all over again I don't think that Society was ready for a mixed marriage, and even in the military there were those who held those very same views. Yes in the Philippines there were some who didn't even like it.

Don't come over here and marry OUR women! Marry your OWN women, and your own COLOR.

You know it was kind of crazy about the rules of the military when you married someone from overseas, but yet I could go down town and marry a Camp Fire woman and DON'T even need permission to marry her. That's life, but mean while about that marriage to someone from overseas, now here comes the ass-kicker of them all about Society" Yes, good old Society! You see when a person in the military married a woman/man from overseas Society looked at that person as a Gold Digger or just wanting to get that GREEN CARD and get that FREE PASS and come to the United States of America, here to the PROMISED LAND. Society thought that they would drop his/her ass like a HOT POTATO once they got to the states. Even this BULL-SHIT way of thinking is still going on today.

You know, the most pain and deep down words of HATE came from the Black Woman. Yes the Black Woman. N--------er you aren't SHIT. What's wrong with US? Why didn't you marry a Black Woman> Just tell me one thing mother F-------er why did you marry one of them

Those words have been spoken over and over throughout time. When a man or woman marry out of their own race. I and my wife got married on February 14, 1959 while I was in the 6200 Food Service Squadron, later I received orders sending me to the 6208 Hospital Squadron, where I was discharged from the U.S. Air Force. I return back to Detroit, Michigan.

Before I go on, I am wondering have I really opened the door on my life for you to try and understand "Who I Am"!

One never knows, maybe by the time that we reach the end of this book, you will know "Who I am" In the mean time let's move on, because I have so much more to tell you about myself and the life that I have lived. Now where was I? Oh yes! Back in Detroit, Michigan.

In April of 1959, everyone was looking for me and Red to get married, but it was not to be, because I was already married to Lucia Manelese Armour. Now that was a shock to everyone and even to Red herself. Once again I have hurt this woman, only thinking about myself. There was restlessness inside of me, I had to get away. My sister-in-law was going to Louisiana because her baby sister was graduation from high school. She ask me if I want to come alone and help drive. I said sure, because I had nothing better to do, besides getting out of town would take some heat off of me and let things cool down about me and Red not getting married.

While there in Louisiana I end up going downtown, and I saw this logo about joining the Navy, and see the world. I did join the Navy on that day. Not telling anyone what I had done, that I had join the Navy, so when we got to Detroit I told my mother and Red what I had done that I had join the Navy No one said to much about this, but members of my family had that look on their face, like saying man you don't know what the F----K you want to do. My family didn't understand me; I was feeling like there wasn't anything there in Detroit for me.

First of all I chose the military over my girlfriend, and another woman had taken her place in my life and she became the mother of my children and not her. On July the 9th, I left Detroit going to San Diego, California, starting my Navy life for the next eighteen years; after training there in San Diego, I received orders to report aboard the USS Coral Sea an Aircraft carrier station in Alameda, California. This ship would become my home for the next four years. (1959-1963) I just need to fill you in on just one thing! The Navy is not the place for anyone. You had to be a special type of person. As I unfold things you will understand what I mean by being a special person to live the life of a SAILOR for twenty years or more.

Man, being in the Navy you were here today and gone tomorrow. Time away from your Love ones. That shit took a toll on you and your mind and sometimes you would spend days out there on the water, which got next to you after being out there for thirty to forty days at a time. I saw that look on the faces of some sailors wanting to be home with their love ones.

Sometimes we went without mail for weeks at a time and when we did have mail call, one of four things would happen? (1) You would have lots of mail waiting on you. (2) There would not be any mail for you, because no one had called out your name. (3) The BITCH of them all that F----king "Dear John" (4) the news telling you that you are about to become a father, because she is two months gone. The ass-kicker of all is that you have been away from home going on five and a half months out here on the water?

Now please don't tell me that you got her knocked up through the mail? Nothing eats your ass up more than getting that "Dear John" or I am having a baby. I have seen shit like this and have seen many grown men "CRY". This type of shit is a TWO way street! Because when I was in the Air Force, I knew guys who wrote letters to their love ones, telling them that they wanted out, because they had met someone else and wanted to marry that other woman.

Man, life can be a BITCH when this kind of SHIT hits you in the face. Hell man in some of those letters someone had spoken those very words that I LOVE YOU AND MISS YOU EVER SO much, but behind the door there is SOMEONE ELSE. That's the ASS-KICKER that makes you want to get that drink, shit not just one, but a hella lot more drinks.

I have known guys go out of their rabbit-ass-mind behind this kind of shit. Now you see and understand why you had to be a Special type of person to be in the Navy, and must have that Very Special person to understand that the life of a sailor is and will always be Hell on "EVERYONE" I'm not saying that I am Superman because there were times that I had gone with mail from my family, but all I could do was hope and pray that WE both were strong and knowing that this too shall pass, because WE were as of ONE,

Now please, don't get me wrong about the Navy, because if I had to do this all over again! Yes! I would join the Navy, but like I said before the Navy is not the place for everyone.

I was an E-3 next to the last on the poll. I was assigned to Harris crew, this guy was sharp. I do mean sharp. There was something about him; he kind of reminded me of Johnny, the Italian who I used to work for when I was in high school back there in Detroit. Harris took a liking to me. Maybe he saw something in me that I didn't see. He (Harris) found out that I was married with a wife and two sons, and also that I had been in the Air Force for four years. One day Harris said to me what in the HELL is wrong with you man? Do you think that you can support a family on an E-3 pay. Man I was not thinking all I wanted to do was party and I do mean party. Let me run it down to you just what I was doing.

Me and my side-kick would go to town night after night and get down, for those of you who don't know anything about Alameda, California or where it's located at. It's just outside of Oakland, California, we would walk from the base to down town Oakland, and own the way to town we would stop by the store and buy us a bag of RIPPLE and drink it on the way to town. My friend had an old lady in town, and sometimes I would spend the weekend there and get down with a cold COCKTAIL. What I'm talking about is THUNDER BIRD! You do remember that? What's the word, and what's the price! That was it back in the day, the drink of the town.

Man that shit was so good, that it made you want to slap your mama. Now the women that I ran with were the butt-sisters? They had to be the plus size, and if one was thin, she wasn't in. On the weekends when you went to town and didn't have any place to sleep; you did that (sleep) in the movies, the all night ones. Hey! Even in those movies one knew just where to sit and where not to sit. The dirty old men set in the front rows, because you could hear them getting down with Annie-Pawn. (The hand job.) Anyway Harris began torturing me, he would ask me questions about cooking, you see I was a cook and the Navy wasn't like the Air Force. At that time the Navy was on the TEST system. The machine, didn't know who you were or what color you were all it wanted was the right answers.

(The Air Force was who you knew, and who you drank with) With the Navy's test system all it wanted was the right answer. If you made a high score and you fell in the percentage range of being promoted you got it. There was just one thing; you were going up against others throughout the Navy in your field. The Navy Times (newspaper) would tell you just how many cooks would be taking the test and just how many would be promoted. Lets' say that three thousand cooks would be taking the test, but only six hundred were going to be promoted to the next pay grade. Now you see in the Navy, you were not just a cook; you were a Jack-of-all-trade.

You were a Cook, Butcher, Salad Maker and a Baker and you had to know how to keep records for Storage and know about Food-Born-Disease. Petty Officer Harris knew the book, from the front to the back. He could tell you just what page to look up for the answer to that question. One day I ask him (Harris) why he was doing this to me, and why are you so damn hard on me? I tell you what the next time that you visit the head (rest room) look in that "GLASS" in front of you and come back and tell me what you saw? At first I didn't understand what he was trying to say. He never asked me for the answer to that question. I didn't think about it I kept on hitting the books.

I learned a lot from Harris about cooking that were not in the books. One day I got the answer to the question while I was in the head (rest room) Harris father was from the old country and he knew just how hard it was when he came to the United States (being Italian and not speaking English at all) One day when I was out on the Fantail having a smoke, Harris came up to me and ask me what did I see when I looked into that mirror? Damn man, I felt like I had been kicked in the ass by a mule. I not only saw a Sailor, but I saw was a Black Sailor. Harris just smile and said "Sailors' might not like you because of your COLOR, but they do RESPECT your RANK. I would write to my wife who was still in the Philippines. When my ship arrived in the P.I. (Philippines) I took some leave and went home to see my wife and my sons. I made E-4 thanks to Harris. I aced that boy, but I wanted more. Man, I kept my crazy ass in the books. You see I wanted my family to be with me here in the states.

Now, I felt good, a little more money in the pot. However, like all things, there was a catch to it! One had to be an E-5 or above before the government would ship your family and household goods for you. Then on the other side my wife was having some trouble there in the P.I. It came from the GOOD old Americans at the Embassy, because I was Black and they tried to fill her head with all kinds of BULL-SHIT. One of the round eyes (That's the name that was given to the Americans who worked in the Embassy) said to her once she got there to the states, I would leave her and the kids and that they would become award of the state.

Now, that shit really did get to me, so I started the paper work to bring them to the states in San Francisco, California. Damn, I had to go through hell to obtain the correct papers for them; also other shit was going on; if you don't ask no one will tell you SHIT or what to do or say. I'm here to help you. "It's like some people are saying F-----k you that's your problem. Shit even in her home land "RACISM" was hard at work. Now I can really see why some people says "life can be a BITCH"

Again, it's one of those times that someone has come into my life for a reason; like I have said before I was trying to fix the papers for my family to join me here in the states. Thinking about those that played a roll so far in my journey to find out "who I am". But I didn't tell you about Amanda (whose name means Worthy to be loved) until now with her tall fine ass-self. When I speak of her being tall, I'm talking about 5' 11 ½. It was funny in away why or how we crossed paths. I needed her, and she wanted me.

What I mean is that I needed her in order to get those papers fixed, what steps I should take in order for me to complete those papers. Amanda, wanted me to become her Boy-Toy Amanda was getting on up there in age, maybe she was thinking that she needed someone, but why not get herself a Young One and bring him up the way that she wanted and teach this young boy to do the things that she like and wanted someone to please her the way she like it. Amanda was about fifty-two years old, twenty-nine years older than I, but what she didn't know that I had been down this road two times before her, and what she was really doing and that was to let "The dog out"

I had two very good teachers before her, and what could she teach me that I haven't already learned? Like the say F------K me dead that you do learn something every day and Amanda did have a bag of tricks. Man that's the second time that a woman has brought Smoke to my ass and Tears to my eyes. Those Sweet tears of Joy. Now, I can see why she is "Worthy to be loved." I'm sorry but I can't help from saying this, because I'm sure that some of you have heard that old saying! "That the Blacker the berry the Sweeter the JUICE." I was just a young puppy back then, now that I have gotten older, it's true about the old saying the Blacker the Berry, the Sweeter the juice, and damn this is something that I want lie about.

In the end Amanda and I both got just what we wanted, for me it was he paper work to bring my family to the states, and for her it was that Young Puppy who had some tricks of his very own, and like they say," you pay for what you get, and isn't nothing in life that's FREE.

Before I go on, I would like to say at times I find myself on a New Adventure or perhaps doing a bit of Soul searching to understand "WHO I AM" and just what my needs are. It may also cause me to figure out things that likely need some changing and maybe the need to be more compassionate with others, like wanting to sit and spend time with others.

Maybe this is what I need to bring about some very spiritually uplifting conversations and stop day dreaming about things in life but to share this knowledge about life with others. Maybe by you reading this book of who I Am." You'll get a better understanding just who I am, not just another person who wonders this earth, but to get an understanding on what my life is about.

Sometimes my wave of thought make it difficult for me to FOCUS on my story and explain what is REAL and share and I try not to let FEAR stop me from reaching out to you, because I am not alone in trying to find out and understand "WHO I AM."

After getting those papers that I needed in order to bring my family to the states, I could not use them at that time; so I just file them away for another time. There was still something that I must do; you see I still needed to become and E-5 in order for the government to ship my household goods and bring my family to the states. I could not take the test for E-5 until six months after I had made E-4, so I had to wait for October before I could take that test. This gave me many days and nights to study for that test, and knowing that I must keep my head in those books, if I wanted to pass that test and make E-5 in order to bring my family to the states.

Yet, there was just one thing that was eating away inside of me and that was what went down between Amanda and I. What did we both gain? I became her boy-toy, to wash her back at nights and rub her down with Hot Oil; Only to hear hr say "Not like that, take your time or Right there.; Yes that's it. For me I got that paper work and yes I did learn some new moves and tricks that only a much older woman could have taught me to do.

Now, I have had three teachers, teaching me about Sex and what to do and what not to do. Only to hear one of my teachers say "KID" you are, learning, and that you are Mamas Baby, and when I get through with you, in the end I'll make a man out of you. Now come on over to mama and learn something "NEW" That was Amanda speaking. I have asked myself did I "SELL" my soul to become a Boy-Toy in order for me to complete my task?

Now, I remember something that my grandmother once told me "SON" never sell your soul for "SEX" because in the very end you want be happy, plus you will be the "ONE" that's getting F----KED

Yes, I did learn some moves from this woman, but when I took a bath it was like I could not clean myself good enough. I would always smell her (Amanda) odor, even if I had wash myself every day, that smell was always there' No matter what kind of soap I used. It's like she was the DEVIL and laughing at me, knowing that I had sold myself to her for some paper work. Damn, for days this ate at me, who could I tell that I sold my soul to this older woman for some help in obtaining some paper work that I needed in order to bring my family to the states?

What could I say! Hell some people have done this for less, but did they enjoy it on one hand and felt like a FOOL on the other hand? That bitter taste remains with me for days at a time. I had to keep telling myself that it was for the good of the family. That I had allowed that WILD CHERRY to become VICTORIOUS by bring Smoke to my Ass and Tears to my EYES?

After that encounter with Amanda, I said to myself, "Armour" you did what you had to do, now get over it and move on with your life and one day you will thank yourself for this and NEVER AGAIN ALLOW THAT Wild Cherry to get you down and become VICTORIOUS over you in a fight that you know that you can't win, because better men then you have fallen by the way-side, and many rivers have run RED because of that Wild Cherry. What can I say, it was a hard but a good lesson to learn, that YOU don't get nothing FREE.

Now as time moves on, then one day a door closed in my life and that was the start on my Rain and Pain. That's the time that I lost my step-father, the man that I wanted to become. Remembering that the Red Cross had found where I was stationed at and contact the ship and expressing that I had lost my step-father and the family had request that I come home. That day was a very sad day for me. When I arrived home (there in Detroit) I ask my mother what had happened to "POPS," that's the name that all of us called him. We never spoke of his first name. Mom, said that he was in an accident, his body was brought back to the house for those who wish to view his body, you see mom had this thing about when one passed away the body would come back to the house and rest, the last stop before going to the cemetery.

I cried seeing my step-father laying there in the front room as people came and went after seeing his body for the very last time. That's when the RAIN and PAIN took over my life. It was July of 1961 that I lost "Pops and for some reason I would not allow those that I loved to come into my world and share my feeling, yet only to suck up that pain all alone not sharing it with anyone. Even today as I sit here trying to express myself it's still there. I would not allow myself to feel anything (not even pain or even cry) after being there in Detroit to see Pops for the very last time, before he was sent safely home. I return back to San Diego, California to my ship; after serving a few more years on that ship, making E-5. I received orders for Great Lakes, Illinois in 1963. My family came to the states, because I was an E-5 with over four years in the service, the government shipped y household goods from the Philippines to Great Lakes.

Hell! The family arrived in the states in the dead of winter. The base was a training center for new recruits coming into the Navy for the first time. I'm sure that a lot of you are aware of the cold weather in this area (Chicago) just think here you are coming from a place that's hot all of the time. In the summer time you didn't want to go outside and face all of that heat

Now my sons they loved the snow, for they had never seen it or felt that cold White stuff. Wow! Now my wife, that was another story, going out into that cold stuff didn't fly with her. I tried to stay away from Detroit. I just wanted to enjoy my family. I knew if I didn't go over to Detroit, it wouldn't be fair to my mother, because she would not have gotten to meet her grandsons and see her last daughter-in-law. You see I was the baby of the family and the last one who got married.

My mother accepted Lucia (her new daughter-in-law) because she was my wife, after being married for some time, I finely told my girlfriend that I was married; she met my wife and sons; at that time my wife was not aware of who she was, and that she was that other woman in my life.; but it came to light later on. It' funny how life or fate can play a trick on you! You see after being stationed there at Great Lakes I received orders for Vietnam. Now this was a kick in the ass, once again I had to leave my family, but this time I had to leave them therein Detroit with my family, knowing my wife, hell no this wasn't going to work out. There was this language thing my wife spoke "Tagalog."

Before going to Vietnam I had to undergo Special Survival Training in Behavior and Self-Discipline. This training took place in the upper part of Washington State. Right about the time that the rain comes. Man, that rain was cold to the bone. Shit this was pure HELL, living in the woods, eating only what you could find, Bugs, Snake, oh yes! I have eaten Dog. Yes, Dog! All this was getting you ready for the Nam, and if for some reason or something did happen to you while out there in the jungle of Vietnam, you knew what to do and what to eat or not eat.

I'm sure that what I am about to say might sound like some off the wall shit, but if you ever get or got lost and trying to understand what you should eat, well all you had to do was watch and see what a "Monkey eats. They will only eat those things that are good for them to eat.

(HELL IN VIETNAM)

I remember the very first day that I arrived there in Vietnam at the Air Base in Danang. It was January of 1966. It was Hot and one could smell death in the air from different directions. I got my gear off a pallet from the C-130 and walked to the bus bound for Danang where I was to spend the next twelve months of my tour of duty; but it was not the case to be, after a few months on the base. I was re-assign to a YFU boat running up and down the Delta with supplies for other troops; as I recall it that most of the time you were always wondering who was out there waiting for you or if your boat would get hit while you are out there on the water. I have talk with my fellow Vets and heard their very own stories from those who had endured those hellish days and nights out in the jungle not aware that the seed of Shared Trauma had been planted into them (PTSD) Post-Traumatic-Stress-Disorder.

Some of US came back home to a country that we felt didn't understand where we had been or how the "WAR" had affected us. "What they do know is that we are different, yet they don't know why it is or how it happened. For some of us when we returned back home we felt Emotional Numbness, lack of Interest in Activities and Difficulty feeling love and joy. The reason that I speak of this, it's because when I returned back from Vietnam, I saw the people out there speaking out about the war in the Nam. The news with its stories of what's going on, like in my book "Coming Home" I spoke about this very same thing, but in a different way.

When I came home from the Nam, I stayed alone and tried to make it the best I could, but still there was a part of me that wasn't me. I was not the same person! Man, war is hell and it takes something from us and that it adds something to our lives. The STIGMA of appearing Weak and the lack of knowledge and the mental effects of COMBAT. I can only speak for Armour, but there are many other Vets, who could tell you their very own story; and some of that will bring HURT to the HEART, if you think that this is all a lie, man or woman go out there and talk with those Vets, who suffer from PTSD or just ask any Vet. And they will tell you that "War is Hell,"

Thinking back over the years about all of these men who were in Vietnam, man they were ALL looking for the very same thing as I was, and that was to return back home to those that we miss and love very much, but the ONE thing that "WE" didn't want was for people asking us "Why did you have to go over there."

Man, let me tell you this, people would not have understood it, if we would have told them why we went over there! Now it's 1967 and I am on my way back to the states. To face something new, and leave those things over there one question has been on my mind for so many years? "Why Vietnam." The one thing of this, it made me understand that life was SWEET or did it cause me to remain behind CLOSED DOORS! Not feeling anything and not letting those that I loved become close to me. Those memories of Vietnam I cannot forget. I look back at the person that I was and wonder how I kept my SANITY?

Yet, with all of this I received something from Vietnam that I shall never forget this it will always be a part of me FOREVER. That medal which I received was STAGE THREE LUNG CANCER. How can I explain this place to somebody who haven't even been there? When I came back home you couldn't even tell anybody that you'd been there, because you thought about ALL of those "WAR" resisters, who ran off to Vancouver, Toronto, and Montreal or who's family had money and kept them here in the states or those sorry ass ones who claim to have a medical problem. The very same ones that said that they Loved the U.S.A, or have spoken out about "Make America Great Again."

I'm thinking about home, what would I see and what will be there waiting for me, besides my family who was in Berkeley, California. The draft resisters marching at People's Park just down the street from where I lived. The country seethed with controversy over the war. Shit in 1968 was the height of the anti-war protest and this time I found myself on a carrier going back to the seas of Vietnam, once again in another part of the war... It's crazy as hell even today I wish to return back to Vietnam, to see that pace

I have seen Vietnam on the TV; it's not the same old place. It has been built back up and if I did return back there would I find her? Yes, I met a woman while I was there in the Nam. Would she be the same person or would she have aged because of the war? Or would she be F-----ked up because our government had used AGENT ORANGE on the people there or would she be suffering the effects of that Agent Orange like I have

Yes! That place left its make on me and what Our Government had done to me and so many other military troops. I want talk about this for now, but

I shall return back to Vietnam and tell my story and explain why I said that this place left a mark on me and how my government let me and so many others down and put SHIT in the game, because what they did and fail to tell the American people and also kept the troops in the dark for so many years,

Sometimes when I have nothing to do, I sit down and go through the Family History Books. The one of my family there in Detroit, Michigan and the other one that I and my wife Lucia have put together over the years. To my amazement from the moment I see those photos tears flow freely from my eyes. I must say that I'll be the first one to admit that I never dreamed that I would overcome so much adversity.

(THE UNCONTROLLED FIRE)

I would overcome so much adversity like the way that I and other G.I's were treated when we returned back to the states from the Nam, like we were "SHIT". We didn't ask to go over there, being in the military it was a job. Now what had America come to? My question is, what if things were going on in a America? How would we have been treated then? I bet that there would have been lots of Ass kissing and the Red Rug would have been rolled out with "Welcome guys" on it, you boys did a good job. While there in the Nam, something happened to me while spending those months in Hell Land with my life going down a new road. A road that turned my life around. While there in Vietnam I made Petty Officer First Class (E-6) more respect because of my rank and more responsibility as a father.

It was time for me to start thinking of what I wanted out of life? What was I to do after getting out of the military? Where were we going to settle down at? Man, I have seen guys in the military doing this and that, Some of those very same guys didn't have a POT to piss in or a window to throw it out off. The door was closed on my old life. Detroit was in another space and in another world; after all she too was married. One day I was looking through some old papers and there was a picture of her. Damn, I thought that I had clean out everything from my past.

I was living in Berkeley, California at that time. I would wonder down to People's Park just down the street from my house on the weekends. Wow! It was just like going to the "What's happening now Church" The Flower Children, Black Panthers, Davis, and Lewis all speaking out against the Wrong of Society and the War in Vietnam. About this time I received orders for Guam. There's not much to say about this place. The only good thing was that I and the family were together with each other. After spending eighteen months there in Guam and off to my next duty station in Pensacola, Florida.

I didn't think that my life would make a major turn sending me down a "Hell of a Dark Road" for the next six years. I would have to deal with "RACISM". Damn, this shit was running crazy (like a fire out of control burning a path to Hell and back) throughout the Navy; Just about this time one of the Navy ships whose home port was on the West Coast, had a Racial problem. Fights between White and Black sailor ran throughout the ship. Well we all know that when ABC, NBC, and CNN gets wind of something like this. Wow! The word ran faster than when Grant ran through Richmond. Man, this uncontrolled fire spread from one place to another, and it began to have a great effect on other parts of the military.

The Department of Defense began to act quickly, and I do mean quickly. This uncontrolled fire was running wild and didn't know where or when to stop, burning the hearts and souls out of so many good men and women who loved the military. The Department of Defense set up the Race Relations Institute at Patrick Air Force Base in Florida. Men and women from the Army, Air Force and the Navy were sent there for training. We spent hours and hours in the class room seven days a week, from sun-up until sun down.

Man it was hell, the truth came out about the military and some of its people. We had our ass on the Hot Seat for more than three weeks. I spent more time there, than the 120 hours that it takes to get an AA Degree in most colleges. Upon graduation from the Race Relations Institute at Patrick Air Force Base there in Florida. The U.S. Navy felt that I needed more training, so the Navy sent me too the Navy Race Relations School in order for me to become an R.R.E.S. (Race Relations Education Specialist) for the Navy. I conduct seminars for the Navy from 1972 until 1976.

These seminars were given to members of the Navy, to give them a Rich and meaningful experience in the struggle to control or understand that HUMANS are delicate, and show them that "RACISM" could and would turn you inside and out, and burn your hearts out.

One had to deal with those who had hate in their eyes and deep down in their souls, because they didn't want "CHANGE" and some military bases would not roll out the Red Rug for you. This fire was eating my ass alive and the pressure was so great that at times I thought that I would go out of my rabbit-ass-mind and needed that drink to help put that fire out that was burning inside of my soul. Shit, for four years I lost a part of me! I lock my true feelings away behind a steel door, not allowing that dog to come forward, knowing all alone that there were those who wanted me to crack; Yes! They wanted me to crack, so that they could sit back and have a good laugh, saying that he (that N----r) couldn't handle it. That's why you always had a TEAM mate to work with you.

My co-worker, now he was something else, he was a young White fellow, born in the Deep South of Mississippi, in the heart of Red Neck Land. He was married and he had one child and a mix-marriage, his wife was Black.

His voice was that old down home Southern tone. Man, when he spoke with that tone, I just wanted to shoot him that Red Neck tone sent chills down my back.

He would tell stories that brought tears in some of the class member's eyes. He told them about the story of his wife, and just what his family had said after they had seen her picture. Shit, it even hurt me, and I could not hold back the tears in my own eyes, as they rolled down into my mouth.

He told the class that he had sent a picture home to his family showing his mother and father a picture of their grandchild and his wife. He just stood there for a minute or more the class room was still, so still that if a rat had piss on cotton you would have heard him from the start of that piss until the very end. He took out a letter and said that I would like for each and every one of you to hear the welcome party that my family have waiting for my wife and their grandson!

Dear Son:

> Hows you doing? Got your letter and that picture of that gal and boy. Just want to say that "WE" hung that picture and now we are waiting for their BLACK ASS to get here, so that we can hang their Black Ass too. Not one person said a word. You could see it in their faces, and some of the tears that came from my eyes. The tears that I could not hold back, because those were tears of hate.

When my side-kick got discharged from the Navy. I never got another team member again, because when he left, it was like a part of me left with him. One month after my partner left I received another set of orders, sending me deeper into the South. This time it was for Gulfport, Mississippi, deep into Red-Neck- land.

I knew that I was up the creek, because those Good-Old-Boys didn't play around. Shit, I tried to get those orders change, but the Navy said that no-can-do, because I was needed there on that base. What could I do but pack my bags and move on. All I said was the hell with it because my time was getting short, ready to get out of the Navy.

When I arrived there on the base in Gulfport, Mississippi. I wasn't ready for what took place; it blew my ass out of the water. You see I was assign to a Seabee outfit, a Construction Battalion. This was something that I was not ready for. This was the crazy part of the Navy. These sailors were builders. They love building things along with drinking and fighting. There is this old saying if you can't beat them, then join them. That's just what I did. I put my class room skills down and picked up some tools. This went on for about one year. Moving from place to place building things for the Navy and repairing the air strip in Bermuda.

Wow! What a place this was, I felt just like I was at home, blend right in with this group of Seabees in NMCB-71. I left my wife and sons there in Gulfport while I was in Bermuda because we had brought a home there. I was really amazed about being in the Seabees. They took care of their own. A far cry from the other part of the Navy. Someone was there to help your family, and if the wife or any other family members had car trouble there was someone there to make the repairs for them

This place (Gulfport, Mississippi) wasn't what I thought it to be. The White Sand Beach and going down to the pier to buy fresh seafood. Like a good thing all must come to an end. I received my next to last set of orders sending me to my next duty station up to Bremerton Washington. On the way to Washington we made a stop at a friend's place in Richmond, California, because I had thirty-days before reporting to my ship. We started to look around for a home there in Richmond. I knew that it would be easier to buy my home while I was in the military, then when I got out of the military. I had a job (the Navy) and also I had my G.I. Bill to fall back on. Any way some of the homes that we saw, man, I wouldn't let my dog live in that shit. I don't know what in the hell that this lady was thinking by showing me this shit.

Maybe she was thinking that because I was Black and that I didn't have any money that I would go for that house. We kept on looking around and we found a nice one on Lowell Ave there in Richmond. It's funny how some people will judge you by the color of your skin. While looking at that house one of the Good neighbors, this "BITCH" just walk right up to me and said "WE don't like renters moving into this neighborhood." Now F----k me dead, this lady didn't know anything about me. Now this BITCH wasn't aware that I had just brought this place.

Wow! Here was another case where someone White, and this BITCH was from overseas, and had the "BALLS" to judge me. Now this lady was from Australia you see I had been in the Land of down under before and I knew how things went over there. Man, I just stood there looking at her while waiting for the moving van to arrive with my house hold goods. Dismissing her in a cool way, by saying to her, nice to have met you and I do hope that you have a wonderful day, and I just walked right back into the house, leaving her sorry ass just standing there, because nothing else needed to be said to her.

After getting my family set up, I left for Bremerton, Washington. Now my sons were at the age where they could help their mother out and drive her where ever she needed to go. Both of my sons were attending Richmond High School about that time. The school wasn't too far from our home; in fact you could walk from the house to their high school. Mean while I began to send out applications seeking employment so when I got out of the Navy. I found out that there was an opening for a state job in Woodland, California; it was too far away from Richmond.

They were looking for a Race Relations Specialist. Man this was right up my alley, because I had been doing this type of work for the Navy for the last six years, with countless hours in the class room and also out in the field, with over three-hundred hours of training. I faxed my application to Woodland, and also to other places in the area seeking this kind of work. I received my first reply from Woodland concerning my application; it went on to read, thank you ever so much Mr. Armour for your interest in # 42 for the Race Relation Specialist position Sorry to inform you that you may have the training, however Mr. Armour you lack the education requirements needed for this position.

Damn, what is a poor boy to do, with over three hundred hours of training in the field, and years in the class room! More hours than what's required to get a B.A. from most Universities. Oh well, that's the way that it goes. Well it's February and the 9th of April will be here soon and I shall be "FREE, after twenty-one years of giving myself to the U.S. Military" and returning back home to my family. Well as the guys would say I'm "Fig-mo, which means that I am getting short, and now it's really only a matter of time and I'll be leaving the Washington area going home to California.

Man, can't wait to get those papers in my hands and my things in my car for that wonderful drive back home. Right now what I'm doing is just reporting into the Master-of-Arms office just to let them know that I'm still alive. Since being here I have met some of the guys from the base, and have been going over to Fort Lewis the Army base to the NCO Club.

Shit, there are some fine looking sisters over here, that's all alone, it's because their old man's were overseas in Korea. I met Betty, her old man had been over there in Korea for eighteen months according to her, and he didn't want to return back to the states. That told me something that he had someone over there. Me and Betty would hang out and I really wanted to get off into her panties, but it was too late to be going off into some woman's cherry box when you are about to be going home soon. Damn, it hurt me to my heart, but I turn that Wild Cherry down for three reasons. First: I didn't know who she had been running with over the last eighteen months.

Plus I look at it this way, if she wanted to give me a shot of that tang? Who else had she given it up too? The second reason: I didn't know if her ass was on FIRE or not, so I let that one alone. The third reason if you are going home and you have been telling your wife/husband that you haven't had any in a long time. Well you were only supposed to be in there and out quick like. I do mean quick, but if you got off into that tang and last a long time, your mate can tell that you have been getting something from someplace else and it wasn't from home or through the mail.

Hell, if I had maybe about four months before I was to go home, hell yes I would have got off into that Wild Cherry. Just like those times that I had spent while there in Vancouver, Canada... Now that was something else, plus the women were out of sight over there. Wow! Just two and a half more days and I'll be free of this military life. I can see myself walking into the front door of my home. Damn, that word really does sound good. "My Home" I know that sleep will be hard to come by knowing that after twenty-one years your "FREE, like a bird.

I thought I'll call the family and let them know that on July the 9th I'll be free and on my way home, never ever have to worry about getting another set of orders going to someplace else and they wouldn't have to worry about pulling up roots and off to a new place and a new school.

Man this shit is hard on your kids, here at this new school today and next year they find their self's in another school. I knew that this shit was starting to get next to my wife also. Home alone again just her and my sons. I might have stayed in the Air Force, but that ass sucking got next to me and besides back then it was hard to make rank if you were Black and didn't kiss someone's ass. I couldn't do it, that's why I end up in the Navy.

Then if I had stayed home I would have had to deal with that old crazy ass factory life; and maybe the factory life wouldn't be the only other thing that I would have had to deal with. You see there was this other woman? Could I have stayed away from her? Or would I have become one of those guys who went to the store of Friday to buy some milk, and not return back home until Monday with a loaf of bread in place of that milk? Who knows?

Maybe it was best that I had kept my ass in the military! That alone could have saved me from having a wife and two sons on this side of town and a girl friend and another baby on the other side of town I need to put you down for a while, because I need to start getting my things in order to get out of here. So I'll catch you at check-out-time.

Well today is that day! Got my papers in my hand and out the door on the way home. As I drive down 1-5 towards California, feeling kind of funny in one way, but Happy as HELL because that twenty-one year old door is closed, and now out to the new world and to my family. The drive from Washington to Portland, Oregon. Wow! The sights are just so beautiful this time of the year.

Now not going to rush it, sure I'm in a hurry to reach home, but might as well enjoy this drive. Who knows I might not never come back this way again, because like they say "Life is short, but it's all so "Sweet."

MILITARY LIFE

(Thinking Back)

You know it's kind of crazy, but sometime I find myself thinking about some of the things that I have done in my life time. Man, some of the that shit I laugh about it and then on the other hand, I say to myself, "Armour" you were either Crazy or a damn Fool for what you have done while in the military. Yet, some of it brings a smile of Joy to the old face. Like being with my teachers:

Luna: You made the cake.

Lee: You put the Icing on that cake.

Amanda: You lit the candle.

Each of these women played a role in my life, for two of these women, I was just a boy-toy to be used without any feelings or any love. Just pleasure for them and a lesson for me. Yet one of these women there was love in the mix and pleasure for both of us. Even today I find myself looking for that picture of Lee that's in bedded in my mind. Yes! Sleeping on that mat which covered the warm floor, where that fire was built to keep the house warm and you would burn your ass if you rolled off of that mat, because you were not watching what you were doing. Would you sleep on that mat again?

Yes, it was all good, if I had to do it all over again would I? Yes! Oh hell yes. As the old people might say, that there is pleasure in pain; before I go on, I have this bug up my ass. So I would like to tell you about someone who is close to me and they keep on telling me that they know me and all about my life. (Mr. no it all) I keep on telling this person that there is a dark side of me; that you don't even know. For I am the only one who knows me (I think) in a nice way, I'm trying to tell them that they are full of shit and to F------k off.

What I'm really trying to tell this person, man if you really knew everything about me, and if you really understood me and know me like you said that you do. My man, then you knew why I ran the Rice fields of Korea, Walk the back alley-ways of Japan, and played on the roof tops f Hong

Kong, and most of ALL why I cross the dusty roads into Mexico and made the streets of Oakland California my home.

Well my men, then you knew that I was born in a village in Detroit, Michigan. Where I got me some hand-me-downs and got things from the Good Fellows and those Red ASS long Johns with the flap in the back. You also knew that I had to be in the house when the street lights came on, and also Mrs., Wilson who lived five blocks away, knew my grandmother and also she knew every kids name that lived on East Euclid. Nick, the watch dog, he knew who was who.

People in the village would sit out in the front yard and talk with each other and those across the street at night; we would leave our back doors wide open. Yes, Mr. no-it-all we would sleep outside at night when it got too hot in the house and played ball in the streets without worrying about anything (I mean not getting shot) Man, the village that I grew up in was "GOOD". Now when I do come back to Detroit, I look for that village, and it's not there! Like so many other things are gone. Where have all of them gone off to? I miss it, because in My Village there was something that WE had that's missing in many parts of the city, or in some towns. You see we had!

"LOVE and TOGETERNESS."

I'm sure that you have heard that OLD saying that it takes a Village to raise a child. Where are those places like the one that I grew up in back in the day? They have gone to Shit. You see I left my village on April 25, 1955 going out into the JUNGLE. Yes! The jungle where you can't leave your doors OPEN or play ball out in the streets without worrying about being shot. Damn, some places one had to sleep in the bath-tub, because some Fool was trying to poke holes in the walls of your house.

So my good friend you don't know SHIT about me for if you did, then you knew that when I was young, Wild and Crazy I did lots of things because I was trying to get off into some ladies panties and get me a shot of the Wild Cherry. Yet, in the very end I was all most eaten alive by the lioness and damn near step in Quick Sand, all because I had forgot the "RULES of the JUNGLE."

My reader's right about now, I need to tell you something about THREE things that did change me and had such a hold on me and even in my life, most of all how they came about.

1. My Rain of Pain
2. The Dark Years
3. When my Well ran Dry,

I shall try and tell you about them as they took place in my life. Right now I need to turn back the clock to deal with the very First event, and the two events other events will fall in place when the time comes. I do hope that you can re-call when I spoke of those words that my grandmother had spoke to me, and those words were. "Son we are all of TWO people." Yet it's true, because I have only told you about one side of me and my life from 1935 up until 1976 from the time that I was born and until the time for me to retire from the U.S. Military.

I have never spoken of that side of me which has caused me so much pain in my life and those "BLUES." It was that "Rain of Pain" which ate my ass up 24/7, and even as I sit here today that crazy ass pain is still here within me, locked away deep down inside of me and my soul. Lets back up to the year of 1961 the 15th of July? I remember this day, oh so well, because that's the very same day that this Rain of Pain all got started. You see on this day "POPS" my step-father was called away to go home by the good Lord. I was in the military at that time. I was stationed on the USS Coral Sea CVA-43 an Aircraft Carrier outside of San Francisco, California, when I received word from the Red Cross about my step-father death.

People, before we open this door, let me tell you something about my step-father? Some of us have had step-fathers or step-mothers come into our lives that we don't give a "Rat Ass" about them. Yet some of you have had a step-father like mine! Tall, a strong man, but on the hand low-key, never betting you or saying those crazy ass words to you! "Boy you are just like your F----K-up daddy.

"You ain't shit."

Oh no! This never happened to me. He was kind and a soft spoken man. Now when the time came for someone to get off into your ass, now that was moms job (in my family that's the way that it went) I knew this because when my mom got down into my ass, she always said those crazy ass words "Boy" this going to HURT me more than its going to hurt you." Hell, now that I think about it, I smile and laugh about those words. "It's going to hurt me more than it will hurt you."

Hell man I was the one that was getting my ass beat with those very same switch that she made me go out into the back yard and cut them Now don' act crazy and bring back one of those switches that the RATS would laugh at and say "Fool I could have done better than that. Now who knows just what I'm talking about? I bet some of you are saying "AMEN to that" because I too had been down that very same road that you are speaking of. My step-father's death really hit me, man I cried and I cried, it was just like I was hearing Bobby B. saying those words "Cry, Cry Cry, like you have never done before. I'm sure that some of you just who I am speaking of, for those of you who don't even know who Bobby B. was, he was a Blues singer, and at that time I had the Blues.

I will not talk about the "BLUES" because you'll never understand the BLUES unless you have lived "The Blues."

What I'm trying to say is that those blues turn into my Rain and Pain for me. What it really came down to is that on July 15, 1961 was the very last time that I have cried. I'm eighty years old now, so I have NOT cried from the age of Twenty-Six which was fifty-Four years ago that this Rain and Pain was there, never going away, because it was locked behind Steel Doors and I had lost that key to that damn door. Not even talking with anyone about how I felt.

Why am I speaking of this now Fifty-Four years later? There is something holding me back from crying. I just suck that pain up and deal with it and not allow anyone to share that pain with me. Its 2015 now and in a few more weeks 2016 will be here with us and my Rain and Pain is still here with me. Maybe one day I shall learn how to "CRY". Until that day, I'll have to deal with it, just as I have been doing over the years. In fact Fifty-Four of those years.

Maybe his death (Pops) and Vietnam and other events has cause me to become this way, that my pain is my pain! Again, it might be that I'm not one of those people who will sit down and open up and let others get into my world and tell them what's going on in my life and what makes me tick. Then again maybe I don't want others running around like my half- ass-good-friend talking that crazy ass shit that they know me. I'll tell you the very same thing that I have told to others "You don't know me, you ONLY know of me."

I will get off of this Rain and Pain for now, because there are other events where this Pain and Pain will be there kicking my sorry ass from Left to Right, because I had F-----K-up but I had found away to deal with it.

BLOCK THREE

U.S. POSTAL SERVICE

1976 – 1997

U.S. POSTAL SERVICE

I felt so good being home with the family; know more orders from the military, only those orders from my wife. I sat around for a while waiting for that unemployment check, after a while this got to me, because I wasn't use to sitting around on my ass. I got to thinking where was I going to work at, and what shall I do! A friend of mine said to me Armour, why don't you check out the Post Office, because they were looking for people. I said to myself, why not; so I got off of my ass and went down to Oakland (Oakland, California) on 13th and Alice for the test. Mean while I had been doing some studying about the Post Office and its test system. I took the test for the Postal Service, not knowing at that time, that for the next twenty-Two years I would be an employee there.

I received a letter from the Post Office in Oakland California down on Seventh St. I turned this job down, because it was only temporary; I was looking for a full-time job. However I received a letter again from the Post Office three weeks later it was for a full-time job in the Richmond BMC (Bulk Mail Center) one of those places where the mail just kept on coming. I didn't care because now I had a full-time job I was working on the South Dock loading mail into trucks. One day Rick my supervisor asks me if I would like to train to become a Supervisor and get out of those trucks.

Now this was the second time that someone had given me a helping hand to move up the leader. First there was Harris my watch captain when I was stationed on the USS Coral Sea, when I was in the Navy; Now I thought that I had gotten away from all of that bull-shit, back-stabbing and ass kissing when I left the military "LORD" coming into the Postal Service here it was all over again, but a whole lot more of that shit. Back-stabbing and ass-kissing and damn, so much more that I had never dream of seeing or hearing about, because this shit was out there in the OPEN for all to SEE and Hear about.

Man, it wasn't just the back-stabbing, but who you were sleeping with or who was F------king who? It was that sleeping and F-------King that got you over. Well things were going good for me. I had a job and a check each month from the government from the Navy. Yet there was something missing from my life, and that was an Education. So here its twenty-Two years later after graduation from Northern High School in Detroit, Michigan That I returned back to school. I felt a little out of place in Junior College, because I had sons older than some of the students that were in my class.

It wasn't easy for me because I was working eight or ten hours a night I went to work at 6 pm until 2:30 or until 4:30 in the morning if we had overtime. I had to be in school by 8:00 am I received Associate of Arts from Contra Costa College in Richmond, California in 1997. Now I was on the right track in getting that education that I had dream of having. We began working six days a week to ten hours a night. I would hang out with some of the guys and started going out to the Race Track with them. This was a new thing for me, at first I would just watch because I didn't know anything about the Race Track.

At first I would just watch the people, and their Behavior was something else. Man, I could see it in their eyes, the joy of winning the upset when they lost. Tearing up tickets and the words that some of them said. Shit it was like a spell had come over them. I return back to work after my outing out there at the Race Track. Man! I took a good look at some of my co-workers and their actions, the kissing-up. Right then and there, I knew what I wanted to major in. I was in the right place to study people and human behavior. I kept on going to the Track, at first taking notes, but before long I became one of those fans at the Race Track.

In the fall of 1997, I started back to college at San Francisco State University. My major was Human Behavior; after all I had some training under my belt from serving in the U.S. Navy and now with the U.S. Postal Service. This was my lab to do my work and study, a live show five days or six days a week from a cross section of people and mix of different races.

The year of 1980 was a dark year in my life? sometimes when I have nothing to do, I would get out the Family History Books. That's just what I'm saying Family History Books, I see pictures of my father who passed away when I was just eight years old. There's grandfather, a fine looking man. Standing tall, a ladies' man by the looks of him; for some reason I use to think that he was my father, because there was something about him. The way that he stood, but to my surprise I found out that this man was only my grandfather and not my father.

Now there was grandmother, a wise old lady who I wish that I had spent more time with her, because this old lady had it going on. I still can remember the things that she would tell me about life. Yet, I didn't hear those words, like most kids all I had on my mind was playing, but when one is young you don't have the time to hear those words, but as time goes on those words are like A GHOST coming back from the dark to give us a wake-up-call, which would kick you in the ass and say "Fool what's wrong with you."

Even if you were not really close to some of those folks. You remember things and those words have away to find its way back into your life and eat away at your soul. I don't know about you, but for me, I felt that I have lost something that would have made me a much better person, because I keep on hearing those words from my grandmother; It's always at that time when I'm about to make a mistake or about to step-in shit.

I remember that old saying that you had an Angle walking with you all of the time. Is my grandmother my Angle who's always there with me, warning me that I am about to F-----K-up? And that I should get my shit in one bag. Yes, 1980 was a dark year, like that day when mother and I were talking; She said "son" if anything should ever happen to me, Fella (that's the name that she called me by and also other members of the family did) please take the Family Books and hold on to them. Promise me that you will take then and past them on will you! Shit, something did happen to her.

I'm, really, really glad that I took those books, and because some years later I found out that those books did cause some problems in the family. No one knew just what had happened to them or where they went or who had the family books and records for the Armour family.

On September 17, 1981, I lost my sister, it hurt me. You see sometimes her and I got into it, even if she was older than I. The door re-opens for me and I found Red back into my life once again. In August of 1985 almost four years later after the lost of my sister, I lost my mother. It was on August the 25th when my mother's house was sold. It looked like those things that had been left in the house got "Legs" and just up and took flight.

We were all there; I do mean ALL of us were there at the church. The Seventeen-grand children, the twenty-nine great-grand children that my mother had. Reds love, her support and open arms were also there to hold me tight and dry my tears, telling me "Honey, its okay to cry and that she loved me. Planting a warm kiss on my lips, saying to me that no matter what happens in life, that I would never stop loving you, even if we are both married.

I knew right then that I would love this woman until the Good Lord came for me. Damn, how could I give up and stop loving someone who stood by me, in my darkest hours. Once again I had to return back to Detroit, Michigan on April 11, 1989, because I lost my brother. We weren't really close, because I was in the service and never there in Detroit that much.

Only remembering things even if you and he were not close. I do remember that he helped me to buy a car from Dick Green, and he gave me some money for my plane fare to California when I first join the Navy reporting for duty in San Diego, California.

I knew that she was in the back row. I could feel her and the love and support that she had brought alone with her. That day I wanted to run to this woman and let her hold me close and once again wipe the tears from my eyes and hear her saying "I'm here for you, and I will be there for you no matter come" Hell or High water" I still remember that special day that her and I had. Lord to the day! I left Detroit, it was just before she turned fifty years old, and I didn't return back to the Motor City until August of 2007.

In part one of this story I explained about the ass-kissing and the back stabbing that was going on in the Post Office where I was working at the Richmond BMC there in Richmond, California. As the Action-Supervisor on the South Dock, and back section of the plant; on that night we had light mail and we were letting people go home early. This one Supervisor friend asks if she could leave early. I explained to her that she could not leave early before others who were senior to her. This lady just turned her back to me and said something and just walked right out of the building. A female employee who was standing near us said "damn, Armour did you hear what she said? I said that I didn't hear her. What did she say I ask that employee what did she say? She something like "kiss her monkey. I wrote her ass up for being AWOL; some of the guys said to me "Armourr" your butt is in trouble" Don't you know who she is? Man, she and this one Supervisor have a thing-going-on. Shit, to me she was just another employee, plus I had a job to do, and I did my job.

About six months later the Post Office began to promote people for full-time Supervisor. When the list was posted my name and some other employees name were on that list, but later that list was "REVISED" and my name and others were replaced with other employee's names.

When we asked what was going on, management came up with some crap, saying that none of us were qualified to become Supervisors. The bull was that those on Tour two were more qualified then we were. You see we were working on Tour Three the night crew, and not around the Big Wheels in the day time. We felt that some SHIT was going on, so we went and got ourselves a lawyer. Man, we kept this under cover (so we thought) but one of the "YES MEN" ran and informed the managers about what we were up to.

We didn't file the EEO Complaint because they said that we were not qualified, so we based it on "Age Discrimination. The fact was that ALL of those other employees (the new list) were under the age of THIRTY. The Post Office saved face by making two employees from Tour Three as Supervisors" One person was promoted to Supervisor because of "Age" (which was I) and the other one because he was "White", because there was just only one White Supervisor on our tour and he worked sometimes up stairs in training.

Now we were on the "HIT" list. They got me! The post Office began cutting back on Supervisors, I was cut! It was pay-back-time. The past came back to bite me in the ass. You remember that lady who I wrote up from being AWOL! Well her friend was acting manager wrote me up on some crazy ass-shit, saying that I had allowed an employee to bring a "DRINK" onto a keying station (where you key letter mail to another place)

I was working two sections that night, one section was on the WEST end of the building and the other section was on the EAST section of the building. I could not watch both sections at the same time. I had a letter put into my records (which this acting manager somehow forgot to have that letter removed from my records, like he said that he would do) I was sent to work in Concord at one of the stations. Later I was reassigned to the Post Office in Oakland, California down on Seventh Street. Another one of those Ass-Kissing Post Office.

I was placed into the training office (now f--k-me-dead) another one of those places who you knew was the thing. Anyway someone must have been watching out for me, because no sooner had I left the Concord Post Office, shit hit the fan, and I do mean that SHIT did hit the fan. Now the shit in Oakland was no better than that shit that was going on in the Richmond Post Office (BMC). Now my job was in the training office I was to train other employees to become Craft Instructor, that was my main job, but I would also set-up classes for upper managers for training. Again this is where shit hit the fan, while setting up these classes my way to get the best cross sections of managers in the class room, some people didn't like the way that I was doing this and that cause a problem (I let it go) I wasn't out to kiss any ones ass.

Now man, what really got to me was when an upper Supervisor was kissing ass with an employee in order for them to look good. Man, that Supervisor thought that they had their shit in one bag. but that person didn't know shit from the time of the day. Man, I got tired of the bull-shit, so after a run-in with that person, I knew that it was time to get my ass on the road. Damn, I had twenty-one years in, so I put my papers in, getting free from the back-stabbing and ass kissing.

On Monday March 27, 1997 my manager asked me if I wanted a going away party, and if I was coming into work on Tuesday? I said to her, thank you, but I do not wish to have a going away party and I told her that I want lie, I will not be in for work of Tuesday, because I am going to call in sick and take the rest of the week off. Hell! What could they (the Post Office) say or do? I already had my date. She understood where I was coming from; all she said was "Good Luck Armour"

Man, I felt good the next day when I called into the office with a smile on my face. I said hello "This is Armour calling in to let you know that I am sick. My friend who was on the other end of the phone knew what was coming, all he said was "Good Luck man" and I can't wait to get out of this shit house. I also said I shall not be coming in for the rest of the week.

I am sure that the Military and the Post office are not the ONLY places where this is going on. All I can say is those words that Dr. King spoke "Free at last, Free at last thank God I am free at last."

BLOCK FOUR

RETIREMENT

1997 - PRESENT

COULD I

Last night I had another one of those dreams? It came from my grandmother! Wow, this is out of sight, because this is the very first time that I have had a dream about her in a number of years. Now this one really has me sitting here wondering why her? What's wrong with my life, that grandmother should come to me with some kind of word! Is this a good thing or a bad thing When she spoke it was always with a word of wisdom.

That I should do something or look out for someone who's trying to enter into my life for the wrong reason, or is there a Red Flag out there that I don't see? It's been a while that I haven't dream about anything or anyone. What could she be trying to tell me? Damn, there is someone calling me, so I'll be right back with you. I need to take this call. Shit this is one of those phone calls that I don't want; its bad news, someone crying to you about this and that and bull-shit. Whenever this one lady calls me she's up to something or wants something from me. Now this call blew my ass out of the water. All she said Hi Armour, just call to say hello and find out how you are doing? Now that's bull-shit.

I don't want you to think that I'm a ladies' man, and when I speak they come. Far from that, at this age of life I have what some of them want, and in return they have what I desire. Some of these women are looking for security, and I am looking for a "Road-Dog" It's all good that we want something from each other, but like grandmother said "One should not sell his or her soul just to have someone in your bed." Its hell out there and no one gives up something for nothing... That's why I must find that special person who understands this.

I look back to that one woman that I have cared about for over the years, and even at times with the things that's going on in her life, I do ask myself that in the end will I be selling my soul just to have her or will she be selling her soul just to get that security?

Now is this a dream or is it that Red Flag that comes from grandmother! Boy watch your ass, and do remember what I have told you "if that's not your cup of TEA don't put NO sugar in it. Wow! it has been five years ago that was the last time that I had any dealings with this mother, because there is some bad blood between her and I.

What I mean is that she was in need of some help, that's about the time when I was running around wild and acting crazy, but most of all I had forgot the rules of the jungle in that I was looking for love in all of the wrong places.

I came to her aid, and that mother got out of town without saying a word and didn't even say thank you. Now my ass pocket is saying "Armour" zip me up and forget all about me man; because her sorry ass wants something again, and you do remember just what happened the last time when you put your hand into my back pocket and let her have something? Her ass hit the freeway, and damn her ass didn't even look back!

Sometimes people ask you a question and you give them an answer to that question, and at that time you really don't think too much about that question, but later on that very same question began to eat away at your soul and you think about it. What I'm trying to say that one day me and my friend was just sitting around and kicking it, and out of the blue she said "Armour do you think that you could love a Black Woman? I said to her what do you mean by that! Could I ever love a Black Woman? Well Armour since you have been married out of your own race and married someone who was not Black! That's why I am asking this question, could you Love a Black Woman?

You see I had a mix marriage. I married a woman from oversees who was not Black. My wife was born in the Philippines and we were married for Forty-Seven years. I knew just what she was really looking for? Could I love a Black Woman or would I want to have another mix marriage to another woman not of my own race. My answer to her was, "yes" I could love a Black Woman; yet another question has been eating away at me and that question was "HOW DO I LOVE A BLACK WOMAN"?

I'm sure that someone is saying "man" you got to be shitting me about how do you love a Black Woman? "NO" I'm not blowing smoke up your ass or shitting you. Now tell me how do you love somebody from your very own race after you had not loved or had any kind of contract with a woman from your own race in over Forty-Seven years? Now talk to me? I know that at times a Black Woman can get the Ass. I have seen this from some of my lady friends and her girl-friends and also from wives of some of my friends.

Yes, at times some Black Women are quick to get the ASS, "it's BECAUSE some of US BLACK MEN have made them this way! "Staying out all night and not coming home for hours or days at a time and DAMN, man throwing that baby mama UP into her face and now some of US BLACK men have SUGAR in our gas tanks and even SWITCH hitters. I know that there is lots of Beautiful Black Woman out there, but some of US wonder down another road. When I speak of US, yes I'm talking about MYSELF also.

I want to love a Black Woman, but not just any Black Woman, but that ONE who got away, and the very same ONE that I can't forget. "How do I love her as a Black Woman?

I'm sure that some of you are "Saying", man she is a WOMAN? Yes she is, but when you have not really loved or spent time with a Black Woman how do you love her? All alone knowing that the LOVE that you have had and now this new love want be the same, because NO two women from two different races are the same when it comes right down to LOVING and UNDERSTANDING.

I read a book once call "How to Love a Black Woman? That book really did open up my eyes to things that I have never thought about being a Black man.! When it came right down to loving a Black Woman. Maybe I should re-read that book over and over again, because I have learned more about my sister, when it comes down to loving them. Now my ONE question is, when my friend asks me that question was she afraid that I could not love her because she was BLACK? I want lie to you, because the last time that I had REALLY been in Love with a Black woman or had anything special to do with a Black woman was back in 1955 and that was before I had set out to see the WORLD, maybe if I had taken the time out to UNDERSTAND the BLACK woman I would NOT be asking these questions now.

I have met and even seen some Beautiful Black Sisters and I have learned so many things about my sisters, and yet I STILL NEED TO LEARN

MORE ABOUT THEM (the Black woman) to really be able to answer my friend's question of could I love a Black woman? Maybe I need to get my head out of my Ass and understand that LOVE is LOVE no matter what COLOR that other person is; the ONLY thing that should matter is that you BOTH really do love each other.

Well maybe me and my friend need to sit down and talk about this and let her NO that I love her for WHO she is, and not BECAUSE she is a Black woman.

WHO YOU WERE

One day I was sitting around eating some candy, I chocked on it. I tried to bring it up, but the only thing that was coming up was blood. I went to the hospital to get a check-up and while the doctor was checking me up and did some lab work I found out TWO things! One was that I had HEPATITIS-B and there was that other thing that I didn't tell anyone about it not even my family. That one word that has cause so many people to fall down and cry out "Lord why me." You see I had just found out that I had" Stage Three Lung Cancer."

November 25th of 2006 that was Thanksgiving weekend. The grand-kids were here at the house, all nine of them and we had a very nice time and a very wonderful dinner, we all were just kicking back and talking about the old times. We all helped to clean up the kitchen and put away everything. It was about that time so everyone said good-night and went home. No sooner had the kids left you fell to the floor and couldn't get up, and all you said was Honey "take me to the hospital please."

Shit, I knew for sure that something was wrong. Lucia you hate going to the hospital. I called 911 for some help. They arrived and took you to the North Bay Hospital which was close to the house. While there in North Bay sometime that night your heart stopped and they had to shock you in order to get your heart going gain. Lucia for two, you just lay there not saying a word with your eyes closed. Several times they had to use the paddle on you and Honey each time it took a toll on your body.

Lucia, as you lay there blood began to run down from your nose, I would wipe it away, not knowing why there was blood coming from your nose. I was hurting just standing there looking at you. Praying that you would open your eyes and say something to me; wanting to hear you say I'm okay, but nothing came from your lips, and your eyes didn't open. For two days you just lay there not moving or saying anything, and then on the third day, the doctor called me to the side and explained things to me about how you were doing. Honey, just the way that those words flow out of his mouth. I knew that something was wrong!

Mr. Armour:

The only thing that's keeping your wife going is this machine and the paddle was not helping at all. Mr. Armour, in fact the paddle was causing more harm than good. Wow! Here I am sitting here watching my wife slip away from me, knowing that it's only a matter of time and knowing all alone that you might have to do something that you don't want to do it!

Something was holding me back, I stood there with tears in my eyes (not crying, because I could not cry) telling myself that she will come out of it and that she will be okay. I think about those things that some people have said "that when it comes to that time, they'll pull that plug from their love one or love ones.

"Man that's Bull-shit"

Man you don't want to let go of that person, because of the LOVE that you have for them. I stood there finding myself talking to her, the words came but they are slow to leave my lips.

Then a warm feeling came over me, it was very still in the room, but yet I could feel a "BREEZE" along with a very soft voice saying "It's okay Honey, it's okay to let go of me "I could feel my hand move slowly towards that plug, knowing that I must do what I have too, because she has told you that it's okay to let go of her, because she wants to go home to a better place.

LUCIA MANELSE ARMOUR

Lucia Manelse born in the Philippines on the 7th day of January 1934. The first child of a family of seven, four girls and three boys. Honey you know it's kind of funny that people come into our life and we NEVER say to them "Thanks or Appreciate Them" for they come and go, here today and gone tomorrow.

Lucia you made me who I am and you played a MAJOR role in making me "Who I am". Thinking back when I first met you, there was a "MYSTERY" about you. You were warm, and with fire in your touch. Your eyes sparkled with Joy and said "comes drink of me, for I am what you desire." Lucia you were comfortable with yourself and where you were in life.

The glass of water that I long to drink of, knowing that I would keep on coming back to drink out of that glass. Our lives began on the 14th of February of 1959 on that day you became Mrs. Lucia Manelse Armour. You were more than words could ever express. The mother of our children. Lucia most of all you were from a Special breed of women. The military wife. I can remember that day when I told you that I was going to stay in the military for twenty years. Honey, not asking you how you felt about this. All you said was Mr. Armour, if that's what you want. Here in my hand is a letter that was for you. One that you never got to read or hold in your hands. It came later after you had gone home.

I put that letter in a frame for the ENTIRE world to see, just who you were. It was a Certificate of Appreciation from the United States Navy. Honey that Certificate went on to read:

Lucia Manelese Armour has earned Grateful Appreciation for her Unselfish, Faithful and devoted service during her husband naval career.

Her unfailing support and understanding helped to make possible her husband lasting contribution to the United States Navy.

L.F. Eggert, Capt, USN

Commanding Officer

I didn't tuck this away in any of my books (your letter of Appreciation) its here on the wall for all to see who came into our home. Lucia you were more than words could ever express. Love sitting here and looking at the calendar soon it will have been TEN (10) years now that you have gone to that resting place home. I still can't get used to your absence, you being snuggled up next to me. I have gone out and brought me one of those things, a body pillow which helps a little bit, but it's not the same.

The truth is there's no replacement for you my love that very special person that you are to me and into my heart. Soon that very Special day for me will be here, I'm talking about Valentines' Day. OUR DAY February the 14th. Our wedding day which took place in 1959, fifty-seven years ago. I only wish that you were here with me right now; than I wouldn't have to sit here and try to find the words that I need to say." Lucia thank you for everything, but yet sometimes words need not be spoken, just the touch of a hand or the Warm and Wonderful kiss is all that's really needed to take place

Mrs. Armour, sometimes I feel abandoned, it's funny that we all need somebody, even if it's only for that "touch" baby anyone who says that they don't need someone isn't telling the truth. They are telling a DAMN LIE, because we ALL want to be touched, it does not matter what our age is or who we are, that TOUCH is like music to the soul.

Mrs. Armour, you were the answer to my prayers, the partner that I could spend the rest of my life with. In my dreams you were a 100% match.; I am not sure what a 100% means or is, but never the less our relationship hit a high on the 14th day of February of 1959, when we became as of "ONE" and then on November 27, 2006 you were taken away from me. God dispatched his Special Angle to see you safely home.

My Darling we had those bad times, but you and I made it, we put those bad times to the side and made good ones out of them What can I say, only that there was a reason that you and I became of one. Lucia in this letter it holds "a message" that delivers the exact way that I feel about you. The things that we spoke of, our Hopes, Dreams, and plans for the future, and our conviction that things do happen for a reason. Mrs. Armour, thank you for being my wife, but most of all THANK you for those Forty-Seven years of your WONDERFUL LOVE.

Lucia, when I first met you there was something about you that words can't explain. You taught me how to love and what it means to love someone. There you were with that warm smile, hair shinning as Black as Coal. Your eyes with that glow of a soft warm light, saying I'm yours FOREVER. Your name was Lucia Manelse. I said to myself, damn I got to have her.

Love sometimes when I sit there in the dark thinking about OUR life together, one minute I'm laughing and the very next minute I'm crying, feeling the hurt and pain, because I can't reach out and touch you. I can't even feel you lying next to me. Yes! Darling there were so many things that

I didn't get to say, and there were so many places that you and I didn't get to see and the warm sun set off to the West over the mountain tops. Honey I remember when you used to read to me "Who will be with you" I can hear you saying those words right now...

Love is like spring
It grows on you,
Seduces you slowly and gently,
But it holes tight,
That's the FEELING tell me,
That LOVE is GOOD.

If I would only stop to listen to that wind knowing of the power that is within love, that has been embedded into my Heart and Soul. Lucia Honey, your memory will be the FUEL that will keep me moving on. Lucia you brought life into my life. I thank you for all that you have given to me. Mrs. Armour, after I lost you, I found myself sitting in our bedroom in the dark, night after night dealing with this pain and hurt not wanting to go to any place, just wanting to stay in the house.

Nothing mattered to me, because you were gone out of my life, but never from my heart... Now I'm in this cold house all by myself with no one to talk with or touch, but most of all there is "NO" one to speak those words to me and say!

"Honey I love you ever so much."

Now it's just me and our dogs, Kathy and Lady. How could I tell them (the dogs) that I had just lost you? That very wonderful person who I had spent the last forty-seven years of my life with. Now that my "WELL" has run dry, but at times I find myself seeing you in my dreams. Wondering if you were trying to tell me something.

Lucia it is like I said in my very first book "How Strong is Your Love" That your love from the grave is still holding on to me! Is this the reason that those dreams of you keep returning back to me or is it saying "Mr. Armour" you belong to me, and only to me.

BLEW MY MIND

Lucia one night I found myself putting on a CD by Aretha Franklin, the next thing I felt were tears coming from my eyes. Yes, I was crying! Why! This song I had flash-backs. You see the last time that I felt like this was when I lost my sep-father. All other times I just put that pain behind my shield and said Armour deal with it; about this time I became friends with a group of people who really help me out. They were a comfort to me and my soul. I understood just what they were telling me. We became close, very close. Man; all I had to do was just reach out to them. I'm talking about James Cleveland, Shirley Caesar, Vickie Winn and many more others, about that time was when I came up with that Dog Day thing.

My wife was gone and now all I had left were my two girls. I'm speaking of Kathy and Lady (my two dogs) I would tell my friends not to call me on that day, because that was my dog day. I did not answer the phone nor did I go out. Hell I even told my doctor about this (no I am not crazy) Yes, I even told Red about this. I knew that she world understand just what I was going through and what was happening with me. Yet I found myself reaching out to this lady more and more. The phone calls, the dreams. That's what kept me going.

I tried going out to meet someone, but it didn't work out for me. Maybe it's because I was pushing myself. I think that the main reason this didn't work was because they don't make them like they used to do. Please don't get me wrong, there are lots of good women out there, but they are not in my age group. I see those kind of women in the malls, in church or just passing by not saying a word, only just that HI type of smile and they would keep on walking by. Hell I was going through so much at that time that I didn't know to shit or go blind.

I went away to Mexico high up into the mountains to get my head together. This was one of those special places where people would retreat off to in order for them to gain wisdom and some answers. When I return back from my trip I called Red. You see she was that other woman that was in my life; but there was a Wall blocking her and me from being with each other, you see Red was a married woman.

Red was that one that got away, and the ONE that I was in Love with for over fifty years. Damn, hearing he words "Armour" I am going through a lot of things, and my plate is full, and you don't know me and you might not like it? So I want blame you if you walked away and found someone else. Deep down inside of her she knew that I would not walk away from her.

We spoke about this and that, knowing that she was a married woman, who could not just up and walk away from her husband, because he was very sick, and he needed her, besides she loved this man, even through their love was on the down side. She just said "Armour" if you found happiness with someone else, not to wait for me... That was in 2007 and I have not packed my bags yet. I'm still here waiting for this lady. I know that this sounds kind of crazy, but sometimes love will make one do some crazy things.

Maybe one day when you find that true love, you'll understand just where I'm coming from and you will also have learned just "How Strong Love is." It's been quite some time since my well has run dry. I am slowly getting back on track, but at times I find myself still running back to the past, wishing that I had done lots of things right the very first time' but like they say "don't cry over spit milk." Yet it hurts knowing that I'm in love with a married woman and can't do anything about it.

There is just one question that I need an answer too? Am I just a fool in love or have I gone out of my rabbit-ass-mind? Stay with me! Because there is so much that I have to tell you and then maybe you can answer that question about me being out of my rabbit-ass-mind. Where am I today? Well to tell the truth about it, at times I am unsure how it feels, is it the feeling of Joy or Happiness? Yet I keep on asking myself "How Strong is Love?

As I look back over my life it has been good. I had the Honor of being married to a very wonderful woman. She was there for me when I was only getting paid $ 141.00 dollars a month, until we were able to obtain part of the American Dream.

Now a part of that dream is gone forever, and a part of me is also gone. Only the dream keeps on coming back to me. Maybe that's just what is keeping me from moving on, knowing that soon I must close that door and move on. Only to open another door, that one door which has been with me for over fifty years. I find myself looking into the mirror asking myself that one question of where I am today. I'm still in love with that married woman. Hey, I'm not sitting around with my fingers up my ass. I have tried to meet someone but I have had some bad luck in meeting that person. I want say the right person, because who is that right person?

One day when I was at the Race Track my second home four days out of a week. When I met Tess, a nice looking sister, who was into game playing. I was not looking to get married; it was just to have someone around as a friend. Man, Tess was looking for a Milk Cow so that she could milk his ass dry and then take off. I told this woman that she need to take her sorry ass on and go kick some rocks, about two weeks later after Tess was gone from my life. I met Nancy at a party; this lady was sitting on a kid's bike sucking on a rib bone. Damn, about this time I was ready to get off into the valley and get me a shot of that Wild Cherry.

My right hand man pulled my coat and said Armour before you do anything crazy, man I saw what you have your eyes on, man we need to talk I was down for that, thinking maybe he could put in a good word for me, and I could get a shot of that Wild Cherry. He said watch your back with Nancy, because she is a switch-hitter! Hell with someone like that you'll be wondering if you might be the one who's getting stabbed in return.

I was getting to that point that I wanted a shot, man it has been so long when the last time that I got me some, hell I didn't know what it looked like, felt like, or smell like. I just wanted me some.

Sandra, man she had lots of things going for her, I could see myself into that, but there was one thing that kept my ass from getting some of that! Damn, she had some problems? Her personal "Hygiene". If that lady didn't hit the rain locker (shower) her ass can just keep on walking. Shit there's "NO" way in the world that I was going to allow my Dog to play with her KITTY!

Man, let me tell you something I have been all over the world and met many women and there's one thing that I have learned from those women, who ALL have one thing in common, and that's "NO" woman wants to lay next to ANY MAN that smell worse than they do. I feel the very same way when it comes to me getting off into the valley and getting a shot of that Wild Cherry. I don't mind fighting that Tang, but having to fight that smell also, that shit want work for me... I was getting close, I do mean close to that danger zone, where I wanted to go out and tap anything, because that boy was betting me out of the bed in the morning.

We all have heard that story about the Big Bad Wolf, who met Little Red Riding Hood, that boy was looking at his dinner. Well I was like that when I met Jennifer. I was in the mall and there she was. Lord to the day, just looking at her. I wanted to take her to the Post Office and stamp Air Mail on her ass and send her home to me. Damn, just looking at her, she stood about five-four, 120 pounds, Brown Eyes, jet-Black Hair, skin so smooth that water would just run off of her skin. I would say that she was about 34-28-36, now that's just right. Not to heavy up stairs, anything over a mouth full would be a waste. Just looking at her I could tell that she was mixed in between Black and something else. Yes, she was DELIOIOYS! Just looking at her. I was like a man who was on death row DEVOURING his last meal.

In my mind knowing that it was good, so good that I could taste the Wild Cherry; so we sat down and start talking, I explained my issues to her, and got that CODE number to her heart. We went out a few times for dinner and drinks and that Sunday drive, I was comfortable and at ease around Jennifer. I start to have dreams about this lady, she was that flower that I wanted in my garden; about nine months or more, when we were out for a moon night walk, I said to her "lady" you really don't know me and you might not like it, but most of all I can't give you 100% of me, or my love. I asked her how she felt about this and I said that I don't mean to lead you on nor do I want to hurt you, lady you are that candy bar that I want.

This lady took my hand into hers, and I could feel the heat starting to burn into my body, never have I felt like this before. My soul was on fire just from her holding onto my hands. Damn, what would that body heat be like, could I stand it or would I cry out, asking her to put out that fire that's burning the hell out of me.

All she did was to look at me with those soft Brown eyes, she just started to laugh and she said something that blew my sorry ass out of the water?

Horace I don't want to sleep with you, nor do I want to F----k you, all I want from you is your friendship. In my mind I was saying you got to be shitting me. Why hold on to that Wild Cherry, just give me a little. She could see that I was a little taken back about what she had just drop on me. Hell, what could I say, it was her thing, and if that's what she wanted? By that time the boy was also taken by those words that he went limp and went to sleep on me; before I could say another word, she planted a warm kiss on the side of my face and said let's sit over here, because I need to tell you why I don't want to F----k you?

You see Horace, in the past I have had a very hard life with men! I have been beating on, pissed on and even shit on by men. Horace my step-father has cut my body with a razor and forced himself on me and made me do things to him that I just wanted to die. You are the first man that I have met who didn't want to jump right into the bed with me. (Damn, there goes the Chocolate-coated Strawberry Candy) you have been up front with me in this short time that we have been kicking it. I hope that you want give up our friendship. I respect you and the love that you have for that other woman, who's miles away. Horace, love her if she is all that you say she is.

Jennifer went on to say that I'm very sorry that you have lost your wife. You must have loved her very much, because after you lost her you weren't running all over town trying to get into some ladies panties. (Wow! little did she know) Wow! This lady was one in a million, better than a roll in the hey or a one night stand. Looking back about all of those other women that I have been with, maybe that old saying is true.

"Things happen for a reason. ALL I can say why me, why now. Damn life sucks.

WHAT AM I LOOKING FOR

Right now, I want someone to talk too. I want someone in this house with me, even if she spends all of the time on the couch watching soaps. I'm sick of being along with no one for company or to hold tight and feel her soft skin and smooth as silk and softer then Georgia Cotton, but most of all to feel the heat from her body. I hate to cut out on you, but its Sunday Morning and I must get ready for church. I have this feeling that I must attend church today, because something is not right and I do need the word. The last time that I felt this way was when I lost my wife. Maybe some of you have also felt like this too.

I found myself unlocking that door and tuning to that other man's wife. For comfort, love and someone just to reach out to, and lay my head on her shoulder, and let my tears flow. Now you can understand the real reason that I need to get out and attend church today. Those of you who are just like me, who have really felt love, but you couldn't" have that love that you longed for because that love belonged to someone else, her husband. It hurts like hell; just like it did when I found out that I had Stage Three Lung Cancer. That day when my doctor gave me the word, I felt like I had been kicked by a Big-Red-Ass-Mule. I found myself like so many others, Crying out "Why me, Why me Lord. Now all kinds of thoughts went through my head? How long have this shit been eating away at my Lung? How did I get it?

It has been over thirty five years when the last time that I had a smoke. Has this shit been in me for all of this time? I'm sure that some of you might understand just where I'm coming from. You just might have friends, love ones or maybe even you have had to deal with some form of cancer and praying each night that you will make it; so you can wear that Pink or Yellow band on your right wrist. "Saying live strong." Each time that I look at that yellow band of mine I thank God that I made it.

I never told Red about my cancer, she had her own problems, and some people said that I was wrong for not telling her about my cancer. She was another man's wife, did I have the right to have this lady worry about me, when she had a husband that was sick also. I don't think so; I know that old saying about the truth will set you free. It just might set me free, but then again it could just eat my ass up, just like quick silver.

Again I found myself returning back to the mountain top, that long ass bus ride, over dirt roads having to deal with chickens and other things that were on the bus There were some people who were wondering what was I doing out here? Where was I going to and what did I want? You don't see many Americans out here, and for damn sure you didn't see any Black people walking around and going to the mountain top. I was like a fish out of water to some of the people or a puppy dog looking for a bone.

I kept on going my way, because I had been here before looking for some answers and also some healing to the mind. The morning came quickly, the Red glow of the Sun coming over the mountain. One could tell it was going to be a hot one by the rays from the sun. Here you are in a place like this cut off from the outside. However news reaches you about the bull-shit that's taking place in Washington, D.C. and other places. Makes one say the HELL with it all, sell everything that you own and come live in a place like this. The people do with what they have.

I have found peace here in the valley; also I have found some ammo that I need to help me get out of the rain. There are tons of things going through my mind, as I sit here in my room in the dark I ask myself; "Horace" are you crazy? I'm not sure about this, but let me ask you something or just put yourself in my place and ask yourself these questions. Please be real about what you feel and your answers to these questions:

1. Am I crazy to want someone to love me?
2. Am I crazy because I hunger for that Special Love?
3. Am I crazy because I want someone to hold me tight and dry my eyes when I'm hurting?
4. Am I crazy to be in Love with a married woman?

These are some of the questions that I have come here seeking answers for, you see my STRUGGLE is to "FREE" myself from this web and stop this Rain and Pain.

I realized that this web had me bound to the love of two women! One Love was for my wife who was in the grave and to the other one was Red, who was married, but now she too is free. There is one thing that I would like to say before I close this door to my room! I'm not sure that this will be my last trip down this road, but no matter how many times that I come back here I'll always be asking myself!

1. Who I Am?
2. What do I want?
3. What's my purpose?

I can only get the answer that I'm seeking if I can answer these three questions truthfully. I just want you to understand that some of the things that I encounter or undertake it's for me to find my way, and put things in the right place and try understanding "Who I am?" I do believe that each and every one of us needs to ask ourselves these three questions. Hey! I would like for you to do something. Close your eyes and ask yourself "Who I am?

I need answers to this question.; Thinking back when I wrote my very first book "How Strong is Your Love, now I ask myself why was I writing that book or WHO was I writing that book too? Who knows maybe one day I'll find that answer. Mean while I need to move on, I need to get back home, because there is something that's eating away at my ass about Jennifer?

In the months that Jennifer and I have been together we have become close and friends. Yet I feel that deep down inside of this lady there is a FIRE that's hot as hell... The kind that shows nothing but hate? When she and I talk about her family, I can feel the danger in her tone. I would hate like HELL to be on her bad side, because I feel that if one would push this lady to far she would become a BITCH.

Maybe one of these days, I'll ask her what's up. What are you hiding or hiding from? I guess in a way of speaking she is just like me, because I too am hiding something from myself. And do I really need to find out what it is? I feed good, but at the same time I feel kind of sad that I'll be leaving here and the people here have been good to me and also a great help in getting my head clear. I have gained some knowledge and information to help me as I move on down this long road seeking more information to that one question that I and millions of others are looking for.

You know it's funny but like I and so many others before me have said that people comes into our life for a reason. I am speaking about Jennifer, when she first came into my life, looking sweet like Twilight Delight, and all I wanted to do was to get her sweet ass to that chopping block. Now, it's a new me, and this lady has become my true friend, someone who I can turn to, when I'm deep in shit. If you don't mind I really like to move away from Jennifer for now, but I shall return back to her, because this woman has become a part of me, my life and family.

Right now I need to find something else to do, because I find myself on the phone with this other woman, the one that's married while I'm trying to write this book, and that want work.

THE DEVIL

Hi, there, just wondering if you received that birthday car that I sent to you on Monday? I was just thinking of you and your upcoming birthday which is coming up soon. I thought that I would let you know that I have not forgotten about the big day. Wow! Just think how a phone call could lift you up and make you feel good and could bring sunshine to your day. Damn, that was just what I needed.

Right now I need to get myself a bath and be off to church. Well here I am sitting in now number 8 from the front, because I wanted to hear him. A man who could and would put fire into your soul. The speaker stood there looking out at the congregation. I alone with others was waiting for the message from him which was how Devil worked his way into our life through "DISTRACTION". You could feel that he was about to speak. He paused and took a sip of water. He began speaking about how Peter had been distracted; he turns that into an everyday life thing and how we are distracted, and even in church that some of us are "Distracted" away from the word onto something else.

One could feel the power in his voice, where those words got to you. It was good that some of the sisters couldn't hold it back. I got distracted, because I saw her. "The Devil in the Blue Dress." Saying come to me" and when I touched this lady hand in giving her a tissue to dry her tears that was flowing from her eyes. Man, I could feel the fire that was coming from deep down inside of her soul. I should have run for cover, but I didn't do it, because I was exposed to the Devil in the Blue Dress.

Maybe this was about the time when I began to take on Emotions, Loneliness and needing someone in my life, and that warm body to hold at night.

I once read that Happiness was the key to a fulfilling life? Is this something that I have been looking for after I had lost my wife; but somehow I just can't find it? Am I going about it the wrong way? Wow! Was that before I forgot the rules of the jungle, because I was looking for Love in the wrong places?

Am I doing this again? Allowing history to repeat its crazy self once more? Man! Just knowing that in the end of it all, my ass will be eaten alive by the lioness, who is just sitting out there waiting for my ass to come alone.

Is this her? The Devil in the Blue Dress. I had been kicking it with this lady for about six and a half months then one night she got a cramp in her left leg, being a good guy I start to rub her leg. My God! This woman had hair on her legs. Now, please don't get me wrong, I wasn't upset about seeing all of that hair on her legs. You see I had a weakness about me, when it came to women with hair on their legs. I was afraid, not of her, but it was her body. There's that old s saying "those women who had hair on their legs, could make a blind man see, and make a cripple man walk"

Lord to the day. I was looking at one of those women sitting there in front of me. Maybe she was really the Devil in the Blue Dress.

I began to spend more and more time with her, but always getting out of her place by midnight. I didn't want to stay past mid-night, because just thinking of it (that Wild Cherry) I was getting weaker and weaker. I wasn't ready to fall into that trap, and for damn sure I wasn't ready to walk into the valley of the shadow of death just yet. I found out that Carol (that was her name) had been married twice, and I wasn't about to become number three on her list. So I got my hat and just walked way, and I have not been back to her house or nor have I seen her in over three year.

I'm sure that you aren't buying this story about me just up and walking out of her life. To tell you the truth, when I was wild and acting crazy back in the day. I was going with a lady like Carol; she too had hair on her legs. I could feel her body heat and those hairs on her legs had me bound to her, and after being with her I was unable to walk, because she P_____y whip me, and sent my ass to the hospital. Now you see why I run from women who have hair on their legs.

Damn, that was the time when those hairs got to working on me that I had tears in my eyes Yes I cried; I do mean cried and I said to myself "Armour Boy" if I lived to reach the age of 105 years old; Shit I never, ever want to cry like that again. That's why I'm afraid of ANY woman that has hair on their legs... For now all I can do is sit here at the cross road waiting for the light to turn green, allowing me to ease on down the road. Oh yes! Sitting here with Johnnie Taylor in the back ground, sometimes when we sit down and hear those Blues, they make one think. Those very songs bring back the past. There's something about the Blues that reaches deep down into the soul.

As I told you before that I would return back to Jennifer? I think that now would be a very good time for that, because those blues are starting to get next to me and creep down into my soul; man when you have those Blues, at times you don't know to Shit or go Blind. Well if you have never had the Blues, then you wouldn't understand me, or what I'm talking about. To understand them, you would have had to live them. One night Jennifer came to me and said "Horace", please sit down, because we need to have a talk. You do remember that time when you and I first met? I told you that I didn't want to F---K you and that I had been shit on, piss on by some men who were in my life.

It all got started when I was about Fourteen years old. Horace I didn't know it at that time, but my father came from a family, who had some money, and he had set aside something for me. My mother learned that he was killed; so we moved from Washington State to San Francisco, California. That's when my mother married this drunken sorry-ass man. My step father. Horace one night after my fourteen birthday, this man ended up in my bed and he was drunk. The first time, he said that he was sorry, and thought that he was in his own bed.

One night after drinking a lot he came into my bed room and forced himself on me. Each night after drinking and his drunken ass would come into my room and have his way with me and make me do things to him, which made me sick. Horace he would cut my body with a razor and said that I was his and that he would kill me if I ever told anyone about this. What really hurt me was that my OWN mother knew just what his this man was up to and what he was doing and she didn't say not one F-----King word to him about this.

Now I can understand why she had this thing about men, and why she didn't want to sleep with me, because of what her step-father had done to her as a child who was only fourteen years old

I sat there not believing that this shit took place, and like she had said her own mother knew that this dog was having his way with her daughter; the child that she carried for nine months. I guess "LOVE" will make one do some crazy ass shit. Man, this kind of shit is enough to piss off a dead man.

WHAT YOU DID

As time moved on, I didn't see too much of Jennifer, but she did call and check to see how I was doing. One day I received a call from her saying "Dad" we need to talk! I said to myself "DAD" what this dad shit is? I didn't know that she had given up her family name and took my last name she is now Jennifer C. Armour. It' in the court records. Now I am her adopted father. I don't believe this, I'm kicking the hell out of seventy-eight and now I have a daughter.

About three weeks later there was a knock at my door and there stood Jennifer's grandmother I knew that there was something wrong, because this old lady had never been to my house before. All she said was "Sir" your daughter is in the hospital, she passed out at work and they rushed her to the hospital on 22nd street in San Francisco. I tried to see her, but they would not let me see her, only the family would be able to go in and see her. I need to see my baby. Sir, so that's why I am here at your place. Mr. Armour, I want to go with you to the hospital and find out what's wrong with my baby.

When we got to the hospital, we had to sit around and wait for the doctor. You know how it is in those places No one wants to tell you shit. You'll have to talk with her doctor is all they would tell us, it's the same old shit, sir, you'll have to talk with her doctor. I have been down that road before, sit there half the night before the doctor comes around. Now here he comes, sir are you the father and mother of Jennifer, before the grandmother could say a word, I said yes she is our daughter.

I got this look from her grandmother, who wasn't a bad looking old girl.

There she was just lying there. I said, baby are you okay? What happen to you? The doctor said that my blood pressure had drop so low that I passed out. When I ask him? He gave me that old crazy ass doctor look and said that she isn't getting enough IRON in her body, and that's what cause her to pass out. She will have to stay overnight here in the hospital, so that we can check her out. We stayed for a few hours. Her grandmother could see that Jennifer was tired and needed some rest. I didn't say too much to her grandmother, but I had this feeling that the doctor was not telling me everything about Jennifer and her health. I kissed her good-night and said that I would see you in the morning and that I love you and now you get yourself some rest.

We left and I told her grandmother that I would drop you off at your place. She said Mr. Armour; I want to go back to your place, because you and I need to have a talk. Now I'm saying to myself why do you want to go back to my place and what do you and I have to talk about? When we arrived back at my place. I ask her is she would like a cup of tea or something. No she said, but I would like a drink, because I just want to know have this child ever told you about her child hood and are you F_____King this child? Wow! I wasn't looking for that and didn't really believe what she had said, "Are you F_____king this child?

Now, hell I was the one that needed that drink after that. I said to her lady, first of all she is my daughter, and second of all I'm not like her step-father, and to ease your mind, I'm not F_____King this child as you so put it. You know sometimes after a few drinks that's when a lot of people start shit, damn, this lady didn't have a drink, she came right out saying just what was on her mind. Now, this was my kind of a lady, know game playing, speaking what was on her mind. I knew right then that me and her (Jennifer's grandmother) was going to be okay with each other, because she was up front about things and how she felt when it came right down to her Granddaughter.

Damn, why couldn't other women that I had met be up-front like this lady was with me? She didn't need that drink to express herself and just how she felt about things. Well Jennifer is out of the hospital and I told her that she needed to stay at the house for a while, so that I could watch out for her, and when she felt better she could go home. I did need some sun shine in the house and bring this place back to life. Jennifer stayed at the house for three weeks and then she went home.

That was a very good three weeks for me, because I had someone to talk with and worry about and take care of them. On May 1, 2010, a day that I shall never forget. Jennifer came over and she was crying. I had never seen this woman cry before, and we had known each other for a while, and we had grown on each other as a family. Sometimes I felt that this woman had ICE WATER for blood. She just stood there looking at me. I said baby what's wrong? All she said was that the mother F_____er, mother F_____ was dead. I was trying to understand who she was talking about. She just stood there looking at me with tears in her eyes.

Man! These wasn't those kinds of tears when you are hurting, damn, they were tears of HATE.

I stood there, waiting for her to say something, but she didn't speak, all she did was to turn around and walked right out of the door. Now, I am standing there with my fingers up my ass, wondering just what's going on with this lady. Who I had taken as my daughter and loved her like she was my very own child. One week had gone by and still no answer from her. I was worried, had something happen to her? I kept on calling her place and each time no answer, so I left a voice mail for her to call me. I didn't know what to do who to call to check on this lady.

Three more days has come and gone, still no word from her Then on May 11, at 2:30 in the morning Jennifer shows up at my house. Looking like shit had hit her in the face, and a Mack truck had ran over her ass. All she said was "Dad, hold me please, don't let me go, but I really wanted to let go of her, because she smell like shit, and the only thing that could really help her, was some Dove Soap and some hot water. There was only one thing left for me to do and that was to give this woman a hot shower (damn, I wish that I had some of that soap that grandmother used to make out in the back yard)

I had never seen her body before. I got her things off of her and took off mine also. I didn't want to get all wet while I gave her a bath. I began to soap her down and my mouth flew open, there they were? Those marks that she had told me about. They were old now, but you could still see the marks where they had been. Remembering what she had told me about her stepfather. Damn! What kind of DOG was he?

I finish cleaning her body, all of time that I was washing her and her body; she just stood there like she was lost in space, not saying a word to me. I dried her off, and still looking at those marks. I could feel this pain deep down inside of my gut. I put something's on her and got her into bed. I felt this warm hand holding onto mine, hearing this voice saying "don't leave me." I lay with her, and I could feel the tears as they began to flow from her eyes, onto my skin burning like hell. The next morning when we woke up, she rolled over and looked at me. I could see the question in her yes? I kissed her on the forehead and said "no baby." She just said thank you.

I hugged her and let her know that I cared about her and that she was SAFE in my arms.

We finely got out of bed and all she had on was that tee-shirt without and underwear own. I had never been in a house with a woman walking around without any underwear on. I gave her my bath robe to put on, hell after all I am human, plus that boy had come alive, and this was not the time for that boy to be acting all crazy like. I ask her if she wanted to talk, she said that I have told you that it all started with my step-father, and just what he did to me, and what he made me do to him. Damn, we see and hear about shit like this on TV, it passes by some of us, because it's not our family and we don't even know these people or understand them, and what's going on with them.

We sit there in outer space and ask ourselves! How could a thing like this be? How could it happen to a child in her own home? Then one day that shit hits home... You find out that Uncle George has been doing that to your baby sister, creeping into her bedroom playing like his sorry ass was drunk Now tell me that life don't suck. Man, then you ask yourself that one question that brings tears to your eyes and pain into the HEART? Did mama know about this? Uncle George was tapping on baby sis! Hate like hell to say this, but shit like this has been going on for years, in some homes and WE turn our backs on shit like this. Man if one of my family members had been doing this to my baby sis, his or her sorry ass would be out there on 12 mile road. Better still every time that took a bath and saw those marks that I had cut into their body, they were there to remind them of what they had done to baby sis.

"Better still the WORD was that if you F-----K with baby sis that was like F-----king with me"

Jennifer wanted me to attend the service with her! I ask her" are you sure that you want me there? Hell yes! I want you there so I can show my sorry ass mother just what a real step-father is like, Dad, All I want you to do is just walk with me to the family row. No she didn't have to ask me that twice' because I wanted to see this man, wanting to view the body myself. I left her and found me a seat. A lady sitting next to me asks me, sir how long have you known John? I said that I don't even know this man, I'm here with my daughter Jenifer his step-daughter.

This lady who was sitting next to me was John's second wife; He had been married twice before marring Jennifer's mother. She just looked at me and didn't say a word with her mouth wide open. Man, if looks could kill, then my ass was dead.

Now it was time for the family to view the body, but for some reason my eyes came to rest on Jennifer, she had this little Black bag with her. I could tell that she was speaking some kind of words over him as she dusted his body with some kind of dust. I heard her mother cry out "Oh No!" Jennifer didn't return back to her seat. In fact she just walked right of the service.

As time went by, I didn't see too much of Jennifer. Then one day I got this call from her saying dad we need to talk. Man, when ever this woman used that word "DAD", hell I knew that something was up. Sure baby, come on over, is it something that I should be worried about? Not really. When she got to the house, she put a warm kiss on the forehead and said "Dad I am going to have a baby! Now talk to me child. How long are you? Who is he? Has he got any babies running around town? Is he married? Some of us worry when our daughters come to us saying that soon they shall become a mother. Now I had some concerns! Was this a one night-stand? A weekend type thing or what?

Before I could say another word, she said that he was not married and don't have any kids running all over town. Dad, Fred lost his wife some time ago daddy. (Now this blew my Fruit of the looms off) I want you to give me away. Wow! How could I say no to this woman who had given up her family name and took on my last name of Armour, and who has always had my back.

GONE FROM ME

Well now I'm here out on the open road trying to keep up with the Big Dogs the eighteen Wheelers bound for Detroit with joy in my heart. Now all I have to do is just stay on I-80 East from California until out side of Chicago, and then switch over to I-94 East... Home here I come. As I drive towards Detroit, there is one thing that I have to remember that she and I can't be like Mr. and Mrs. Jones, because she is a married woman.

Now, yet we did find some time to spend with each other, and it was all good, but always looking over our backs to see who is watching us. Now my brother has a place there in Canada, but old crazy ass me didn't think about that place because it just might bring back some of the good times that I had when my ship was in Vancouver when I was in the navy. Wow! A weekend in Canada. Shit what was I thinking about? Take another man's wife over there for the weekend! It would have been all good, because we wouldn't have had to worry about anyone seeing us. It was about that time for me to leave and I was thinking, maybe next year would even be that much better, because I knew just the place for our weekend meeting over there in Canada. I had to be getting back to California had a wedding date.

That day was almost here, I felt good, a father and a grandfather at that. The wedding party wasn't too big, about twenty-five in all, plus I had gain a son-in-law. We left the church to pose for a few pictures outside. Then this Black car came rolling up, and the next thing that I knew the air shattered by gun shots, and a mass panic ensured as everyone was ducking for cover, in all of this madness, nobody was paying any attention to her (Jennifer) I could hear someone calling out "Call 911". Then I saw my daughter in a pool of her own blood from a gaping wound in her side.

I knelt at her side, and she gurgled out the words "Daddy, hold me and I love you. There was no time for a doctor, no time for anything, before I could say a word, her eyes rolled back in her head, and she exhaled a strained breath, my baby was gone.

My baby was gone. She was dead, her White wedding dress and the ground around her that GUSTENED with blood. Her own blood. I cried "my baby is gone, my baby is gone. The image of her laying there. I kept my eyes averted so no one could see my tears. It was too late when the Paramedics came rushing in to take over.

It was all on the Six O'clock news about the drive-by. Once again I found myself sitting in the dark, with drawing, unplugging and disconnecting myself from the rest of the world. That Rain of Pain was once again back in my life. First it was my wife of forty-seven years, and then my youngest son, who was found, shot in his own home, and now this, my baby.

I ask myself "Horace" what do you have left now. What could I say? All I have left now is my Truck, my Dog and the love for a Married woman. I heard those words, "she is gone" but she will never be forgotten.

I thought of all the times that she and I had spent with each other. The talks, the walks, and the times sharing each other's pain. Yet I had never asked her for a picture of herself, and now it's too late to ask her for one now.

About three weeks after the death of Jennifer, her mother came over to the house. Her ass was about three- sheets in the wind, her sorry ass was drunk and she wanted to know if her daughter had left a will? Now kiss my ass on a Sunday morning. This sorry bitch wanted was some money. Mr. Armour I thought you might have known if she had a will and that she had left something for me?

I stood there looking at this drunken ass woman, then I said I'm sorry I don't know if my daughter had made out a will. The "BITCH" got the ass when I said "my daughter" She jumped up tripping over her own two feet trying to get out of the house... Man, I couldn't believe the nerve of that bitch, all she wanted to see if she had anything coming to her. Yes, she had something coming to her, and that was a foot up her sorry ass, now my world had been shot in the ass. Damn, looking back over my life of those that I had lost. It hurt like hell knowing that two members of my family were taken away by the gun.

The sun was fading into an amazing blend of Orange, Yellow and Red hues' I inhaled real deeply, and then I held my breath and exhaling slowly. Here at the water front with Jimmy Smith on and kicking it with him. It's about 64, with a warm sunshine, just a little wind and not too many clouds in the sky. It's just beautiful; the water is still and my man Jimmy is kicking the hell out of that Organ. Makes one just want to throw up your hands, and say kick on Jimmy.

People walking around with their kids, and the kids with their kites, while mom and dad is holding hands; Damn, I wish that I had someone to hold hands with. Looking at all of this makes me look back to when I was a child. I too had a kite, but know dad to share that time with. Right now, I'm going to lay you a side for now, because trying to write this and Jimmy is here doing his thing, can't stand too much more of this.

MAKE A CHOICE

My day started off just great. I got up and went to church this morning. It was not the church that I attend each Sunday, but it was the church that I had walked away from. I went there to pay my respect to them, because I didn't want them to think that I had forgotten about them. I had just finished talking with my girl friend. You know it's funny that sometimes people can say the crazy ass things and it makes you wonder about things and about yourself. We were talking about the past and she just came right out and said that I was prejudice: it's because of the women that I have dated? Now this really got to me like a storm! I ask her why she said a thing like that. All she said was now you think about it? Pat was of light skin, I have light skin and you wife was of Brown skin, but yet you have not dated a Dark skin woman! Now that really got me to really look back over my life at the women that I had dated; maybe she had something there? So let's see. Shirley my first girl friend was of light skin, Carol she too was of light skin, Lee her skin was also of light skin; that's because she was from Korea.

I said to her it's not that I didn't like Dark skin women, it's just that I had never met a Dark skin lady that her and I had a thing for each other. I want say that I would never date a Dark skin woman, because I have seen some Dark skin women who would make you think she was the last supper; and made you wish that you belong to the Clean Plate Club. Hell, besides I have never dated a White woman. I believe that she has this color thing all wrong! Because if I was prejudice and only liked light skin ladies, then I would never dated Betty and married my wife. I didn't say too much about that with her, because the wrong word could have one in deep shit.

It's like they say, you only believe just what you see and think. Hell if she could only have met my Road Dog. Now that's one fine looking Black woman. When I speak of being Black, she is what you might call "blue Black" and I would be just like George Washington' can't tell a lie." I think that I should move on and get away from that skin color thing!

It's funny I can't do it, because that brings back the past about Delta? She was one beautiful Dark skin lady who had "HAIR" on her legs; Shit she had my ass crying; maybe that's why I never dated another Dark skin lady again. Afraid that I might run into another Delta, Damn, I never wish to cry like that again in my life time.

We all have our FEARS about something's, yet my worst fear is of Dark skin women who have hair on their legs or any woman that has hair on their legs. I do find myself looking at ladies arms and legs, if she has lots of hair on her arms and legs, then that bread basket ifs full of hair also, and my ass is running for the hills, too old to cry like that again.

I know that I should get away from things like this, but when I see and met a sister that I might want to get her magic code number, my eyes just wonder to her arms and man if it's hot outside my eyes wonder to those fine brown legs.

Man, if I see something that's there that shouldn't be there. My ass just keeps on going, and run for cover. Maybe right about now someone just might be saying "Old man you must be crazy or out of your rabbit-ass-mind.!

Maybe so, but this is what I feel and have been through in the past.

Right now I'm in the mall doing something that I know for sure that I should not be doing! That shopping. Whenever I get tired of sitting around the house, I hit the malls and find myself buying things even if I don't need them. Today I brought somewhat-knots, now thinking what is I going to do with and where will I put them.

Hell, I think that I should get myself a hobby, and maybe that way I can keep myself out of the mall, and stop spending my money on those things that I really do not need. Then again the mall is a bad place for me to be, because I could hurt my neck by turning it this way and that way checking out the ladies. We are all aware of the different types of women that we run across in the malls. Plus it's a good place to get your thing on. It's Friday, and we all know just what that means? They (the women) are out here doing their thing, spending their money or the old man's money getting ready for the weekend.

I'm here just passing away time, not wanting to go home, because whose there for me, besides Topper my bird, who I find myself talking with him quite often, but always careful of what I say around him, because he has this thing whatever you say around him, he repeats those words and there just might become a time when he just might say the wrong thing when the wrong person is in the house.

Right now I don't have to worry about that because it's only me who's in this house, and I want have to explain why my bird said what he said to her or anyone else. Maybe I'll take in a movie or get me something to eat; it's really no rush to go back to that cold and empty ass house. I have gone that way before and that loneness also ate me alive and once again I found myself out there in the jungle looking for love in all of the wrong places.

Man, let me tell you shit like that can eat your ass alive. Hell, I have run across a hella lot of women out there, some were good and others wanted to take your ass to the Cleaners. Why? All because your dumb ass forgot the rules of the jungle. Some of you understand just where I am coming from because like me you too have been down that road and almost step in quick sand.

Well it's getting kind of late so off to the house. I'm home now playing some songs from the past and remembering a song by Aretha Franklin "Spanish Harlem, Some years ago Red played that song for me and said "Honey do you understand just what she is saying, and what it means? At that time, I didn't understand the message in that song, but after sixty years, now I understand those words, now I'm ready to open that gate and plant that Rose in my garden and watch it grow.

By loving it, honoring it, but most of all respecting it. You no somehow I have never ask this lady to forgive me for the Ultimate Betrayal from walking away from her only to wed another woman and never telling her why I did it. Yet, still hearing those words that have been rolling around inside of my head for over sixty years. "Honey go do what you have to do, but come back to me." Night after night those words has been there, how many nights did those words keep me awake. Wanting to come home to the one that got away, the very one that I can't forget.

Sometimes I want to cry out and say Lord Help me, but like they say that the Lord helps those that help themselves. You know life has away to make one think about the past? How would it had been if I had married Red from the get go? Would it have lasted? Would I had become like so many other young men, not ready to settle down and have a bunch of babies and unable to support those kids. Even while I sit here with that crazy ass smile on my face. I hear those words that some of you just might be saying, Man, it's wrong to be in love with someone else's wife.

Tell me, can you stop drinking water? That's how I felt about this woman. It's like a Fire that's burning inside of me, and no matter what I tried to do, that fire got hotter and hotter. It was that kind of pain which wasn't too bad. But at times it was joyful to the soul. I kept telling myself that the day is coming when she and I shall cross over that line and become as of one. I understand that I have a job to do, discovering ways to do it and get it right the first time.

I'm captivated by her strength and the way her beauty is manifested in her eyes, is this love or am I still here blowing smoke up my ass? I don't know! You tell me? Like so many other times when I look back on my life, I see some of the things that I have done wrong, only wishing that I could go back and correct them. Like I have done with my daughters, given more to one and given less to the other daughter who is of my blood, the very same blood that flows through out my body.

I can still hear those very words that I spoke to you. Francis as a child you never asked for much or asked for anything. Even today, you have not put any demands on me, as a child I wasn't there with you or for you. Baby, your words come to me, the words are of warmth and deep love even if I haven't been in your life.

My other daughter Jennifer, who we are not bound by blood, but by love as a father and a daughter. You were the sunshine of my life; you became that daughter that I so longed to have in my life. I can't forget the guilt that I felt and the hurt that's deep down inside of me. This shitty feeling. It's like a fire that want go out. I know that this sounds crazy, but the back off my throat ached knowing when you were hurting Jennifer my arms were there for you, but away from my other daughter when she was hurting.

Baby, I gave you love, but when Francis needed my love I wasn't there to give her love. Jennifer maybe if I had let those feelings out a long time ago and reached out more to my other daughter, then this pain of GUILT would not have eaten my ass alive. Yet, this is something that I will have to live with.

I need to get away, where can I go to or what will I do when I get to this place where I want to be? So I left California seeing the very wonderful hillsides as I drove to Detroit. Three days out here on the open road. Damn, that drive made me want to change my way of life. I needed this trip, because it told me that I should change my lifestyle. I need to get out more and maybe I just might get me a Road Dog to travel with me when I go out on my weekend runs.

I felt so good just seeing all of those wonderful places, there just for the taking, coasting you nothing but time and some money for your food and gas and a cot and a hot shower. I made a stop at the Salt Flats in Salt Lake City, UT. Man that salt was so White and bright burning into your eyes. Got me some of that Salt had to have it, for who knows when I might pass this way again. My next stop was at the Purple Heart Trail Rest Area. I liked the words that were posted there for all to see and feel those words deep down in your heart.

"FREEDOM IS NOT FREE"

As I drove on my way to Detroit, I could not help but to think back to the time when I had my RV. Me and the wife out seeing the other side of the states. Now here I am in Detroit after that three day drive, need a hot bath and some sleep. I must be ready for Donna Jean Birthday. Last year when I was here in Detroit, I took her to the Race Track, because she had never been to the track before, plus it was her birthday. I want say which one that it was, but it was up there.

I must cut out on you, because I must be off to see her; she was the other reason that I came back home to Detroit. Wow! The last time that I held that woman in my arms, feeling the heat from her body, plus it had been sometime that I have had a shot of the Wild Cherry. Man, I got a nut, just thinking about it. The main reason that I came back here was for me and this lady to sit down and talk about what we should do about our life; now that WE both aren't married. She too had lost her husband, just as I had lost my wife. For some reason I felt that Red, had some doubts about our relationship! She thinks that I'm afraid to get married. I do believe that she's the one that's afraid of getting married. I have tried to tell her that I wouldn't allow myself to wonder off into another woman's arms and end up in her bed.

Maybe it's that move from Detroit out to California and not knowing anyone but me. I can understand that, when you are born in one place and haven't moved to another state, it's hard; besides she has her own home and so-call-family there, and soon she will be kicking the hell out of eighty years old. For me, in a way of speaking its no big deal, because half of my life I have been on the move;

Some of my friends tell me that I should sell my home and move back to Detroit! All that sounds good, but what if this lady starts to act a fool and put my sorry ass out. Now I have sold my home, and where can I go? Maybe it would be better for both of us, if we had a summer and a winter home? She could come stay with me in the winter time, and I could stay with her in the Summer time. Now if SHIT gets crazy we both can just walk away and return back to OUR OWN HOMES. Yet there is still so much more to learn about her and there is a TON of things going through my mind as I sit here writing about my life, and I am still seeking that very important answer Who I am?

Let me ask you something or just put yourself in my place have you ever wondered who you were! Am I crazy for wanting to know the answer to this question? Yet there are other questions that I need an answer for, but I need your help in helping me to understand that one big question. Damn, I have gone to college and done my studies in General Psychology, and other classes in the Psychology field. Man I have all of this heavy stuff in my head and I still can't get that one answer that I am looking for or must I return back to the mountain top?

This will have to wait until I return back to California, so for now, I'll have to put all of that shit on the side line and enjoy myself while I'm here in Detroit. I know that so far I have only told you what I think that you need to know. Just one more question have I really opened the door on my life, in order for you to really understand me and where I am coming from. I need to apologize to you my readers for not being able to really go deep into my life for you to really understand me and my world, for you to do this you will have had to read my other books: "How Strong is Your Love, and Coming Home."

In order to put my life together and maybe, just maybe you would have understood me, my life and just what makes me tick. Right now I have my first book how Strong is Your Love sitting here next to me. I find myself turning the pages looking for something! What it is, I don't know just what I'm looking for, but something has me looking back there for something. Maybe it's because I was thinking about something that I read about what women should not be like? At that time when I wrote about this, I had ask some of my men friends that question; because at that time I didn't give much thought to it, because I wasn't looking for anyone, but now that my girlfriend and I are trying to make it as one. I ask myself that very same question? What women should not be like? Can I use the answers that some of my side-kicks used what they can't be like; these are some of the answers that I received back from them:

I'm sure that some women will become upset with those answers, and again there will be some who will get the ass, and come right out and say, that these men don't know what the F_____K they are talking. Well here they are.

1. Can't be judgmental
2. Can't load me down with lots of Responsibility
3. Only thinking about her?

The main reason that I'm putting this out there, it's because some time ago I had a friend who was starting to act kind of crazy about our relationship and just a pain in the ass. Like I must do this and that I must do that! Let me put it to you this way I used to have what I called "DOG DAY." This was the time that I spent with my dogs, and all other things took a back seat. What I mean is that I told my family, my doctor and friends not to call me on a Tuesday (which was dog day) because I would not answer the phone or even go out to the doctor's office on this day.

Well to make a long story short, I was spending six nights a week with her and I would not go over and see this lady on this day.(Dog Day) Man, she got the ass about this and wanted to know what was up about this Dog Day shit as she called it? All hell, man she went out of her rabbit-ass- mind, and told me that I had to "MAKE A CHOICE" between her and my dogs, because that was her day also. Damn, I was giving her SIX DAYS a week. All I could do was to tell her that I loved her very much and that I would do anything for her and that I would make a "CHOICE" between her and my dogs?

Well I told "HER" that her SORRY ass had to go, because she didn't know what my dog' means to me and what "WE" had gone through together over the years. You know maybe, just maybe if she had understood me and knew how much that I loved those dogs and "ALL" of the Darkness that we had been through, and then she wouldn't have come up with some "Dumb-Ass-Shit like this. May she and I would still be kicking it now. Hey! She is on the outside looking in.

Damn, now I know what I was looking for when I was reading How Strong was your love. It has to do with my girl friend, thinking that I was afraid to re-marry? I really need to ask myself these questions:

1. Do I want to go down that road again (get married)
2. Am I ready for that!
3. Do I still believe in my old saying? Marry just one time?
4. Is there something holding me back?
5. I don't want to re-marry, because I'm still in love with my dead wife?
6. Did she set me free?

These are something's that I must answer, because I see and talk with other people who have been down this road, and they all say "never again." Well I'm here in Detroit just sitting and waiting for a phone call from my girl friend, to see if she wants to kick it or what, I really would like to go over to Big Mamas for something to eat, some of those Wings and Greens. Well here she is at the front door, looking good. I said to her, I was waiting for your call, but wasn't looking for you like this; so off we went to Big Mamas for some take out food and have dinner at her place. Just the two of us. Damn, the one thing that I can say about Detroit is that it has some women who have it all in the right places. Can't help for looking around while waiting for our food

Now back at her place, this feels real good to have someone to talk with while you have your dinner with a warm smile on their face. Not like being isolated, like I am when I'm back in California. This feels good, just what the doctor ordered. You know how it is after you have had a good meal; you just want to lie down. Can't do that because her young daughter is here, part of my meal just got shot in the ass...

Well back to big brothers house I must go. You know how it is when you are staying at someone else's house you can't stay out to late, plus I don't have a door key, not only that, they had to be up early for church. So once again I had to put things on ice for another day.

The next morning my Road Dog ask me if I wanted to go out to see moms grave and the rest of the family. When we got there I spent some time at each grave, but when I went to see my stepfather graves, we could not find it. My Road Dog said Uncle it's here among the rest of the family. I was looking for his head stone, but there was none. Only a round plug in the ground with a number on it. I said Donna are you sure that this is his spot? All she said that she would look into it and check with the office.

I'm sure that some of you know just what I'm saying, when you are first put into the ground. They put a round stone to mark the grave site. Damn, here it is 2013 and pops passed away in 1961, that's fifty-two years with only marker, in my mind; I was asking myself what's going on? Damn, that my stepfather was there and only a round stone to mark the spot where he lay?

Hell, fifty-two years without a head stone? Oh hell no, I had to do something about this, because this man was good to me. So I gave Donna the money for a head stone. It was only fitting that I should do so, because he (pops) was more than a stepfather to me, he was my friend.

LADY IN THE RED DRESS

Friday night me and Donna are out at the Race Track, One Dollar Hot Dogs and two Dollar Beers. What can I say, there she was standing tall in that Red Dress, kind of short, some people might say, but for me it's just right. A find Dark skin sister, some would look at her and they just might say "The Blacker the Berry, the Sweater the Juice."

Wow! Just looking at her, makes me want to take her ass to the Post Office and stamp Air Mail on her ass and send her home to me, out there to California, One gets to thinking about those things when it's just you and you don't have that Special one at your side. Hell let me draw you a picture of her; and you'll see just where I'm coming from.

She was about 5'6 maybe a little bit shorter, because she had those hills on. Skin smooth as silk, a short hair cut, now maybe up stairs. I would say about a 32 and as your eyes move down to a 24 in the waistband you can't help but to let your eyes move on down to those hips, about 36 or 38. God, just right to lay your head on and wonder just what lay down below as your thoughts wonder through your head, saying Lord to the Day, there is Lilly in the valley.

Hell man! Maybe I have been alone to long and this is one of those times that has me wanting to reach out and touch something and hold them, or it close to the soul; but as one gets older you only want that very special one, but looking at her in that Red Dress, remembering what grandmother would say "boy it that's not your cup of "TEA" don't put any sugar in it, but sometimes you just want to put a little "DAB" more in there, so you can say "How sweet it is."

So for the time that I am here in Detroit, I shall get the pleasure of being able to lay back and say those words. Oh! How sweet it is, but come next month September when I return back to California, it will be me and the "Salt Peter Pill'" all over again.

One day soon, I shall walk out into the back yard to that Blue Trash Bin, and open that top and say" bye Salt Peter" and thank you for being with me on those cold and lonely ass nights. Man, maybe if I had not seen that Lady in The Red Dress; I might not be sitting here writing these words, or letting my mind wonder off, thinking just how wonderful to have someone like lady in The Red Dress.

Well in a few minutes me and the family will be off to Canada where my brother has a place, I keep trying to get Red to come with us, but she doesn't have a passport. I keep on telling her that she should get a passport. Just thinking that her and I could come over here on a weekend, just the two of us and enjoy ourselves. No dogs, no phone calls and those crazy ass people who like to drop by at the very wrong time of the day or night just to say hi, how you are doing. Now that's an ass kicker when you are with that special person, trying to get a shot of that Wild Cherry. So we will have to do something about that passport thing.

Well we are off for the weekend, for me it will give me some more time to work on this book while we are here in Canada. Just sit back and checking out things as Donna drives makes me want to get out and see things and enjoy life. Just looking at some of the homes with tin roof on them, makes me think back to those days when I was overseas in Korea and the Philippines.

Wow! Just hearing the rain drops hitting that tin roof while you are getting it on, and that soft breeze coming through the window cooling the two of you off. All hell! That's all good. I guess it will be a long time before I can hear the rain on a tin roof again. Just once if I could talk here (Red) into coming with me for a weekend over to this place, then Please let it rain, let it rain; but mean while I can dream can't I? Just thinking if I had not came over here where the land looks green for miles, I would be in the Dream Cruise moving down Woodard Ave, with all of the others in their Old Classic Cars, but there comes a time that one must give up something for the greater good.

It has been sometime that I had been over here to Windsor. This is the place to be, out here in the open space. I could go for this. Well we are on our way back to Detroit, so my dream trip is over with, until the next time that I return back to the Motor City. Maybe by that time Red will have gotten that passport.

GOOD NEWS/ BAD NEWS

Sometimes news comes in twos? The Good news and then the Bad news. Today is one of those days that the news came twice? The bad news is that a good friend is down and out, with his wife standing at the cross road, of not knowing what to do! I'm here in Detroit kicking back when that call came. My friend who I can't speak of his name, because I don't have permission to speak of his name out loud. So let's call him Willie. I and Willie go way back over fifty years. First I received a phone call from Baby-girl, (that's the name that I will address her by) she called me and said that Willie was sick and not doing too well.

You know how we do! Say thank you for calling me and not give it much thought. Then I received a phone call from his wife, telling me that he was gone. I could feel that it was more to it then what she was trying to explain. What was going on? All she said Armour, I need to talk with you, because there is no one else that I could turn too but you, because of my English; people might not understand me in what I am trying to say. I knew where she was coming from because of her broken English.

I could understand her, because I was married to someone from overseas in her home town. Knowing how some of us state siders are, we have that off the wall shitty way of looking down on those who do not speak English, or the correct English. Anyway, she has more worries than that English thing! You see she don't drive, and don't know how to get around town, her big problem is this lady is new here in the states.

Man, that's am ass-kicker in its self not speaking good English and not knowing how to get around town. Plus I'm not sure how she and the in-laws are getting alone? I am really worried about this lady, now that her husband has passed away. Now who will be there for her? I truly understand all of this, because my wife might have gone through the very same thing as this lady is facing now, but we had two grown sons.

Yet, one night when I and my wife were lying in bed checking out the TV, out of the blue she (my wife) said "Honey" if something ever happen between us, I hope that I shall go first? Man that's a trip, you laying there next to your love one and they start speaking of death. I said Lucia, why do you speak of this.

She just held my hand and looked me right into the eyes and said "if something ever happen to you! Who will take care of me? I could understand all of this, because one thinks about these things when you are far away from home and in a land that you don't even know anything about.

Now, for some good news, because that bad-ass news sometimes makes some of us want to go down to the board walk and drown in our own tears. (The board walk in which I'm speaking of it's the BAR) I had just had an inter-view with a radio station concerning one of my books, and all went well with that inter-view. Wow! That blew my mind, they wish to have a second review of my book call "How Strong is Your Love". Man, I didn't know if I should shit or go blind.

There was a very nice story in the Daily Republic News Paper in my home town in Fairfield, California, and then a TV inter-view. Damn, all of this makes me feel ever so good, plus when I wrote that book "How Strong is Your Love" I never dream that something like this would happen to me, or that my Special Angle would allow something this wonderful to come my way.

Like they say, "good things come to those that wait" and this is the second GOOD thing that has happen to me. The very first Good thing that happens to me took place on February 14, 1959. That's the day that I married Lucia Manelse who became my wife Lucia Manelse Armour for the next forty-seven years. Now this! Two very wonderful events in my life. What more could I ask for? Now I must play the wait and see game. All of this is just incredible events for me to deal with at one time. Like that old saying! "A good thing does come to those that wait."

Damn, part of that NEWS was just what I needed, but that other news,

I could have done without. Well that's the only news that I have for you right now, but I shall let you in on the reviews from the radio station when I receive them back.

Today was one of those days! First off I Had an appointment to be placed into the tube for my CT scram, it's because by me having Stage Three Lung Cancer sometime ago, I have to take this type of check-up alone with my lab works, Anyway after my test something told me to go see that movie "War Room". Not wanting to go by myself, I called my Road Dog and ask her if she would like to attend the movie with me. Not really understanding what the movie may be like, off we went to see this movie that many people have spoke about it. Even those in the church have spoken of this movie also.

So here we are fighting this crowed of people, you know how it is when you and your road-dog are out at the movies, and you see someone that you don't want to see, knowing that later on, the question will come up? "Who was that lady with you at the movies Armour? Damn can't I go out to a movie with someone, but when that person turns out to be someone from your church, well you just know what the Sunday talk will be all about?

Girl did you see who Brother Armour was with! Child I didn't know that he was running around after Sister Brown. That old dog should be ashamed of himself out with that young woman like that. Little did they know that Sister Brown was not a spring chicken, she might look young, but she is really up there in age, plus she has been around the block a few times?

You have seen some of those women, who could pass for around forty, but they are up there in age, but if you really knew her, she is kicking the hell out of seventy-five. Hell let them talk, this just might be one of those cases when someone is thinking or wishing 'that should have been me."

Yet some of those church people have a way of turning water into FIRE.

Well like I have said before you do your thing and I'll do my thing, but watch out for which way that the water flows. That was on September 24, 2015, this morning my doctor called and said Armour your test was looking good, and remember that we will have to repeat this test again next year Anyway let's return back to the movie "War Room. Wow it was good. I do mean good. It's one of those movies that I feel that many of us should see, and understand how the Lord works in OUR life everyday of the week. 365 days a year. Go see it if you can or just get it on a DVD. When it comes out, and then you'll understand just what I'm talking about, and what the War Room is all about.

I'm just sitting around kicking it after the movie at my road-dog place, out of left field she ask me why don't I get married or why aren't you married yet? You know where I'm coming from? Well that's one hell of a question? Why I'm not married? It's that I want to be sure of this, is this what I really want! The question is Will I get married just to be doing it! Or will I marry the right one, and not someone who's looking for what I can do for them?

Speaking about getting married why aren't you married yet? Hell Armour it's a jungle out there, some sorry ass dude comes alone and wants to play games. You know just what I mean, the ones who are always sticking their hands out or those who thinks you are that sugar-mama. Shit, the one that's there even before Christmas time comes around thinking that you need a man Armour, let me tell you something, I have been out here and almost step in quick sand and I have seen those sorry men sitting on the side line licking their chops waiting for you to come their way. They know that you are retired and have your own home, with a few coins in the bank.

Shit, I don't understand why I have to get married just to be happy. Armour, I look at some of my girlfriends and hear their story about the second time around of doing that thing. Sometime I ask myself do I want to go through all of that bull-shit again. Hell no. I don't think so. Sweets I can understand that, you see I have tried to meet someone new, but have had some damn bad luck in meeting the right one, like Tess with her crazy ass, she was only out for what she could get, and her ass would be off in a heartbeat, in places of the unknown.

Armour, I will tell you the truth, I like kicking it with you, because you aren't asking me for anything. We do what we want and if we don't like it, it's no big thing... We just go our own way and hook up somewhere down the road. Like a dog in heat, I said to myself Armour, man give it one more try. Hell what do you have to lose? So here I am off again looking for love in all of the wrong places; again it wasn't to be for me, after all of those events, got me thinking damn this isn't for me so go back home to your cage, because it's a bitch out here and this jungle will eat your ass alive.

Like so many others when you reach that age you ask yourself what I want. Well I want someone in this house, I'm sick of being alone, with no one for company or to hold tight and feel her soft skin which is smooth as silk and softer than Georgia cotton, and the heat from her body drives you right out of your rabbit-ass-mind. The big question is do I have to get married just to receive all of this? Or will the jungle eat my ass up before I can reach the first water hole?

Oh, how I wish that I had someone to talk too or tell me just what I must do. You see I had someone once like that before, but she is gone from my life. Her name was Jennifer. Well that's another story and for another time.

I got a double-ass kicking that day. One ass kicking was by this girl and the second ass kicking was for fighting in school. Now don't you laugh, you see back in the day there were some girls that could hold their own with the best of the boys. You see I had seen her (that girl who kick my ass) get it on with other girls and had seen her take on two boys at one time. These guy were some of the best around. I knew that if I could take down the "Queen Bee" I had it made, but as it turned out I became second to the "Queen Bee" in school.

Even as I write this story with that shit eating smile on my face. I wonder what ever happen to her! Did she ever marry and stop running around kicking some ass. If she did marry how many kids does she have and where is she at now?

It's funny that all of the time that I was in Detroit, I never thought of this lady. She was just someone from my past. Maybe I'll go out there on Face Book or call some of my old Class mates and ask about her.

Maybe someone will remember her and knows just where she is or just what has happen to her. I think that it would be funny talking with her about old times. Now that really would be something to laugh about, speaking with that girl who whip your ass, but most of all to let you NO that your Shit didn't STINK.

Sometime the past has a way of easing back into our life, just thinking about the one girl that kicked my ass! I think that this is one part of my life that I should let it be still, because the past is the past; after all that was back in 1948, a lot of my old classmates may have gone-by-the-way-side and she just might be one of them.

Then on the other hand, if I did run across this lady, would she remember me? And that she kicked my ass when we were in Moore School back then? Or would it be the other way around! Yo! Armour man remember that time when we were in Moore School, that I kicked your sorry ass on the play ground, and I was still the "Queen Bee." It's funny how some of the things from the past can bring a smile to ones face and a laugh from the heart when we were only kids at that time, but after that she and I became the very best of friends.

Now, "today" if something like that did take place man, there would be hell to pay, because some of these young kids today would shoot first and not even ask a question. Oh! How things have change from back then to now. I don't know what has happen to this world or to OUR kids today? Shit, I just can't leave some of the Adults out, because in some places it's like the "OLD WEST" with Billy the Kid running wild as hell.

Well let's get off of that kick, because I'm sure that I have much better things to talk about, but that shit is a part of our world and like they say "man we have to live with it." AS for me, I'm back on that old path running through the jungle still looking for something? But this time I walk slowly and carry a "Big, Big Stick" because some of those lionesses have learn some new tricks just to suck your ass in; but this time I am ready to hit and run. I do mean run like hell. Man, I'm tired of playing games and hearing that same old "BULL-SHIT"

Yes baby, what CAN you do for me or they are coming to the table with X and Y, but wanting your ass to leave with Z (zip) I know that this don't sound like that old Armour, but it's a ""NEW DAY" and a new game. Maybe that trip to Detroit had me thinking and knowing that I must change my life style. Yes, I have a girl friend, but I have to make sure that she is in the same "BOAT" with me. You know what I mean?

Today it looks like getting married is "NO" big thing anymore. This time I have gone down this road only looking for was a "ROAD DOG, and NOT A GIRLFRIEND OR A WIFE."

I have had this talk with my girl friend about the summer and winter home, but I'll have to sit back and see just what she really thinks about this. Now, please don't get me wrong. I love this woman, but she and I have a small problem and it's that WE know of each other, but we don't really know each other? The question is has she really gotten over her husband yet? It has only been three years that he has passed away. Now is that enough time for her to really say "Yes" let's have that summer and winter home.

I'm not getting cold feet, but I have to look at the big picture, would she want to give up her home and move out here to California? What about me!

Am I ready to deal with those cold ass winters that they have in Detroit? That's why I say that she and I must be in the same boat. No, I don't have anyone (for sure in my life) here, but when one gets about my age, one wants to be sure if this is what one really wants. Lives is too short to F---K-up and open the wrong door, plus I have something that I must clear up and it's not marriage. I had this thing about if I ever got married it would be for keeps and only marry for just "One time." I need to know am I still thinking about that ONLY one time marriage and one time only. Now you can see why I say that this lady and I really do need to know each other.

I feel that we should live together for sometime before we make that very big move. That's why I told her that we should have that summer and winter home. That way we could learn so much about each other. Is all of this just me? Because I have seen and met so many people around my age who have gone down that road, and don't want to return back down that road again. Some people say that it's better the second time around. Am I worried that my second time around want be as good as my first marriage! The thing is I'm worried that I can't love someone new as much as I did my wife.

The one question that I must face is the real reason that I don't want to re-marry it's because I'm still in love with my wife? Lucia has been gone for almost ten years now, but is this love for her that strong? That I don't want to give it up! This is the question that has really been getting to me! Is that's when I wrote my very first book "How Strong is Your Love" was this what I spoke of? That the love that I and Lucia (my wife) had for each other! Is this why I can't allow myself to really LOVE someone else?

Will Lucia be that second person in my life, like it was in the past or will it be like that "SONG" saying three people in my bed? Me and my woman and my wife who is still in my head? Maybe I need to return back to the mountain top, one more time in order to get my shit in one bag, because at the age of eighty-one only to wake up and find out that the grass wasn't as Green as you thought it was, or say to oneself, man you really did F_____k up this time.

It's funny in a way that we all just run around in life, doing this and that. Somehow we never think about tomorrow, or the very next day. Then here it comes, not to you but to a friend. "DEATH" We all know that one day death will come knocking at our door. Are we ready for it? I don't think so, but what about our love ones? Did we look out for them! Did we put that Golden

Egg aside and say that this is for my wife, daughter or that crazy ass one that has been running all around town acting crazy and being that damn fool! Somehow we don't think about these things. We have seen this on the TV, when something goes down and there is no "Insurance" for that person; we are asking others to help carry the load.

Why am I speaking of this! Is there something that I have not done? I don't think so. I believe that I have put things in order and what I want done in the end. Then why must I speak of "Death" at a time like this? You see I lost someone and the family didn't know which way to turn and where to go too... It's sad that when you have lost that love one, you are in the dark not knowing what to do or how about getting things done; my good friend is gone, and did he look out for her? Who will be there for her? I don't know what he has done for her, speaking as a friend, but I do hope that he has put that GOLDEN EGG up for her, because those other things do come up!

What about me! I should have gotten that. He/She was my ex. (I know that this is crazy but things like this does come up in some cases) I knew that I have something coming to me! I can understand this because this very THING was placed on my door step by my daughter's mother. Did my baby leave me anything; this lady thinking that she will get something, but only to leave with nothing at all?

My friends this is what ONE speak of as a "WAKE UP CALL" because that call can bring joy or it can be a Bitch, for those of you who are sitting around with your fingers up your ass and have not sat down and got your THINGS in order, Please do so now.

Sitting here looking back over my life, man many things come running through my head. Like the times when I wondered if I would ever see a Black man in the White House? Not the one who is walking around cleaning the dishes off of the tables or setting them up, but one who's there as the President of the United States of America.

Man, not only that, but to hear about some of the other crazy ass-bull-shit that's going on in the world. Like that Pastor in Brazil who had the congregant sucks his D_____K in church. (Wow! in all the places, the church) saying it was his "Holy Milk" and convince women to take his sperm in the name of God.

Now if you think that shit was crazy, what about that other one who Strips females church members down on the river front praying for them to get a husband. Shit like that takes the cake. This might sound crazy to some of you, but these are TRUE facts that this world has gone to hell.

So for some of you that think that I am blowing smoke up your ass, well baby just check out the news on the TV, and please come back and tell me just what SEE or HEAR.

THE QUESTION

Here I am out here at the Cemetery a very wonderful day and the Sun is out and there is a still in the air. For some of you here in Detroit know this place or maybe you have been out here, because of family or friends; it's a place where we all will one day call home. I'm here to pay my respect to the family. Grandfather, all of my brothers, my sister, mom, and my stepfather (Pops) there are others, but I don't know where they lay, because some of them were before my time and some of the records have been lost or that round marker has been removed.

I wish to thank my family for coming out here and keeping things up. Looking around I see very few people here today, but maybe there will be more because of the Labor Day Weekend coming up; about that time I should be almost ready to return back to California, knowing that I did pay my respect to members of my family saying that "I have not forgotten you and that Love you all". Looking at the other graves, wondering will someone come out to just say "I miss you?

Sometimes we don't take the time out and come here, because they are gone and they are not a part of our life any more. This makes me think about Jennifer my daughter, who I lost by the gun. I find myself going out to visit her every week. Sometimes twice a week. Just sitting there and talking with her.; knowing that she can't answer me back, but it's a way of getting things off of my chest. Yet there are some things that you just don't want to talk with others about, because they just might not understand you or they just might tell the world what's going on in your little world.

Man, talking with the dead, it's only you and them, plus they (the dead) want run around and put your stuff in the wind; because you know how we do it, because there are some things that we just can't keep to our self. Any way lets return back to why I or you came out here in the first place. That's to pay Our respect to the ones that we lost; as I look around I see head stones on one side and markers or flat stones on the other side with grass that has almost covered them up, or because the lack of T.L.C.

I'm not trying to knock people for not coming out here, because some might not have a ride, and again there could be other reasons for this.

Well I'm at grandfathers resting place which is right across from my dad, brothers and near my stepdad. Mom and my sister and other brother and sister-in-law are on the other side of the grave yard with that Black stone and Red Rose on it. Hey man! Can't stay to long because we have other things to do, besides the sun will be going down soon, this place want look the same and a crazy ass feeling comes over one when you are out here after dark Some people says that's the time when the dead comes alive and walk around and talk with each other.

I don't know if this is true or not, but I don't want to be around to find out about this, if the dead do walk around and talk to each other. Well I'm sure that you have other things to do, besides talk about this place and those tales that the dead do walk around and talk with each other.

I am sitting in the car with family on the way back home, and was thinking that somewhere down the line, I had told you that things do happen for a reason. I can't remember if I made that statement in my first book "How strong is you love, or did I speak those words in "Coming home? Yet! I do recall saying that "things happen for a reason. What I mean about this is that I met this lady when I was out there "CRYING" for help on one of those chat lines.

We talk and got to know a little about each other, and I explain to her that I had just written a book covering my life. One day I got this email from her and I could tell by her actions that this lady was Hot and upset by the things that she said in that email. Maybe at that time she didn't understand that I was "crying" out for help, and wanting someone to hear my cry! Oh yes she did! Yet from her emails I learn so very much about her. We would call each other and talk about my book and why I wrote it. This lady wanted to know did I feel sorry about the things that I had written concerning my life.

Any way as time went on this lady and I became very close, yet there was a mystery about this lady! I wish that I could tell you who she is but I can't do that, but I can tell you that she is warm, smart and will tell you where to get off of the train at. Sometimes when I call this lady I lie to her, saying just checking to see how you are doing, but the truth I just wanted to hear her voice. I don't quite understand what's happening in my life, but something is crazy going on and has me wondering? What I mean by this whenever I go on Face Book and deal with those things like who is your love one, or what is your number one color, or who will you marry.

She is there in my life and my Astrology Zodiac reading, my trips, close friends, and the one that I am thinking of. Hell, all of this has me wondering what's going on. I have never said anything to this lady or wondered about her being in my life or my love life. Yet, she is there. It looks like we are always coming up together in all kinds of events. I don't have the time actually to read through all of those emails and absorb what it's trying to tell me. Yet, these events have my attention.

Is there an indication that there is something "at play" in my life, which is driving me to seek some answers or some type of guidance in preparation for a big change that might take place in my life? Is it quite possible that I have been swimming up the stream against the currents in my love life.

When I had those dreams about my wife, is this what she has been telling me in those dreams, "Honey swim downstream with the current? Wow! Have I noticed that obstacles and challenges that I now face are becoming too much to ignore. Am I about to enter into a BIG period of change in my life, am I prepared for it? Is it about time for the fog that I have been drifting through has been lifted to unveil the path that I need to take? Do I think so? Man that is one hell of a question.

Now, I am asking myself what does all of this has to do with me when I went back to Detroit in July of 2015? Shit something happened to me or came over me, making me want to change my life and life style. Sometimes when you aren't around people for a long time, but when you have some time to spend with them, you learn so much about them that you didn't know before. How they think, or act or what's important in their life,. Now I ask myself "armour" where do you fit into picture? What part of the pie will you end up with? Or are you coming to the table with X & Y, and that you will leave with???

Now I'm sorry that I got off track about this lady that has become a part of my life, well the ass kicker of all of this, you see this lady is my play-sister. We both have so much in common. Born in the same month, on the same day, but different years, yet I feel close to this lady. Is my play-sister the wrecking ball in my life? Is this what they mean when one speaks of that "Things happen for a reason? Like that time when me and my girlfriend was sitting around and she said "Armour" I want to ask you a question!

Do you love me as a Black woman? Damn, now where did that come from, and damn sure didn't see that one coming. Now that might sound like a crazy ass question, so I gave it some thought! How does one love a Black woman? Well I am going to say something, and I'm sure that someone will get the ass about what I am going to say, but it has been said that the "Black Woman" is the hardest woman in the world to love!!!! Is this because of that Stereotype that has been said about Black Women!!! Is it because some Black women have an Air about them and you can't please them.

Now, this is a question that I have asked myself also? You see that my wife who I was married to for quite some time was not Black? Now I find myself in love with a Black woman. Man, I want lie about this (that marriage thing) I have ask myself time after time and my girlfriend has also ask me could I love and marry a Black woman now that you have lost your wife. I'm sure that she had a reason for asking that question. Maybe thinking that if I should ever love another woman that I would return back to marry a non-Black woman? I want lie about this, but there is something about being married to someone from overseas.

Sometimes when we write about one self, we want to keep it clean and tell the readers just what they should know or hear. I'm trying to be real about this and up front. Yes! There will be some dirt that will come up about my life; after all we are of TWO PEOPLE. The One that we want you to know and the other ONE that we DON'T want you to know about. Armour, what is it that you don't want US to know about you? Is it your feelings about Black Women? I'm sure that there is someone out there who is wondering how to ask me about dealing with Black women! If it's you, hell speak up! The one question that has always been on your mind ask it of me. "Armour (someone asking a question)" Armour, when was the last time that you have ever loved a Black woman? Well my friends the last time that I have loved a Black woman was in 1958, fifty-eight years ago, and its 2016, and I do find myself back in love with a Black woman. I'm sure that as YOU read this book, one of you might be saying "damn, he is talking about me and this man is TELLING MY STORY, just as it did unfold in my life. "Is he me?" The one side of me that I don't want to come out, for the ENTIRE world to see about who I am!

I can't speak for you, for I can only speak for myself, and tell you my story. Most of all I'm still looking for that answer which has been eating away at my soul, day and night for as long as I can remember, which has been about eighty-one years. That one question is:

"WHO I AM?"

FEELING ASHAME

I don't know just what's going on with me, but sometimes when I try to do the right thing, the wrong things began to unfold in my life with me and the church. Man, I don't know what it is about me and the church, but this is the second time that I have been distracted by a lady in the church. Let me fill you in, some churches when they have Altar call one comes down to the Altar or remain in your row and hold hands with the person standing next to you. There wasn't anyone seated on my left at that time being. Yet I felt this very warm hand holding onto mine. The longer that I held onto this ladies warm hand the hotter it got.

I could feel that heat burning all the way from my hand up my arms and into my body. Here I was trying to pray, but I couldn't because that heat took control of me body. I had seen this lady in church, but never said a word to her; but now I need to learn who she is and more about her. The one thing about a woman that can get my blood flowing and set my body on fire and that's "HAIR" on her legs, and that burning fire that flow from her body into mine. I am sure that this up-coming Sunday that I shall be looking for her, wanting to learn more about her and why the heat from her body has me wanting to "CRY" out loud.

It has been a very long time that a woman has made me cry, and I have said that I never wanted to cry like that again; because she brought smoke to my ass and tears to my eyes. Is history about to repeat it's self or is it that I wish to cry out again. Just like a baby wanting its milk. Knowing that it will be good. Now my question, am I returning back to my old self? Wanting to check that grass out that's across the street.

Not worrying about how much water that it will take just to keep it green, and don't care about the water bill. All of this was running through my mind while I was there in church. Now, the big question is how I get to met her? I have spoken to her on a number of Sunday mornings, but why now! Is it that this lady, not knowing it has made me ready to wonder off into the valley and knowing that I shall enjoy that Wild Cherry?

Wow! Is this another one of those traps or is this the word telling me to wake up and open my eyes to the truth. What if I get to know this lady and as time goes on, she makes me cry and cry because this Wild Cherry just might be the death of me. Hell what better way to go out. There is an old saying that if "P-----y brought me into this world, then let P-----Y take me out of this world."

It's funny that I am saying this, because years ago I had said those very same words. "If P-----Y brought me into this world, than let P_____Y take me out of this world." Is this what I was thinking when I said that I need to change my life style? When I was there in Detroit, knowing that I needed someone in my life. Not a WIFE or a GIRLFRIEND but a "ROAD DOG". You see when it's all over we both can say "Catch you later." Knowing that the next meeting will be just as good or even better because life is so very short and that there is "joy in Life."

Well all I can do now is to wait for Sunday to come, because this gives me another reason to be attending church besides to hear the world from the Pastor and the word from this lady. That will lead me into the alley and like Bobby Blue Bland would say "cry, cry, cry and cry me a river. I need to put you down for a while because I need to go do something which is very important to me.

Well here I am. I can hear your words as I slowly walk towards your grave. (Jennifer speaking) Wow, here comes my dad, and he walks like he is in another world. As I lay here not saying a word, he sits there trying to find something to say with a smile on his face, looking down on me without a care in this entire world. Then she says (Jennifer speaking) those words daddy I'm in a better place now. It's nice here and not having to deal with all of that stuff down there on earth. Dad, you are here not only to see me, but wanting to talk with me.

Daddy is it because there is no one down there on earth that you can talk with. Hell dad, when you come here to my grave more than four days a week. Hell I know that there is something wrong? Well baby to tell the truth about it Yes, I have done or I am doing just what you have said that I would do? Once again I feel ashamed because I am allowing the church to become my play ground, I'm not there to receive the word, but there to see just what I can catch.

I'm starting to slip back into my old ways of doing things, you remember before when I was out there in the jungle looking for LOVE, and now it appears that I'm in church doing the very same thing and for getting the rules of the jungle, where I almost step in quick sand and got my ass eaten up by the Queen of the jungle. Now how many queens are sitting up here in the church waiting for me to come forth or are they saying "I can answer all of your prayers if you come to me and tell me what's on your mind."

Now back home sitting here with Jonnie Taylor kicking and that hot sun outside keeps telling me to stay in the house and let that outside go for another day. Hell I have been putting this yard work off for over two weeks, with a cold one sitting beside me, there is something about the blues that makes one sit and think about the good times and the bad time. This kind of music has a way of digging down into your soul which brings pain to the heart, for me sometimes I think about the times that I had and the wife had. Those nights sitting out in the back yard with a full moon, and a slight wind.

The two of us holding hands with a cold one at your side. Words need not be said, it's just the two of us with the dogs lying at our feet in our own little world. Those thoughts bring pain to my heart, thinking of those forty-seven yeas, that I had and now they are gone leaving me with an empty heart and a home without warmth of love and someone to hold me tight, and say "Baby I love you" Damn, that's what those blues bring into my life.

Man, this is one of the reason that I don't want to go down that road again, maybe it's like my girlfriend said, that I'm afraid to get married again, but maybe I just want someone to make me cry, yet could this be that she is the one who is afraid to re-marry, but always saying yes to the ideal of a summer and winter home. Hell I could go for that.

Damn, its 2016 now, one doesn't have to buy the whole pie, just to get a slice of that pie. This is not my way of thinking there are others that feel as I do about things like this,

; Man, years ago one never questions the word of getting married. Some have been there and done that and don't want to return back down that road again. Yet, for good or bad reasons, we will ONLY settle for a SLICE of that pie.

Here once again in the house with those four walls closing in on me. I find myself sitting here with the blues working on me and that one song "If you don't know me by now" brings some more hurt and pain to me. As I sit here writing this letter to my daughter. The one that was absent from my life and not being able to spend some time with her. Most of all thinking about that letter that I had written to her, which went something like this:

Sometimes we fathers sit there thinking about you, and it's not that we don't know those words or use the right ones to say. It's kind of funny in a way, until one day when we are sitting there trying to fix our mouth to say those words. Someone comes along and ask us that One Big question that has been so very hard to say at times. They stand there in front of US and say "Who's that beautiful little girl sitting next to you? Aba-Boom, we shit and get off of the pot and say out loud, "that's my Daughter."

I say this because I feel that I'm not the ONLY father who has been absent from the lives of our children. There are so many homes without a father. Some of US because the lack of a job to support that child. Some of US are out there doing OUR thing or having that child and just walk away from them. Maybe it's DRUGS or being in JAIL, because we went down the wrong road. Some of US feel that Our Man Hood has been taking away from us, because we could not support that child. Whatever the reason was WE all had our very own reasons for doing what we did.

That letter that I spoke of, the one that I wrote to my daughter went something like this: My Darling Daughter, as a child you never asked me for much or ask for anything. Even today you have NOT put any demands on me. Baby, as a child, I wasn't there with you. Now a grown woman and still I find myself away from you. People talk about the Blues, and how they feel. I tell them that you can't feel the Blues unless you have lived them.

Baby-Girl, I have lived those Blues and at times I have felt those Hot Tears as they came slowly running from my eyes.

Baby, I sit here with FOUR things in front of me:

1. A Mirror
2. A Glass of Wine

3. A Picture
4. A Letter

As I look into that MIRROR, I see a SORRY ass dad, who walked out of his daughters life when she was just three years old, not seeing her again until she became a young woman and that was for only a short period of time. Now you are a grown woman the mother of two young boys.

The glass of WINE that I have here is to drown my sorrow, that which I have been living in for so many year, trying to drown away that pain that I felt when I left you in the care of others who was not of your own blood.

The PICTURE, of a very beautiful child with those brown eyes, saying hold me "DADDY" and wrap those strong arms of yours around me and never let me go.

Honey, I can still see those words that I wrote in "Letters to my Daughters." I don't have that letter with me, but the words are embedded in my Heart. They went something like this: Honey, you are of my own flesh and blood, as a child I wasn't there with you. I wasn't there to walk with you to school to keep all those other kids from making fun of you and asking that Old crazy ass question! "WHO'S YOUR DADDY'?" Honey those kids were looking at you all crazy like because you weren't like them, you were of a mix family, and your daddy was Black.

Maybe you couldn't really understand what was really going on at the time. All you knew that the kids would pick on you. Baby you were what would say a mix-breed. Your mother was non-black and your father was Black. Honey you were not alone there are other kids just like you throughout Korea, Japan, Vietnam, and yes her in the United States of America. I wasn't there to protect you from those kids and those words. I wasn't there to hold you tight and say it' okay, and even in the darkest of night when you had those dreams.

Francis, my two grandsons that I have never held them in my arms when they were small. Today I only have the pictures of them to look at. It's crazy but your emails and letters come to me with Warmth and deep Love. The REAL love, not that other kind of love that we give to people who haven't been in our life, just like me. I wasn't there in your life. We give them that "BULL-SHIT kind of love." What can I say? Still we are miles away from each other.

What I really want right now is just a little more time for us to get with each other. I'm sure that this will be hard, because you have never said if you hate me for not being there with you and in your life, and for running out of your life like I did. Baby those last words that you spoke to me still burn deep in side of my heart. I can see you now as you spoke these words. "Daddy no matter what I do or what I might become, just always LOVE me and never stop loving me for WHO I AM.

It's so funny in a way that one never thinks about all of those things that we were ashamed of. Jennifer you never met your step-mother, baby you would have liked her, because you and her had so much in common. You both were strong and beautiful women of color (Non-Black that is) you both had that enter power which allows you to do things or deal with the things that others lay at their feet.

Jennifer what I'm trying to say is that when I first got married to your step-mother, I never sat down and spoke about the real world, about me being Black and about the world and even about my own race, when it came to marrying a Non-Black woman, and not a Black woman. It can be a BITCH at times. I'm sure that your own mother who wasn't Black and your father who was Black had to deal with this bull-shit also. Honey, what I mean is that your step-mother was from overseas. A land ten thousand miles away from here. Lucia was born in the Philippines. I met her when I was station over there. We became as of one on February 14, 1959.

There were people who were not ready for this type of marriage, a mix one at that; Baby you do remember Mikeo, that's what she spoke of when she said she would NEVER be FREE because of the color of her skin and she also was of a mix-marriage, one that brought shame to her as it did to your own mother, because she too married out of her own race. Honey, why do I feel ashamed! It's not because I married this woman, but it's because I never sat down and talk with her about SOCIETY and its views on this type of marriage.

Like everything else, I kept this all to myself, not even letting her know what she must face down the road, about being married to a Black man. Now you see why I said that I felt shame, not only about that, but not sitting down and talk with her; even feeling ashamed about things in my life that I didn't even tell you, like being in love with a married woman.

Well another month is about shot in the ass, it's now November, because one could tell by the weather, plus I had to set my clock back one hour. Don't want to be late for church, wanting to see her again, and sit next to her; knowing what some members will be saying, those that know me! "What that old man up to now? Girl for three years he has been sitting over here and now he has moved over there next to that young lady." Old Dog should be ashamed of his-self trying to hit on that child.

Hell I'm not married and don't have to report to anyone about my actions, besides this bed is getting cold at night and it's always nice to have someone to hold on too and keep you warm. Well it's only a matter of time that I should be asking myself "Armour" are you sure that you want to play that waiting game or do you want to go out there and meet someone and enjoy yourself and life, because what's here today, just might be gone tomorrow, because time does not wait for ANYONE.

Man, you do remember just what happen to your ass when you were playing that game? You almost stepped in quick sand and got your ass eaten by that lioness that's out there waiting for you, because you had forgot the rules of the jungle. Now ask yourself, do you want to go through that all over again! What if you run into another Tess or Flo, most of all your ass just might run into the one that you "FEAR" the most! The one with HAIR on her legs, and make your crazy ass cry, cry like you have never done before? Now what? Are you sure that's what you want? Man remember those words that grandmother spoke of! "Boy, if that's not your cup of tea, don't put any sugar in it."

Man, I'm telling you this, if there's nothing like an OLD FOOL? Armour, it its meant for you and this church lady to get together it will be, but if not, shit happens. Armour, think back you do remember what you did on April 25, 1955 Your sorry ass walked right out of that women's life.; are you ready to do that again! What if this is really what you are waiting for! You and her! I'm not saying that you shouldn't go out there and get yourself a shot of that Wild Cherry. All I can say is that this "Wild Cherry has caused many of men to shit and go blind" so Walk softly and Carry a big Stick. Armour, this woman that you are in love with, how will she take this knowing that she has been down this road with you before?

Now history has shown its crazy ass up once again. What about her man! You need to think about this and talk with someone else. Now if you think that I'm blowing smoke up your ass, why don't you go and have a talk with her about this. Your ass knows who I'm talking about? Your daughter. The one who will tell you the truth about this, besides she is the only one that you talk too when you are deep in shit.

Well its getting kind of late so let's call it another day and talk about this at a later time. It's now Monday and I'm on my way out to the grave yard to see my daughter. I guess she is the only one that I can talk with concerning my problems; everyone else doesn't have the time to sit with me and hear what I have to say.

The very first thing that they would say is "man that is your problem" and I don't have the time to hear about your bull-shit!

Those are my so call friends, but when they want something from me, they are my friends. Baby that's why I come to you, because you will be up front with me and tell me like it is and the truth about things.

SACRIFICEING YOUR SOUL

Baby I need to take a step back and say something to my readers. I just wish to say to you my readers that so far everything that you have read in this book is true. I'm not trying to paint myself as a good guy or a person that has walked on water. That isn't me, plus I could have gone out in the back yard and open that container with the Blue Top and pulled stuff out of there to add to the pages of this book I didn't do so, because I want to be true to myself and also true to you in what you have read about my life; for I am who I am, just another one of Gods amazing children.

I have wondered the Wilderness of life trying to find out "Who I Am" It's a very nice fall day outside, somewhere around 62 with a light wind, and all one needs is a light jacket that is if you are going to sit with me here on the water front. It's funny when one is all alone, you have nothing but time and sometimes that eats at your soul and makes one to remember that life isn't worth anything unless you enjoy it to the up most. Wow! Remembering something that my niece asked me one day she said "Uncle" are you okay and are you happy?

Well I look at it this way, Happiness is what one wishes it to be and just what one do with himself or herself. You see I look at things as Happiness being just Wonderful and the Joy of it all, but it's that loneness that's a BITCH, and makes some of US go out of our rabbit-ass-mine. Man, maybe that's why I have gotten to the place that I don't worry about shit anymore, Because I have myself a Road-Dog and just like she say sometimes "let's go some place and get lost for a day or two and just you and I, and tell the world to kiss our ass.

With a Road-Dog you don't have to worry or put up with all of that other bull-shit, and hope like hell that things stay as they are and not "One of US going off the deep-end of things. I am talking about that bull-shit "Friends with Benefits" which is all nothing but a CRAP of bull.

Took some time off so that I could get my mind and clear my head. It's something that we all should do, because at times we are running around trying to do this and that, but we don't really know what takes place in our life; you see my readers I need that time in order for me to get my shit into one bag. A HDX Extra Large one, because that last bag had a hole in it and I found that my shit had gone by the way side.

Damn, I'm at that age Eighty-One and in that thing call "Fiends with Benefits"? I'M SURE THAT SOME OF YOU HAVE FOUND YOURSELF IN THIS SPOT! Friends with Benefits. Hell ain't anything wrong with that, but the only thing that I worry about is if I can be in a relationship call "Friends with Benefits", without one of us wanting more? I remember sometime ago, when I was in the Navy, that an old man once told me "Son SEX has a habit of Creating Desire for Emotional Connection, so watch out for that "GREAT BONK". Wow just thinking that we are so blessed to have an amazing life, so let's enjoy oneself just for time that we have. Yes that was me when I was young wild and crazy and the jungle was my play ground.

I was willing to sell my soul just to have someone in my bed and in my life. Yes, I even sold my soul for some paper work in order for Amerada to help fix the paper work to bring my family to the states. Thinking back I remember grandmother telling me "Boy never sell your soul just to have a bed warmer and someone in your life. This might sound crazy, but there are so many of US doing just that.

I can only speak for myself, for I have done that and been there. I'm so glad and thankful that the dog came alone and bit me in the ass, because had it not; I would still be in that shape right now. A man without a soul, because I gave it all up in the name of love (I thought) I do hope that someone hears my voice, because life can be a BITCH when you end up with that WRONG PERSON, because you sacrifice your soul in the name of LOVE. Like I said I was there and the ass kicker was that I didn't care what she looked like, I just wanted that BED WARMER.

Shit, I need to move away from this, because those were some hell of days back then, but that's not the only reason that I need to move on besides failing to listen to grandmother. The real reason for this was because I had F------K up from the start in writing this letter. What I mean is that I was playing me some Blues and now those Blues are kicking my ass. Those were the days right after MY WELL ran dry (lost my wife) I was hurting so bad because I had just lost that Wonderful woman who had given me herself and her love.

I hope like hell that I never have to go down that road again, but one never knows that someone just might come alone and turn my world upside-down, and make me think twice about life, and what I want, but most of all who I wish to spend my life with.

Sometimes people love it when they see you looking at them, because just last night while shopping I found myself looking at this one lady, because there was something about her. Thinking that she had wanted me to say something to her; yet I held back because the old Armour had come back to life again. The one that I had put under lock and key; knowing that all he wanted was for her to become a member of "The Three F Club"

1. Find them
2. F----K them
3. Forget them

I wanted to start all over again with the one that got away. The very one that I could not forget. Right then I felt a lot of things Hurt, Frustration, but more than anything else I felt a crazy amount of Love for this woman. Who I have been in love with for a number of years. I just can't get her out of my mind, plus I look at other women in another way, that they are there but not for me. In spite of all of this, I was able to get up this morning with a smile on my face and I thank God for allowing my Special Angle to watch over me, as I lay there in my bed thinking just how Lucky I am to have you in my life Lord.

Lord, maybe it was because when I was young and Wild, running around acting crazy, I didn't look at things as I do now. Maybe with age come wisdom (for some of us) and I did stop and smell the Rose Bush. Oh! How sweet it is. Wow it's so beautiful here on the water front, with the Sun casting its self out there for all to see and feel its wonderful heat.

Thank you for this day, sometimes we never sit down and see how things are and say THANK YOU. Maybe this is what's been missing in my life, not sitting down and take a look at all of those things that I have not done before and now I ask myself what have I done with my life? Have I ever looked at life in the whole? Or looking at life the way that I think that it should be. All I can say is that Life is good and that we "ALL" must enjoy every day of it.

I want say that my life before was all wrong, but there was something that did need fixing. Like when I was out there trying to get into every woman's panties that I met, not

Really not caring who she was or whatever she looked like. Man, all I wanted was the Wild Cherry which causes me to run around Drinking and Pop a pill every now and then.

Then there was that Dark side of me, which I'd didn't share with others only going out to the grave yard to share it with her. Yes! To the grave yard sitting besides my daughter's grave and talking to her, knowing all alone that she would not be able to say those words. "What's up daddy? What did you F_____K up this time or who got into your ass, because you were out there in the jungle and not playing by the rules? Who was she? Better yet who is she? Is it that same old lady who has been after you trying to give you a shot of that TANG? Or is it like what has happened to so many of those other old men? You have gotten yourself some of that Young Cherry and it's kicking your ass, and driving you out of your rabbit ass mind?

Now dad, tell me what is it? Dad, let me ask you this, when was the last time that you got yourself a shot? I think that I know what it is? It's her again, she is back into your life again, and you want some of that Wild Cherry, but you are afraid of it (Ha, Ha, Ha) because deep down in your soul you think that she might make you CRY and you don't want to ever cry again like you did when you were with that other woman. You know who I am talking about, that lady who had HAIR on her legs.

Damn, daddy you are afraid of women who have HAIR on their legs. Is she one of them? All I can say daddy if you want some of the Wild Cherry go get it and then daddy cry, cry, and cry like you have never done before, because life is so short. I'm glad that you are here even if there is something kicking your ass. It has been weeks now and you haven't been out here to see me until now.

That's how I knew that something was wrong and that there was something was eating your ass up, because you never stayed away like this. I was worried about you, but now I understand what the problem is. All I can say is go home and take a bath and call her. Daddy let her know that you want to come over and take her out for dinner. Now dad, be sure to take some of those Blue and White pills that you have in the bathroom,; By the way dad go enjoy yourself, so when that hair and Wild Cherry gets to acting a fool, those pills should have kicked in by that time, and do remember dad, you can't wear that TANG out.

Now that was all good! Have not slept like that in years. It's a wonderful day here at the water front. I'm really here to kick back, after last night. Yes I did! I cried, and hearing Shirley kicking on the CD hearing her voice as she sings "You're going to make it." Didn't think that way last night.

It's a very up-lifting song, makes one think and to be thankful that one is a live, to enjoy this Special Sunday that's full of warmth. You know sometimes when you are all by yourself, you have so much time to sit and think, but all at the very same time, loneness can come along and set in and it brings that very sad feeling into one's life. Oh! That feeling of not having someone there in your life to hold you close and tight and say to you "Baby I love you." This kind of feeling can drive one mad as hell.

Damn, maybe I'm human after all, because before I didn't feel anything. I just held all of my feelings in check, not letting them come out; because I would not "allow myself to cry." And stop my Rain and Pain that which ate at my soul.

Yet, as I sit here trying to write this story, I can hear someone saying Wow! He is talking about me.

THANKSGIVING WEEKEND

What does this day mean to you? Each of US has a different meaning for this word or should I say this day? For some of us having a hot meal or a place to get out of the cold with a fire to help keep us warm. Yet some of US never think about this day! Only that mom will be cooking for us and the table will be set, because Aunt May is coming over, alone with all of those other family members, Yak, they too, the ones that give you a pain in the ass, but it's Thanksgiving.

Well let's see what my man has to say about this day or what does that word mean? IM speaking about the man that lots of us turn too when we want to find about a word, but most of all how do we Spell that word or what does that do means.

THANKSGIVING?
1. The ACT of Giving
2. A Prayer expressing Gratitude
3. A Public acknowledgment or Celebration of Divine Goodness.

That's what He (WEBSTER) says "Thanksgiving means."

Yet, we all see it as "Thanksgiving Day" a day appointed for Giving Thanks for Divine Goodness, yes, it's a day for ALL of that, but to others there is a deeper meaning for it. Like I said before I can only speak for myself about this or why this Weekend is a part of me. In a way I and my wife had OUR Last Supper together on this day and that's why "Thanksgiving" means so very much to me. In order for me to explain all of this, I must once again turn back the hands of time to the year of 2006 nine years ago.

November 25, 2006, that was the Thanksgiving Weekend, the grandkids were here, all nine of them, along with my two sons and daughter-in-laws. We had a very nice time and a very wonderful dinner. Just kicking back and talking about old times. You know how we do it, when all of the family is there. The laughter and the smiles, thanking god that we were all there with each other on this very Special Day.

We all helped to clean up the kitchen and put away the dishes. You know in most families that's what we do, before everyone hit the door and say good night. My wife wasn't feeling too good, later on that night, she said to me "Honey" take me to the hospital. Shit, I knew that something was wrong; because my wife was one of those who didn't like going to the hospital, and that was the last thing on her mind.

Sometime that night her heart stopped and they had to shock her, for two days she lay there with her eyes closed, several times they had to use that procedure, and it took a toll on her. Blood began to run from her nose, I would wipe it away. Then on the third day, the doctor called me to the side and explains things to me. Mr. Armour, the only thing that's keeping your wife going is the machine and the paddle was not helping, if fact it was causing more harm than good. Here I am sitting there watching my wife slip away from me. Knowing what I have to do.

Man, something is holding me back; I stood there with tears in my eyes. As I stood there finding myself talking to her. Than a warm feeling came over me. It was still in the room and I could hear this soft voice saying to me. "Its okay honey, it's okay to let go of me now.

Now that Thanksgiving of November of 2006 was that last supper for me. Looking back into history I wasn't the only one that had that last supper, for the Bible spoke of the last supper for someone else long before my time. Now this day and weekend of the 25th of November until the 27th of November has become a Special time in my life, besides February 14, 1959. That's the day that I married Lucia Manelse who became my wife "Mrs. Lucia Manelse Armourr; after I lost Lucia (my wife) I found myself sitting in the bedroom in the dark dealing with that pain in my own way,

Now the weekend of Thanksgiving has become my 'AMVERSIETY', it has become the time that I'm thankful for what I had for those forty-seven years. A wife that gave herself to the family and her love to her husband. She (Lucia) stood at my side for all of those years. While I gave my life to the military for twenty-one years. Those days and nights that I wasn't there, she became the head of the house, as the Mother and the Father.

The Breed of Special Women, the military wife for over twenty-one years. So now you can see and understand why this day is so very important to me, not only because it's a fact of giving but the special expressing Gratitude that I have for her being in my life. That her and I was able to have that "Last Supper" with each other before she was called "HOME", not just called home, but the Good Lord sent his very Special Angle to walk with and see her "HOME."

So I say to "ALL of you" enjoy THANKSGIVING because one never knows when they will have that "Last Supper."

WHEN I'M OLD

Sometime ago I made a statement about people from overseas taking care of their family when they become sick and old. I'm sure that I did piss someone off by saying what I did. I'm sure that someone is or might be saying what about you Armour? When your old ass reach that time who's going to be there for your sorry ass and take care of you? Tell me man, have you ever thought about this, will your ass end up in a home, because your son is in the TV, checking out the football game and he don't have time for you. Now what? I have thought about this for such a very long time. Who will be there for me and take care of my old ass.

Well for me there is only one thing for me to do, and that's to go live with my daughter who lives in the Philippines. She has always been telling me Daddy why don't you come back home and let me take care of you. I have thought about this and maybe that's one of the reasons why I'm not in a hurry to get married. Now the question is, if I do re-marry will she have my back or will it be the case that I don't need your ass any more. It's your MONEY, it's all that I need, but I shall come to see you on the weekends, if I can get out of the TV.

Man, I use to watch my wife's grandmother who was One –Hundred and Five (105) the family, I do mean all of the family was there for her, even I was there also for this old lady, anything that she needed or wanted she got it. Remembering the day that we went to pick her up from the hospital and brought her back to our home which became hers. Baby, I have set up many nights with this lady, feed her and comb her hair and even washed her face.

She was my friend, the very first one to accept me into the family, and my color didn't matter to her. I'm sure that if I did go back to the Philippines, I'll have my daughter plus my two grandsons to look after me. I'm not saying that everyone here in the states will kick the old people out, but those homes are full of the old folks. The son and his wife are both working and don't have the time for them.

Shit! You know what some of those family members would say about the old folks in their home being around their children!! "They use those colorful and backward words and we don't want our kids around them because they don't talk right, plus they are slow and can't remember things. Let me ask you this, have you ever thought about what will happen to you when you get old? Who will be there for you? Where will you stay or will you become one of those that the FOOTBALL game is more important than YOU?

Shit, man that's a hell of a thought that the TV is first and your old ass is Second or maybe Third if the dog is around. I don't know, like I have said many times that I can only speak for myself. Thinking back about those folks who were brought up under the "Old School" of doing things. Baby, those were the ones that put the "Old People" first and all others second. I watch my family look out for my mother. The daughter-in-laws, the grand children and even the great-grand were there for her. I hate to say this, but times have "CHANGE" and in some homes the old folks are sitting in the back seat all alone.

We are working and some of US just can't get out of the F_____king TV, but like they say "it is, what it is". Now baby if you think that I'm blowing smoke up your ass, then man go to one of those places and see just how many old folks that you see who's from overseas? Places like Korea, Japan, Philippines and even from China. Just some food for thought. I'm going to leave you for now and go have myself a nice cold glass of wine. Hell if gets good to me, then I just might have myself a second glass before I call it a night.

In a few hours it will be the 1st of December and soon another year will be shot in the ass, and it will be 2016. Damn, times fly and if you are like me you are looking back and wondering just where have all of that time has gone to. The kids are big and some of them are married and we find ourselves looking at the grand kids or the great grand ones, as they stand there in front of you asking for the Peanut Butter and Jelly Sandwich, the very ones that you used to take to school in that brown paper bag.

It's funny how things like that bring a smile to the old lips; for those of US who didn't have that Peanut Butter and Jelly, there were those Syrup or Sugar Sandwich in those brown bags for us. Those times are gone only waiting for another time to be re-born, like some of us wanting to get away from the OLD ways and discover something new in life

Wow! For me it's only a matter of time and I'll be another year older. Eighty-One, wanting to enjoy each day as they come my way; spending some time with the grand kids, and the great grand ones. Not remembering spending much time with my father, because I was only eight years old when he passed away. Only to hear that he was a truck driver. Yet there was so much about this man that I didn't even know, because I was a small child at that time. Yet, as time went on I did hear stories about this man who was my father, who was a Rolling Stone.

You know some of my friends are asking me Armour, why do you laugh so much? Well I tell them that they don't know what I have been through in life, and if they did, then they would know and understand just why I laugh so much. I have so much to be thankful for. One of those things is that I am "ALIVE". Second thing is that on February 11,2016 is my birthday. Baby just looking back over the years, there has been some good times and hell yes, also those bad days and times. There was also pain that has eaten away at my soul for so many years. If only I had made a movie out of those times and days, WE could sit back and review those times. I'm sure that we could find something to laugh about, and shake one's head and say "man" you were a fool back then.

One can't forget those days and times when those TEARS flow like the great Mississippi River. The birth of a new member to the family and the loss of those that you have loved ever so much. It's a shame that we can't go back and bring back those times and events; but like they say, time moves on, but we do have those Remembrance or Recollection of what had happened back then. Yet for some of US we do not wish to remember those times and days, because that pain was so great that we block it out of our mind, not wishing to remember those events.

You see my friends those are only a few reasons that I have to laugh or smile about; but the Greasiest reason of them all is the "BIG C." Man, you know that word that we wish not to HEAR or SPEAK of. What I'm trying to say that this August of 2016 that it will have been 10 years. "YES" ten long years that I have been "CANCER FREE". In 2006 I found out that I had what they call "Stage Three Lung Cancer" Damn, that word took the wind out of my ass.

Before you turn another page or go on reading this book, I feel that I need to tell you something; the amazing part of my story of "Who I am" is that I am not alone, because there are others out there who have gone down this road. You might be one of those others who are just like me. Wow! Right now I need a cup of tea. If you like please feel free to have a cup alone with me. How can I say this without opening that door on some ones else's life and bring back that Rain and Pain. That we have tried to keep hidden away from ourselves and from others also.

The lost of my daughter was wrenching, that pain reach deep down into my soul and burn the hell out of me. Even when I go out to her grave. I can still see my daughter (Jennifer) as she lay there in the cold street and those burning tears flow from my eyes. I try to overcome this, but one just can't overcome something like this! That event stabbed me in the heart. This took the Sunshine out of my life. A life was taken because of a crazy love for someone. Yet, that crazy love took away a "True Love" and left me with a big hole in my heart.

I am very sorry that if I have cause some pain to return back to someone. I feel that if we don't talk about these things and just hold them in side of us, that shit will eat you up, body and soul. I speak of this from my heart. You see I have been down this road once before.

Man, that shit was so bad that it ate my ass up. You see before this, the last time that I did cry was back in 1961. I shit you not. That was when I lost my step-father and that has been forty-nine years ago. The next time that I cried was in 2006 when I lost my wife and then again in 2013 when I lost my daughter.

Daddy I am not with you and my sister is not there with you also. Yet you wonder about getting old and who's going to take care of you in your time of need. Dads after mom was called home you have been like a dog in heat running around and checking out lots of butts! I speak of this because of your history of or with women. Like that young thing that has milk on her lips. The one who almost set the house on fire, trying to boil some water.

Let's see now, there was the one who you thought was all of that. Dad the reason why I'm saying this is because some of you old men just want to get the Coat Hanger on your arms, so you can run around all over town and say "Look at what I got."

Dad I love you but don't let history repeat its self again. You do re-call what happened to you when you were young wild and crazy? You forgot the rules of the jungle. Now check this out, there are those out there who are waiting for you and "saying that you are old and with one foot in the grave just waiting for someone to come and push your old ass in there."

All at the very same time saying "He's retired, has his own home, and that piggy bank is squirting out more than quarters, and yes there is his SSI. Dad don't rush off into anything, just remember that Francis want you to come home to the Philippines and she will take care of you now that you are getting up there in age.

I think that I should let this go for now; it's because of that look on your face, it's telling me that you are hot enough to F_____K, because of the things that I have said about the type of WOMEM that you have been out with, plus you are worried about getting old.

WHAT'S EATING AT ME

For years my Rain and Pain was eating away my soul, because it would not allow me to cry and letting those that I love get close to me and share my pain. August 5, 2014 I felt like SHIT, because I was not there to be with her! She was only just fourteen years old. I was out of town in Detroit, Mi. I received a call from my son telling me that he had to rush Lady (my dog) to the doctor; after checking her up, he found out that Cancer had spread throughout her body, and she had to be put down.

A part of me was gone and coming home wouldn't be the same; an empty house and her not being there to talk with. Like I have said before I had been down this road before when I lost my wife. The house became cold and empty like someone had just sucked all of the life out of it. Once again I have lost a part of me and my soul. My son Horace Jr. and then my daughter Jennifer and her unborn child and now Lady.

If you re-call somewhere in this book, where I told my friends why I laugh so much, because if they had walked in my shoes, then they would know the answer. You see I have been blessed to have lived a good life and with so much joy coming my way, maybe it's because I have learn to FLY! I don't know just what it is or why I feel this way, so let's say that by me coming to the cross road of life. I have truly found some answers, because life is so very short, that one must enjoy each and every day of it.

Maybe getting older now I understand all of this NOW, it's like something is being pulled from my soul and I feel fresh and clean all over. It's like, I am a new me.

It's a Wonderful day and a very soft wind blowing. The Sun is out, and the sky is clear. I'm at my number one spot, because I had the need to get out of the house and spend some time by myself, just me and the water front. Seeing those small waves roll across the water. It's about 56 here. One of those days that you just want to say the "Hell with everything, because today is my day and my day alone.

Thinking how far we have come as a nation and also as Black people, yet knowing that there is still so much to be done for America and also for a Black person, who still find his/her self still on the front lines at war, not just with Society, but with war among US. Can't help but looking back (I understand that I shouldn't be like "Lott's wife") How far that we have come as a people in a few days WE as a Black person can or should stand tall, because Dr. King birthday is here. As a Black man, I know what it was like back then in the day? When there was a water hole for Whites and a waterhole for Colored.

Hearing those words "Boy" stay in your place and keep your eyes on the ground; even if you were putting your life on the line (in the military) for your country HATE was still there. I recall when I first join the military; it wasn't all Peaches and Cream. We had our place in the military and also in Society. Remembering the stories that my brothers would tell me about WW 11, how it was if you were Black and how you were treated. Man, if you were station overseas and you met someone from France or Germany and married that person man, the shit that one had to go through. I hear that in some cases you could not bring her back to the states if you were Black.

Asking the military could you marry that person? Now that's a bitch that you had to get permission to marry that person. This not only applied to a Black service person, but also to White service members also; but for "US" it was hell. Man in some cases guys stayed overseas after the war. Knowing that they (Blacks) could not bring that person back home to the good old U.S.A. being a small boy at the time I didn't believe that shit yet remembering a movie that I saw back in the early or part of 1950!

This White service member married this lady from Japan and the shit that they went through, but their love for each other was strong, but Racism was a BITCH. If I can re-call one of them end up killing their self. (Or was it both of them) At the time I didn't think too much about it, because it was only a movie.

I didn't understand just how Racism worked and how it could eat your ass up 24/7. It wasn't until I grew older and had to deal with that shit myself, and then I saw how it worked, but most of all I had to live with it 24/7 for forty-seven years. I never spoke of this until now, because that was my other pain, because I "Crossed that line." That line of having a mix marriage and hearing that "bull-shit" it's going to hurt the kids; but I have learn how to say F------K you because this is my life and not yours. I remember that day that my family first came to the states or should I say arrived in California. Shit because that's when the "looks came alive." Even though I was in a military uniform those looks were there and words need not be spoken, it was there in the eyes N_____er what is your Black ass doing with that woman!

Now this did not only come from just the Whites, but the most HATE came from the Black Woman. Yes! The Black woman. N_____er. You ain't shit! Why did you go over there and marry one of them? What's wrong with US, the Black woman? Why couldn't your Black ass love and marry one of us? Your own people. The other reason that I speak of this, is because I had a friend ask me some time ago, I think that it was about six years after I had lost my wife. She asks me Armour do you think that you'll ever get married again. I ask her Mieko why you are asking me this question. I was just wondering if you re-marry would she be Black, and if you could love a Black Woman.

That's all she said to me, Armour I was in a mix marriage like you and I lost my husband, and knowing that if I ever re-marry again, I could NOT marry someone from my own race. I and you have had out talks when you come here to see your daughter and I come here to see him, my late husband. Armour you know that he was White and I'm a Jap. A can of beans that has gone bad, as far as my race is concerned. I married outside of my race and knowing that I could never return back to my people and get married. Now how about you? You too have married outside of your race, can you return back to your race of people and get married?

Armour, the big question is can you love and marry a Black woman? To tell the truth about it, I never really gave much thought to this, if I could love and marry a Black woman. Again this one of those times that the past came rolling back into my life. I never thought much about what it would be like or feel like being married to a Black woman. To tell the truth about it, I never thought about my girl friend being Black or if I could love her because she is a Black woman.

You see I love this woman for who she is and if we ever did get married it will NOT be because she is Black, it's because she is a woman that I'm in love with. Maybe this was the reason why I had to get out of the house and come here to the water. It's that the water has a way to make one feel good and at peace and make you leave all of that bull-shit at home? For me sitting here at the water makes me feel good and clean my soul and thoughts, alone with some soft music, will do the trick.

Damn, I feel good even if some of my past has come to life again. I can't help it because looking at TV and seeing all of this bull-shit that's going down one can't help but to think that society has gone to hell. Well it's Friday and I must be off to spend some time with my daughter. I always feel good when I'm there at her side and hearing her, but not really hearing her words that she is speaking to me from her grave.

I'm here now, as I sit at her side speaking those words. "Honey, sometimes I look around and see others with something that I wish that I had, and that's a mate. I have met some real nice women but there is something holding me back from saying the word. It's the very same thing with all of those other women that's holding me back from getting with them and going out with them on a date. It's not that I'm afraid, it's that I'm not free, and there's still a chain that's bound to me? I ask myself Armour why do you keep on reading your first book that you wrote? How Strong is Your Love. Man you have read that book six times already.

Is there something there in that book or is it the name of that book. Is this why I can't move on in life, but stuck right there thinking that when I wrote that book I was thinking about her? Is that why I named that book what I did? I ask myself have I opened up my eyes after all of these years only to answer that question. Why did I write this book and where did that name come from.

Maybe it all boils down to that Lucia (my late wife) has not set me free and that book was written for her and that love from the grave which stills bounds us, her and I to each other. Is this why I can't move on? Or is it the other way around that I don't want to move on and face another deal of being in love with two women! One from the grave and one that I might end up with? Is all of this because I have not met my cell mate, and right now I'm only living in a dream world without any meaning to it?

Is this one of those things! I need you, but it's because you want me because of what I can do for you? We all sometimes sit around and think about this and we look at the picture and ask one self, man what's wrong with this picture? Or is this the case that one does not give a shit as long as you have her or him at your bed-side, only praying like hell that it will all work out in the end. Damn, that's F-----K-up, because as humans we think one way and act another way.

Am I getting cold feet about making this the second time around or it's that ALL of the very good ones are all gone. Please don't get me wrong, there are lots of good women out there, but there are also that one group of women out there who don't want to go that way again, I have seen some women and men friends of mine, who swear that it will never happen again, because they fear getting another bad apple again.

Hell, I look at it this way; you get out of it, just what you put into it. Well let's move away from this, it was only "food for thought" but a damn good thought at that.

I'm here with my daughter wanting to ask her a question, because she is a woman and I don't have anyone else to turn to for this answer to this question that's eating away at me. You see this lady Mieko and I had this talk about being in a mix-marriage, and the question came up about marriage Mieko said to me Armour could you love and marry a Black woman? At that time I didn't think about it, but this is the second time that someone else has ask that question about if I could love a Black woman.?

You see I was married to a lady from overseas for forty-seven years before she was called away by our Lord. Now I'm in a relationship with a Black woman. Now my question is! "How do I love a Black woman? There are things on my mind and I'm looking for an answer? Dad whenever you come here to see me and you have that crazy ass look on your face, I know that you have a problem? Okay, let me ask you this! Who is she, and is she married? Dad when I see that look, it's always concerning some lady. Dad, please tell me that you'll not up to those things again with a married woman this time? Well baby it's about a woman, but she is not married, but she is Black?

Honey, please tell me "How do I love a Black woman? "Wow"! Damn dad can't answer that question when I'm only half Black myself. You'll have to ask a Black woman that question Dad let me ask you why this question about how to love a Black woman? Well baby me and Mieko had this talk about being in a mix marriage! Damn dad you have been talking with that crazy ass Mieko about this. Damn, you got to be shitting me. You know that Mieko is out of her rabbit-ass -mind. Sorry to talk like this, but I did learn this from you.

Dad this lady is not playing with a full-deck. You do remember how she was speaking the last time that you and she had that talk on Memorial Day. How she went on speaking about that bull-shit about not being free, because she was a Jap and you were Black. Even as I lay there I wanted to speak out and tell her that she should drop that old shit about not being free. Hell daddy, this is America, baby she had her reasons for feeling the way that she did, because of what she and others who were from Japan had to go through and deal with back then.

I could understand her reason for this, as a Black man I know the feeling and I have gone through some of the things that she went through, the only thing was no one pull me from my home and put me on a TRAIN like I was cattle and shipped me out to some camp, like my fore-fathers were done back in the day.

Let's not talk about that, I just want to "NO" how do I love a Black woman? Well daddy I can't answer that question for you, it looks like that you will have to sit down and talk with someone who's Black; all I can say make sure that this person can and will tell you the truth about how to love a Black woman. Daddy, it's all up to you how you feel about this woman, the best thing that I can tell you is please don't look at this woman's color. I understand where you are coming from, because you have not been in a full relationship with a Black woman, and you don't know how to act or go about it.

Dad, there is just one question that I need for you to answer for me? When you and mom got married did you look at her color? She wasn't Black! Did you ask yourself back then how can I love a Non-Black woman? A woman from overseas, not of your culture and of your ways and color! Did you think about that or was it LOVE and her race was no BIG DEAL. Then why are you tripping about color now? Was it because of what that old crazy ass Mieko had to say or is there something else that you are not telling me about! Like something like this.

(a) You don't know how to love a Black woman?
(b) Are you afraid to love a Black woman?
(c) Do you still have your eyes on someone else who is not Black?
(d) What does your heart say?

> Dad, as your daughter and a woman all I can say if she is "Black" love her, then again if she is a "Non-Black woman" from another race, then dad love her also. In the end it's all up to YOU who you marry. Dad, if you ARE NOT SURE that you can't love a Black woman then DON'T, I say DON'T force yourself or try and PROVE a point that you can love this woman JUST BECAUSE SHE IS BLACK.

> Dad, let me tell you this, if you go into this thinking this way, then you have F_____K up from the start. You see I would "NOT WANT" any man to marry me just because I am "HALF-BLACK and you can take that to the bank. I do hope that I was able to answer your question, but most of ALL it comes right down to YOU.

I'm sure that after you have sat down and had a talk with someone who is Black, you'll receive the same answer from that person, but they might not explain it like I have, but I'm sure that in the end it will all come out the same. Follow your heart, and LOVE that woman, because you love her and NOT HER COLOR. Talk with some of your church lady friends and see just what they have to say about "How to Love a Black Woman?

Well dad the Sun has begun to set and I'm sure that you have other things to do. Go home and think about our little talk or better still ask your girl friend to tell you how to love her as a "woman". Daddy deep down inside of you, I know the real reason that you are asking this question it was not only about that talk that and Mieko had, it's deeper than that! You see daddy your reason for not getting married to this lady, it's because you don't know how to love her as a woman. Daddy you have that bull-shit reason in your head and it isn't going to work. Okay baby talk to me, and tell me that reason!

You see I know what it is, but I want to hear it from you. Well baby-girl you think that you know all of the reasons why it want work? Daddy you are trying to love this woman because she is Black. You do re-call sometime ago this very same woman ask you do you think that you could love a Black woman. Did you ever stop and think just why she asks you that question? Dad, I am going to say something that will make you mad as hell, but its better coming from me, then from someone else. Well here goes "Armour" get your head out of your ASS and say to yourself the very reason that you don't want to get married.

Maybe it's because of age or is it that I have stop and smell the Rose Bush! I don't know just what it is or why I feel this way, maybe you are right about this thing of loving someone because of the COLOR of their skin! Or me coming to the cross road of life, where I have learn something about Love that have cause so many hardships to millions of US, yet it has bound some of US together to those that we love.

Baby, I just want to thank you for just being here for me and understanding that question on How to love a Black Woman. Jennifer I don't know what I would do without you, just being here makes me feel that much better.

Honey, you always have the right answer, not just those answers that makes me feel better, but it's those answers that come from your heart.

Love you.

Dad

BLACK HISTORY

I sit here reading the news paper after last night's game between New York and the Warrior's. It was the name that got my eyes, it was a reminder of Black History Month, because some players had tee-shirts on, that on the front of the shirt spoke the words of Black History. I ask myself what is Black History? For years this question was never spoken of. Yet I hear a cry, why not us! Why can't we have a month of History? I can't explain this, maybe it came about because America was ashamed to say I know who you are, and just wanting to say THANK YOU for your service. Is that's what Black History is all about or is there a deeper meaning for this? I don't know nor can I explain it.

Maybe we speak of Black History now is because WE as a Black people are killing each other and that in time there will be nothing to speak of. Maybe then Black History is for the YOUNG, to understand that you have a very Rich History and that you should HONOR this history with RESPECT. When I speak of this, it's because I'm a part of Black History. Not just because I was born in this month that we call Black History. I'm not one of those who just wrote about this event, but I'm one of those people who have lived it.

You see when I speak of Black History, I can't speak about those that came before me, and I can only speak about those that I have seen with my own two eyes. Those that kick down the doors which allowed me and many others to walk through those doors. I could speak about Sports! That one man that made Hitler piss in his pants. Jessie Owens. Others like Wilt, the

Brown Boomer, who I have been to his summer farm there in Detroit when I was a child. Jackie Robinson, Flo-Jo, Author Ash and so many more That young man that song with a Golden voice, which up-set many of men and had some women creaming in their panties.

I speak of Nat King Cole, not that other Nat, who struck fear in many men and had women pissing in their panties. He's in the history books also. Nat Turner is the one that I am speaking of here. What have I done to be a part of Black History? Maybe for now. I haven't done much, but maybe for the years to come my great, great, great grand children can speak of me as have given America 21 years of my life in the military or saying that he help FREE the people of Vietnam.

I'm sure that we all have our very own stories to tell about Black History, Some of us have been to the mountain top and wondered through the jungle of Racism. Only now to sit back and watch our young men walking around with their pants down on their ass and cry out its FASHION and the young girls walking around with those pants that are so tight that the girl is Crying out "please set me free."

Who am I, well just another Black man who's saying Thank you to those that came before me. YOU that kick down doors and allowed me to walk through and not have to ride in the back of the bus, like I have done back in the day. "NO" more two bathrooms or CAN'T come in here to eat and sit wherever you wanted too. I only speak of this for the Young MEN and WOMEN of today; check out your history and understand what those before YOU have done, for many books have not spoken of this (the truth about Black History) That ONE man that I have seen and heard his words that I have been to the mountain top and later spoke those words.

"Free at last, thank God that I'm free at last"

To me that's what Black History is all about. I'm Free to be ME, Free to Understand my History and the History of my people, that came before me and what they have done, but most of ALL what they have given to make this country what it is today.

I speak of this not just because I am a Black American, but I too have been to the mountain top. So to those of you who are sitting around on your ass like I was doing before I learn how to FLY and become "Free" get out there in the "WORLD" it will welcome you with UNRIVALED beauty of what's out there. I hate to say this, but I have set around all of my life doing nothing, now that the doors have been open to me; For it's like I have been in a storm, but now it's over and I can see the light and FLY.

I just want to view the landscape and see the world. I just want to explore the Frontier of History and see ALL of the amazing things out there. People time waits for NO ONE, so get off of your ass and come join me out there.

You see sometimes when I look into the mirror, I ask myself "Armour what you want? Hell I just want to be FREE and be ME. Like I have said before I feel that I have been in a storm too long. This is for those whose blood ran dry on the creek beds in the Deep South and on the battle field, what you have done for me. You see when I speak of Black History, I think of "ALL of this" and I say THANK YOU. This is what Black History means to me.

I would like to share something with you that happened to me on a very special day; you see Black History speaks of the Freedom for or of people. I would like to tell you a story;

It was on a Sunday, a beautiful day outside, one of those days that you want to lay out in the sun and be thankful that you are with no worries. I remember this day all too well, because it was Memorial Day. I had just out to the grave of my daughter Jennifer to spend some time with her. I looked around and I see lots of new faces here today, that I have not seen before. I think that some of those folks only come here once a year to pay their respects to their love ones. This special day really all got started was to pay respect to the men and women of the military who gave their lives for someone to become "FREE"

Here comes Mieko who is Japanese, she is old now, but one could tell that in her day, she would make a blind man see and a crazy man bark at the moon. Her husband's grave site is right next to my daughters. She spoke to me and said Armour you are here because it's Memorial Day like so many others who are here. I said to her, I come here every weekend to sit and talk with my daughter, just as you come here to see your husband and pay respect to him for giving his life to set others free. Yes Armour. She just stood there and looked at me with those eyes that have turned a little gray; and said "Seymour gave his life to help set others free, but he never gave his life to set me "Free."

I wondered about that and just what did she mean, the he never gave his life to set her free.

I had to ask her what you meant by that? I mean that others are free but I will never be free here in America, because I am a Jap, and you'll never be free because you are Black? I didn't see that one coming, but I understood just where she was coming from and understood those words that here in America, even today that people still judge you by the color of your skin and the shape of your eyes.

Yet, for me some people did die to set me free and to cast a vote to use the same rest rooms as others and didn't have to sit in the back of that damn bus. You see my readers this is why Black History means so very much to me. The Blacks that came to the bus station, only to walk away. Those who sat there in my place so that one day I might sit there and hear those words "How may I help you Sir."

I am about to say something and some of you might think that I am out of my rabbit-ass mind or that I am going crazy, and yet someone just might be saying Damn Armour, give me some of that stuff that you have been smoking. Well first of all I don't smoke. I was thinking back about history and I felt that America was the second Egypt? Let me say that again "I felt that America was the second Egypt? I am sure that some of you are wondering why I say a thing like this!

Armour why don't you explain why you made a statement like this? Well my friends I will not give you the answer to this statement, because I want you to do your home work and come up with the answer to this. Maybe some of you will get the answer and maybe some of you will not get the answer.

People if you do your home work right and look back at history, surely you will find that answer. Then you'll see just why I felt that America was the second Egypt. Now you can see why I feel that Black History is "MY MEMORIAL DAY.

SUPER BOWL WEEKEND

It's one of those days, the sun is out and it's close to 50F out today, sitting here on the water front asking myself should I go over to San Francisco for the Super Bowl Party, then again I don't feel like dealing with all of those people that will be there, plus it would be hell driving over there and that boat ride is out of the question.; had enough of that water when I was in the Navy. I think that the TV will be my best bet.

Yet, I need to get out of the house. Man this place has a way of closing in on your ass. I have been down that road before once and man it was a trip. That was the time I got my hat brought to me. Some of it was good and I wanted to go back for seconds. Shit that was how good it was, but what's done and one can't recapture those times over again. So I must be thankful for the time that I did have. Thought I was going to stay in, but that way of thinking didn't last long, because I had some company over and off we went.

Once out there I felt like the world was my play ground and I felt like exploring some new territory. I had been keeping myself on the ropes and not allowing myself to go out and have one good night out there on the town. The very first lady that I saw I just wanted to get to know her and become friends, she was about my age, but a little bit younger.

It's funny while thinking about that, she came up to me and said sir, don't I know you from some place? You know how some of us do, kind of let that slide by, She went on to say, that you look just like this guy who lives close to my house in Fairfield. Sir do you have a twin brother? I smiled and said I do not have a twin brother. Sir you do live in Fairfield? Yes on Concord

144

Ave, in that Gold looking house. Wow, because I live on Concord Court, and she smiled and said now I know you, because one of my home girls who I used to work with lives next to you.

Now I knew just who she was talking about. You know when you are not there looking for something or acting a fool something comes your way when you aren't looking for it. We talked for a while and then she went her way, but did say why we don't get together for a cup of tea. Hell that was my line that she stole from me. We pass each other that code number saying that we shall call each other.

Here comes that party group, the ones that comes with their chairs, just to sit here and have a nice time and wave at the people as they pass by. I want knock them because they have something that I need? That's to belong to someone and have some fun. Yet, I can't find what I'm looking for, maybe I'm reaching to high and need to bring my ass back down to earth where I belong, but they do say that one should reach for the starts.

I really hate to cut out on you like this, but tomorrow is a very special day in my life. It brings back some pain in my life. It was only like yesterday that this happen. It's so clear that I see this right in front of me, just as it took place on that very day here in San Francisco. I would like to talk about this event only if you have the time to hear and feel my pain.

Please close your eyes, now you have become me, sitting there in the court room watching him as he comes into the room. There is no noise in the court room, so still that you would be able to hear a rat piss on cotton. I don't move because my eyes are on him. Yes him! The man that shot and killed my daughter on her wedding day.

I sat there facing him. I didn't see him, because I was having some flash backs. I was back in the jungle of Vietnam and all I saw was a man in the jungle looking for me, trying to keep me from coming home. Sweat began to pour off of me and I found myself wet and cold from that sweat. I had to get away, the next thing I knew that I was back in the court room. Looking at that man who had stamped out my sunshine and took my daughter and my grand-child from me. I felt the tears and the pain and hurt right there in the court room.

When it came time for him to address the court and say why he took this woman's life and the life of her unborn child? This fool didn't even say that he was sorry for what he had done. All this fool said to the court was... If I could not have her, then no one else could have her. "I smoked her ass." Crazy as this shit may sound, there are a lot of fools (men and women) running around the streets thinking about the same old bull-shit. It's like they say this WORLD has gone to HELL and back in a hand basket.

Damn, remembering something that my grandmothers use to say "The Lord gives of it and the Lord take of it. Maybe this fool didn't understand those words. "The Lord gives it, because he (the guy that took my daughter's life) took it. The Sunshine out of my life. That dark cloud still remains inside of me, even as I write these words.

Man, the ass kicker was that sometime later this dog or whatever you might wish to call him found out that he had killed the wrong person. Now open your eyes, and tell me what you felt when the words came "that he had killed the wrong person." Now tell me how you would have felt if that was your "daughter." I start going back to church thinking that this would ease the pain that's cutting me up inside bit by bit at a time. Today is that day. Three years ago on this very day was when I lost her and my grandchild, never knowing if it was a boy or a girl.

Well you know sometimes when something is eating at you when I was in this church, I found myself going to sleep; it was like I was in a fog. This place wasn't for me. I kept on looking around, and then I found this kind of small church where there was around one hundred or a little less. It was a Baptist. I felt right at home there, maybe it's because I am Baptist, and I felt real good when I left there. Rather than bore you with all the details about my church life, let me cut through the chase and ask you one question after sharing my story with you.

"WHO ARE YOU" I'm telling you you've gotta sit down and think about this, and maybe you'll become just like me, trying to find that one answer that I have been looking for, for so many years and that my friends is "Who I am". I mean that WE all need an answer to it! That question that has been eating away at our souls, some of us resist the urge to look for that answer because we might not like what we have found out!

Why? Because the truth can set you FREE or the truth can be a BITCH when it comes right down to finding out "Who I am"

Thinking about the topic that was spoken in church today. "I ain't Done Yet", it kind of goes along with this book that I isn't done yet, because we have many more miles to travel and so much more time together as we ride down this road as of "ONE" Where your thoughts will be come my thoughts and my thoughts will be come your thoughts.

With a light smile on my face as I wonder through another day of life feeling good because I was able to get up and start off to another day. I never got up in the morning thinking how thankful that I was to see the Sun comes up or feel that I'm alive, until now.

I'm sure that you have other things to do, so let's take five and have a cup of tea and talk later.

HATE COMES ALIVE

A few months ago it was December 7, 2016. Maybe some of you young men and women don't remember what that day was or how dark it was on that sunny day of December 7, 1941. What it means to America? Well let me take you back seventy-four years ago. The day that Japan boomed Pearl Harbor on the Sunday morning. America went to war because President Roosevelt felt that Japan was wrong in doing what it did; so from 1941-1945 World War 11 took place America was at war and those who were from the land of Japan were rounded up and was shipped to camps clear across the land. It didn't matter if they were American born of foreign born they were a Jap.

This kind of reminds me of a story that an old lady once told me. The one that I see sometimes when I go to see my daughter Jennifer at that place that one day we all will end up out there. I am speaking of the grave yard; others have another name for it. The "Cemetery" whatever the name might be, and it's the last resting place for all of us. Why am I speaking of this now, because sometimes history has a way of repeating its crazy ass. I watch the TV and I see that fool on there talking crazy and lots of shit. You know whom I am speaking of. Yes! Him, a man that is running for the President of the United States of America.

Lord, help America if this fool becomes the next President? The shit that he is talking about Mexicans, Immigration, women, and now the Muslins. Send them back home; don't allow any of them to come to the states. Hell man, many of our Fore-Fathers were Immigrants and this land was built on the BACKS of the Immigrants, from the White House in Washington, D.C. to the Golden Gate Bridge in San Francisco.

If you would only listen to those words that this man is speaking and hears those that support him. I do hope that "ONE" sees the hand writing on the wall. Shit just the other day two men were praying in the park and this lady comes up to them talking all crazy and going out of her rabbit-ass-mind. Damn, she threw some coffee on them because they were praying, but most of all because they were Muslims.

Now the ass kicker of this, because of what has happened out here in California, where this man went out on a killing run; Are we the good Americans who are starting to allow our hearts to become fill with hate? Or are we playing right into this man's hand! "Don't allow them into this land because as he would put it" they are thugs' murders and unfit to be here in the USA. When this man spoke of Immigrants was he speaking about his father? Whose record wasn't all that clean?

How many Americans out there want to join ISIS? Shit here in California gun stores are pulling in the money and gun ownership is on the rise. Hell what's next, will the Old West return? Even those in the church are packing alone with the schools. I thought we were trying to keep guns out of the schools, but they are there!

I keep on asking myself is there something in the water, because young kids are playing a crazy ass game. Going to school to kill his or her classmates. Hell some Police are running around crazy thinking that they have a license to kill (that is if you are Black) Now please will someone tell me the truth? Is it that America has gone to HELL in a hand basket?

The question that I now ask myself will "WE" or I allow this fear to become a part of my life every time that I walk out of my front door? I look at this Muslim thing like it was back in those days back in 1950, 1951, and so on, even before that when we were colored and Negro. I understood those times; I felt that hate even when I was in the military.

Let me give you a little insight on what I'm talking about and went through. Well you see that the Navy had a Racial problem in the early part of 1972 or it might have been a little before that. So the Department of Defense set up the Race Relations Institute at Patrick Air Force Base in Florida, I was sent there and spent many hours in the class rooms, seven days a week for three weeks for a total of 189 hours; after graduation from the Defense

Race Relations Institute there in Florida. The U.S. Navy felt that I needed more training, so the Navy sent me to the Navy Relations School for another 112 hours.

After graduation from the Navy Race Relations School I became an "R.R.E.S." (a Race Relations Education Specialist) after receiving over Three Hundred Hours of Training, the Navy felt that I was ready to conduct Human Relation Seminars; so from 1972 until 1976 these seminars were given to the men and women of the Navy for a Rich Meaningful Experience in the "STRUGGLE" to control or understand "RACISM"

"I have seen how that shit (Racism) can eat the lives of so many good men and women, who wore that uniform I have also seen how this shit works overseas in places like Japan, Korea, Philippines and many other places, where I had spent some time in those places. Only to return back to the states, seeing just what was going on out there in the streets that hate has return back because of someone's Religion, the color of their skin, or the shape of one's eyes.

Damn, didn't America learn anything from the early years of hate; that very same hate that once again has found its way back into our schools, college and even in the church, police force and now into the political stage. I speak of this as a Black man that has given over twenty-one years to help keep America safe and free. Again is there something in the water making us to become who we aren't!!!!

Now, that I have said those words about that person and his thing which he speaks on the border, Muslims. What or who is next? Will it be women (where this man has already spoken on that when "HE" if you are rich you can do anything) I or someone else that or who don't fit his MOLD or is he that one who has been "REBORN" (from the grave) speaking out that one must be "Blond and have Blue eyes"

I know one thing for sure that if America doesn't wake up, I pray to God that World War 111 is not sitting there just waiting for a fool like him to come alone and push that button. I'm sure that we all have OUR own opinion just like WE all have an ass hole.

This is my opinion, maybe I have just pissed someone of by saying what I did, if so and then so be it, Like they say that the truth will hurt, but it will set you free. Sorry to drop a boat load of shit on you like that, but this is who I am, another person that at times had lived in fear, but on the other hand "life must go on" It's 2016 and there is just one thing that's eating at me ass is "SEGREGATION" on its way back?

WHAT'S NEXT

I believe that this is something that we all must think about. I'm back at the water front here with Pattie Labels signing that song 'If you don't know me" now when you get to that part about ten long years, it's what got to me, it will be ten long years that I have lost my wife in 2006. That's my dark year in my life, when all of the fun and joy was sucked right out of my life, leaving a hole which is still here and no one to fill that hole and bring back joy and laugher into my life.

As I sit here I see others holding hands and that smile on their face, which brings them so much joy, but for me there is no joy, and that smile stays hidden behind a close door. There is no key to open that door, and allow that smile to come forth. Yet you are happy on the outside but it's that enter side that cries out for someone to hold you tight and say those words.

"Baby I got you."

I sit here writing this letter and the blues that's playing on that CD burns deep into the soul and those words are like a big blade cutting into you. Damn, you want to stop that CD, but you can't, it's like something is saying "man" this is just for you and you alone. Those blues that hurt your heart. Now I can see why so many people "cry" when the blues get's to kicking ones ass, like they say you ain't felt the blues until you have lived the blues. Lord knows that I have lived those blues and felt that pain that went along with those blues.

Maybe I should get my ass off of this water front, which at times can bring pain into one's life. I'm not saying that I am Superman and don't feel shit, now that would be a damn lie.

"Lonesomeness in its self has a way of coming into your life and take away all of your Joy and Sun shine.

Man, I had my Sunshine taken away from me once before, can't deal with that a second time.

Damn, that's why I need to put you down, but I shall return, because I have come too far to turn back now; being such a good day I think I'll go for a ride and enjoy this day, because life is so very short and one never knows just what tomorrow might bring to you, it could be Joy or sorrow.

Thinking back over my life for some reason I keep on hearing those words over and over again. The very same words that has been spoken throughout time from the very first day that man became upon the earth? "That it takes a village to raise a child! Yet where has that village gone to? For those of you who were a part of my village, I say THANK YOU, even to those of you that tried to stop me from coming home, the tricks, the games, oh yes! Even those of you that were out there waiting on me when I forgot the rules of the jungle, because I was looking for love in all of the wrong places. I speak of this now, because I am almost at the end of this book, looking back to where it all began in 1935 and up until now.

Like so many others OUR village has gone because of death, divorce, and for many other reasons that we do not wish to talk about. You see my readers you are my village. I need you to walk with me, hear my CRY as it plays music in the air not that cry of the Long Wolf but the CRY of knowing that life has been good to you and that LOVE was SWEET.

I'm sure that some of you are wondering why I speak of "that it takes a village to raise a child" Maybe it's because I see what's going on around US, each and every day, and thinking back to when I was a child growing up in Detroit back in the day, 1935, 1940 1950 and 1960. In my village there in Detroit, it was full of JOY, LOVE and TOGETERNESS. Dinner with the family, sitting around at night listening to the radio. The front door open and people walking up and down the street at night saying hello to those of us who were sitting on the front steps, enjoying the full moon and the cool wind as it came your way.

Man, that's the village that I am speaking of, for we all came from a village, but yet some of us have left that village to go by the way side, and all that's left is an open field in our life. Maybe I'm thinking about this it's because I am getting old, is this why I speak of this? "NO" my brothers and sisters that's NOT the main reason that I speak of this, it's because I miss my village and I say to you HOLD fast to your village and don't allow those "WEEDS" to come into your village and take that "CHILD" away from you.

Now there is still so much more for me to say, and many more dirt roads to travel down before I reach my goal and find that answer that I and so many others have been looking for and that's "Who I am" So don't leave me now, we still have a long ways to travel.

Last night I had a dream. Wow! The last time that I heard those words was when Dr. King spoke those very same words "I had a dream"! In my dream I was in church and she was sitting there next to me a very nice looking lady. I found myself looking at her, and for some reason I spoke these words. Wow! You look just like my girl? "The First Lady of the United States of America. We laughed about that. We sat there in the six rows from the back. We spoke and the next thing that I knew that we were holding hands. I could feel the heat from her hand as it rolled through my fingers.

I said that we shouldn't be doing this, because people might think that there was something going on between us. I had to ask myself, what's going on between me and the church and woman. The last lady that I had met in church she too had fire in her touch. She was the Devil in the Blue Dress. I could not forget her, the one that I was afraid of! Yes I was afraid of that lady?

You see this lady had my WEAKNESS, which could make me cry, cry and I wanted to cry some more. For she too had HAIR on her LEGS which was my down fall.

I don't know why I felt this way about women who has hair on their legs. Maybe it had to do with someone from my past. This lady had hair on her legs. Man not that baby hair, I'm speaking of hair. Maybe it all got started when I saw a woman with hair on her arms. I always said that I bet she is covered with hair down there. The more that I saw women with hair on their arms, I would say to myself, "Armour" you got to get yourself one of those women. I do remember the very first time that I had sex with a lady who had hair on her legs, and that bush was full of hair also. The kind of hair that itch into your soul and that hair on her legs just held me in check.

Shit, I want lie about it! It was good, so good that this lady brought smoke to my ass and tears to my eyes. Hell the very next thing that I knew that I was crying and begging for some more tears to flow. Now you can see why I don't want to deal with ladies that have hair on their legs. What's that saying in Baseball, THREE strikes and you are out? Hell I have already had TWO and not looking for number THREE. You just might think that I'm blowing smoke up your ass! Well let me ask you this, have you EVER had something that was good, but yet you feared that thing because you didn't want to feel like that again?

I guess that we all have something to FEAR about, mine is women that have hair on their legs plus I'm getting to old too be crying like that, but just the JOY in thinking about it. My old ass laying there in bed crying like that, because that Wild Cherry just kicked my ass. I keep on asking myself, what do I really want? Do I want a make believe love because it makes me CRY or a TRUE love.

I feel that when you are in love, at times you are unsure how it feels, but I guess that when you do find that true love, you feel it EMBRACE you. That feeling of Joy and Happiness. Is this why the Church and women keep coming into play in my life. Is she sitting there just waiting for me OR is it that I keep on looking for love in all of the wrong places. Is it that I think that the church is the right place to look for that person? Or am I just looking for a shot of that Wild Cherry?

Maybe it's about that time that I should return back to the mountain top! I need some answers in order for me to move on, and stop looking in the church for what's not there and for what might never be. I think it's best to try and look down the road for that answer. I keep on thinking about women and the church. What if I'm all wrong about this? What if it's the church that's looking for me? I never thought about that! It's because once again I was looking for love in the entire wrong place? I should just leave things the way that they are, because love will find me and not I find love.

Well I think that I should pack my bags and get ready to return back to the mountain top for the answers that I am seeking; so if you don't mind, I need to cut out on you for now, and get ready to make that trip up to the mountain, to clear my head because something is really wrong here, and very wrong in the way that I am thinking.

Sitting here ready for my trip, I ask myself do I really need to return back to the mountain for answers to this problem! Or maybe it's not a problem at all; What if, what's going on with me and the church is not to be. I have heard it said before that when some Black men age they find themselves turning to the church? Is this what's happening to me? Now that I am up there in age... I do find that I need the church in my life.

I never thought of it this way; all I was thinking about how to get over and get off into someone's panties. Hell this is all that I have been thinking about for over the last six years. Have I gotten to the place that I need Wild Cherry in order so that I can go on living or could it be that because I haven't had some of the Wild Cherry in quite a while. I just want to see what it feels like just having a little shot of it? Like the old people would say "hold on" it will happen only with the right person and at the right time; because the two of you will have so much in common, but most of all it was to be....

Last night I was speaking with you about the church? Now it's Sunday morning and I'm getting ready for church, but this time I'm NOT going there looking for her. This time I am going there for myself, because I have this feeling that I must go there. Please don't ask me what it's about, because something isn't right. Well here I am in church, and there are more people her today than any other Sunday, It's that Sunday of the month, its dress down Sunday. It's nice that you can come to church and not have to dress up. I'm here in my jeans and tee shirt. The one that has "How Strong is Your Love" on the front. The color is yellow, which goes right with these jeans.

All is well and for some reason I feel good, just being able to wake-up this morning and come here, and not be worrying about anything, but most of all I'm not looking for anything, all I want today is the word.

That's what I am here for is the "WORD". Wow! I don't know what came over me, but I found myself putting my name on the New Members list for Orientation for the Right Hand of Fellowship. Maybe this is the reason that I had to attend church today. Whatever it was that it had a hold on me; it brought me to this New Road in my life. A road that I must travel until the very end

I'm not getting any younger, maybe this just might be my "CALLING" telling me that I need to change my way of thinking and start a NEW LIFE, because better things a waits for me in the days to come. Last Sunday I spoke of putting my name on the list for New Members list at my church. Today is a wonderful day, it so very nice outside. Yes I'm at my number one place because I just left the house of the Lord. Wow! The church was full of people.

I believe that some came because it was Sunday, and some came to church like me, looking for the word.

Yet, I feel that other's came because it was Easter Sunday? A day that some of us came to pay our Respects to our Lord for what he did for us that was to die for OUR SINS. The service was amazing and the choir was out of sight, because they song from the heart. One could feel the love and warmth that was there in the chuch. People reaching out to one and another, made ONE feel that they were there not only for the word, but for the LOVE that was there in this place. Just waiting for you to reach out and grab it and hold tight to it.

There was something about today's service that made you feel it, and that it was all about you. This was your Sunday and your word, because it was written just for you and with your name on it. All you had to do was just reach out and grab it, and that this is 'MY DAY."

I'm sure that some of you did attend your own church, and you might have felt the same way as I or you might have felt better. Then again you just might have had that very same feeling just like I had. because this was a very Special day in your life and that was a very Special Sunday, that over millions found it to be so very special to them. Like I have said many times before that I can only speak for myself, even as I put my feelings down on paper. Hearing Shirley Caesar on a CD in the back ground makes one be THANKFUL for so many things in life, because tomorrow isn't promise to us.

I do believe that many of you know just where I'm coming from, because You too have felt these things yourself and understand just where I'm coming from, when I speak about life and just how Amazing it is or just how it can become. You see in my Village where I came from we learn about this and what was important in "LIFE" because those in OUR village taught US about life, but most of all THEY were there with us through it ALL.

Mom, Grandmother, Aunt May, and ALL the others who were in my village I do not have the words to say THANK YOU for being there but most of all I just wish to THANK YOU FOR THE LOVE.

IF NOT FORYOU

THE FOUR BLOCKS OF MY LIFE

IF NOT FOR YOU

Sitting here with a cold glass half full of Arbor Mist, Pinto Griglo Island Fruits which has been on ice for quite some time (I think about two months) until today, just waiting for a reason to pop the top. Asking myself should I do it now or wait until 8: pm when I sit down and have that plate of Greens, Corn bread, Rice and those Pig feet. Damn, that's all good. Whatever it will be, I shall be thinking of you.

I just want to say Thank YOU, EVER SO MUCH FOR YOUR TIME WHEN I CAME HOME TO Detroit, to be with you for that very special day of your life. I knew that I must be there in Detroit for that day, your Birthday. Donna, while making that three day drive from California to Detroit, something happened to me. I knew that I had to make a change in my life. Like cleaning the house on Monday and Tuesday, and from Wednesday until Saturday I'm out at the Race Track and on Sunday one could find me in Church.

Hey! Went out and got myself a new Fishing Poll, and asking myself should I go fishing in new Waters or keep on fishing in those waters that my hook has been sitting in for such a long time. Donna, sometimes when one has time to think, it's like they say "one never knows what my happen unless you get your feet wet. "Wow! For two years in a row, if it had not been for you my stay in Detroit would have been like "CRAP."

Donna, sometimes I ask myself why you and I are so close to each other. Maybe it has to do with that you and I are the last two born of the Armour Family. On both sides. And that you are me and I am you... We both have gone down that very same road and at times, yet you and I have been the only two Armour's that have remain close to each other, there for each other. I look at other members of the family, they are there, but apart from each other; sure we speak to each other and get alone sometimes, but if you take a good look at the others there is a distance between each of them.

Hell, like they say that there is a reason for everything? I look at the fun that you and I have and there's "no conflict" between us. Well any way Thanks for everything and those Friday Night. One Dollar Hot Dogs, Two Dollar beers and those "HORSE" kicking your ass. Like on your birthday (smile) those were the fun nights and those other times when I was teaching you how to play the game of Dominoes and I would let you win, because I was in your house, and didn't want you to cry "mama" Uncle Fella is betting on me again and take your Dominoes and run up stairs to your room; Crying I ain't going to play with you anymore."

I must say that you are getting quite good at that game. Donna, no matter how many games that I let you win (smile) I can't fix my mouth to say those words that you want me to say. (Ain't going to do that) I hate to end this so soon, but my Road -Dog is coming over and I think that I'll share a glass or two of this wine with her; but just only a glass, because this one bottle it's special, that's the one that you gave to me.

Donna! Now tell me about it? I'm sure that you got a surprise when you open this book and found your picture in there? It's there because you are special and you belong in there alone with your Aunt Lucia. You see you, and her are the most two wonderful people that has come into my life, and you will "Always" be a part of me and my life. Donna, when I said that you were me and I was you! It's because we both carry that same shield in front of us, only giving love to those that we wish too.

Road-Dog knowing that you were tied when you came home from work after a long day at work dealing with some of those crazy ass people that's there in the school system. The ones that make you want to go out and get yourself a cold one and say to hell with it. I know this, because I too had to deal with some crazy ass people when I was working in the Post Office.

Yet, you always had time for me ensuring that I went to those places and did whatever I had too, even when I was checking out things (the ladies) on the side lines, knowing that you wanted to get back home to enjoy a cold one, and all other things came second. (Like that time when I was trying to talk that lady into buying some shoes for her daughter)

HELL! What can I say, but thank you ever so much, not because you are my NEICE, but because you are my "ROAD-DOG?

Love

Uncle Fella

MOVING ON

It's a Sunday afternoon, and some of you just might know where I have been and where I am at right now. Yes, at the water front just after leaving church. Not really in a hurry to get home, because there is no one waiting there for me. Just Topper my bird, but he's not really missing me, because the only times that he does miss me is when it's feeding time or when it's time for his music lessons.

It's nice here today and so is the view with so much to look at as they stroll by you, can't help but to look because after all you are only human. There is an old saying that my late wife use to say to me. "Honey its okay to watch, but your ass better not try and touch. (I know you have heard that before from your lady friend) I understand that because once you touch it, hell it might get good to you, and you just might want to keep on touching it, and your ass just might forget where your home is. Now that's no lie, because lots of good men and women have gone down that road, and not only lost their homes, but they also lost sight on the world.

Just thinking back when I was there in Detroit last year, we (the family) were on our way over to Canada. It has been sometime that I had been over there. For me the ride was very nice, just seeing the open land and all of those corn fields, which makes one want to get away from the Rat race and come up here to live. We are almost at my brother's place, where we will be doing some cleaning-up around the yard. As we pull up in the drive way, the place stills looks just like it did when I was up here last year. Now just sitting out front and having a cold Bud, which feels good going down, nothing better than a cold Bud and some peace.

Man, if I ever come back this way to live, I would come here to live. It's not that I don't like Detroit or California, but when you find a place that one could feel peace in the air, that's the place to be. I have always wanted to live in the country, with some land around the place. I'm sure that lots of you have been over this way and have seen just what I'm talking about.

For some reason just sitting here and my mind wondered off to my sister who found herself all alone out there in one of those homes. Sometimes not knowing who your family members were Now that the time has come and you understand that you are about ready to leave this place for good, to be off to a better place (they say) You think about all of those times when you were alone and only a few people did show up to see you.

Sis, you lay there like you are a sleep, but hearing those words. "It's so lonely here, is this's killing the old girl? You want to cry out "Hell no, that's not killing me, it's you" that's killing my ass. Coming out here all like this and that but you are know better than some of my church friends; who have taken just about everything that I own, and you are here to finish cleaning house. I look at my sister whose up there in age, knowing that loneness didn't kill her; it was her so-called friends who were stealing from her that did it.

I don't want to be like that when I go out. Man, that's why I have made out my "WILL" and if your name is not there, child you ain't getting shit. You see I have known lots of people that passed away and the things that they had and work so very hard for, those things were gone by the way side and some things got legs and just walked away. I know that this is to be true, because I can look back on my mom's life and her things. Some people got up-set about this and that. Who should get this and who should get that. If things didn't work out like some of them wanted it, Shit, they got the ASS.

Damn, whatever happen to the picture of grandma? Hell man, "DEATH" can bring out the "BITCH" that's in side some of us. I think that I should leave that alone, because I am wondering what shall I do or where shall I go too, but the question is what shall I do when I get there! Well another day has come and gone, I have kind of come down from that high that I was on. That Easter Sunday. A very wonderful day, first of all the service was out of sight. Sorry to use like that, but it was very up-lifting. The Pastor found the right words for this very Special Sunday! This was "OUR DAY" to praise our

Lord who gave his life for you and I. Sitting here thinking about that day. What would it had been like to had been there standing on the side line as he walked past you, wishing that you could reach out and touch him.

Not saying a word as he carried that Cross up that hill, fallen to the grown, with the help of a Black man to help him up so that he might bare that cross.

Yet the history books never speak of or say that a Black man was there at his side, as he walked on not speaking to anyone, the only words that were spoken was when that Black slave spoke out to him saying "WE" are going to make it. No other words were spoken until after he was nailed to that cross, until he spoke out to his father. Those words that I and so many others have forgotten.

Now, time has gone by and it's another month. I am so very thankful that I'm here for another day. Yet so many others can't say those words. We can only think of them. It want be long and some of us will be out there in the back yard, with Ribs, Hot Dogs, kicking on the grill, a holiday will be here, family sitting around shooting the shit and telling it like it is. Yet for this upcoming Holiday in May. I shall be out there spending time with her. Thinking about all of the times that her and I had with each other. No ribs or hot dogs for me.

Those are that time that makes one feel alone. You want that special person to be with you. Yes! As the two of you suck on that rib bone, as that juice flows from your finger tips, with a sweet kiss to the lips to mop up that B.B.Q sauce from the lips of your love one.

Damn, life sucks and loneliness can be a bitch. I speak of this because, just the other day it hit me and I felt it. Wanting to reach out to someone, but there was no one to lay my head on their breast and say to them "Baby, Baby, please hold me tight and never let go of me, and darling I do really love you."

TODAY IS OUR DAY

Laying here looking at my picture when I was in the military and thinking that the 11th of November of any year is "Veterans Day" the day that has been set aside for US! Just received a word from another Veteran, Man it really was a good word and it went something like this:

"It cannot be inherited nor can it ever be Purchased I have earned it with my BLOOD, SWEAT and TEARS. I own it forever for the title "VETERAN".

Those words hit me deep down inside because it's OUR DAY. All through this book I have been looking for that one big question "Who I am". Well my friends today I know who a part of me is, a Veteran. Only one of the millions who stood on the front lines. I alone with my brother's and sister's, who stood on the lands overseas, and spent many days and nights on the open sea.

I don't know just how this day got started or what year that this day was set aside for US... Maybe it's because America was a shame for the way that it treated US, or was it a way to say "Welcome Home". I have seen those movies from the past where the streets were full of people, news stories saying "Welcome Home". Yet there were those who stood on the side line saying that old crazy ass song? "Hell no we want go" Is this the day that we want to say that WE are sorry for closing the door on US, because some of US are sick, some of US are out of a job, out of a home with a warm bed in it, because WE love you and stood fast holding OUE heads high, saying to all of the WORLD that I'm a VETERAN.

We know that some of YOU will come out in the cold or place that flag on your front door, maybe some of you have put that small flag on your car or truck and drove down the streets, letting others know that you CARE about US and in your very own special way you are saying THANK YOU.

My brothers' and sisters', place here on the table as I write this letter, I have THREE things in front of me:

1. A Glass of Orange Juice
1. A cup of Coffee
2. A Glass of Wine

The Orange Juice is for my health. The Coffee is to wake me up and the Wine is for ALL of you my Brothers' and Sisters' because it's "OUR DAY", Veterans Day. To those of you who were there before me and those of you who stood alone with me, and for those of you that must fellow US come on it's your day also.

You see on one hand I have found "Who I am" and can stand and say that I'm a VETERAVN who gave our home land twenty years of service to support and help keep America safe, for those of you I say thank you for thinking of US and standing tall at our side, even when so many of US was committing Suicide. To all of the Veterans far and wide, this was a day that that was set aside just for US. Some of US felt good about OUR DAY, and yet some of us were down and out, because for some of US we have no place to go to, not even a place that we can call home.

Last night the TV with its stories about US. The good ones and the bad ones, like the VA Hospital, how some of my brothers' and sisters' are treated like shit! Yes! I said like "SHIT". I have been there and seen some of their faces of those that walk the streets, asking for a hand out. That little Sign saying I'm a Veteran will work for Food. Damn, each time that I see this, I feel their pain. Damn, putting their life on the line for our country and can't even get in the hospital to see a doctor. Shit, in some cases, I hear that there is a waiting line?

Now you have to be shitting me, because there is a problem of taking care of the staff and not the Vets. Well I'm still in the house, no place to rush off to, plenty of time left before I must I be off to the Race Track. That's my thing, out there enjoying myself, and doing one of the things that I love to do most of all, besides sitting on the Water edge.

Man, now that's the place to be, sitting there watching the tide come in, and feel that wind as it calls out to you, saying today is going to be a good one, because it's "OUR DAY" and WE are alive.

Well it want be long and I'll be putting down this pen, because I'll be at the cross road for good, and by that time I should know "Who I am" My friends this has been a very long ride and it has not been an easy one for me, because not only have I step in quick sand along the way, but there has been so many road blocks out there alone with those lioness who was out there waiting to eat my ass up, because I was on their play ground; but most of all doing some things where I had forgot the RULES of the jungle, and when that happens your ass is fair game.

I know just how this goes, because when I was young and wild I was out there acting a fool. Wow! Just thinking that I have come a very long ways from the womb to the fields of Korea, the back streets of Japan, and the war fields of Vietnam and to the Wilderness of love. Some of you wanted to give up on me, because you thought that I was a Damn Fool for picking up the pen and telling the world my story. Yes, I did that! But what you must understand that my story is the story of so many others. I am only their voice to express that which they don't have the words to say what I have said.

Maybe, they felt ashamed to express just what they went through in life, and what they felt when SHIT hit the fan. We as humans at times don't want people to peep into our back yards, and see just how much trash is kept back there. It's fear of the unknown and the Fear of how people just might judge us.

Yet, at times we all might have walk down this road, but it's so good to have someone to walk with you alone the way and hold your hand in the darkest of your hour. I remember that time when I was out there, a stranger came my way, she didn't judge me, but she stuck out her hand and said "Armour" I'm here for you and will walk with you. This lady is still with me today. Bless her heart for being there for me. I say to you my brothers and sisters I'm here for you, because this is YOUR Story that I'm writing about ALL I ask of you is to walk with me and hold my hand while I tell "OUR STORY.

Maybe, just maybe we all might find out "Who we are" and in return I might find out "Who I am", so those of you who are ready to judge US, please don't do it, because you too just might have a back yard full of shit, because there is one thing that I have learn in these eighty-one years of life "That is to clean up around your OWN back yard first, before you talk about my back yard, or the persons back yard who lives next to you.

So my friends if you see some of "US" out there it's not because we don't have any other place to-go-to or a warm bed to lay our head on at night, ONLY those dark streets, those cold doorways. I can only say maybe we might not have much, but we can still stand tall and say "I'm a VETERAN"

IT'S ALL GOOD

It's another one of those days and my gut is full, just finish off some Pig Feet, with Hot Sauce and Greens and Rice, all I need now is a Cold Bud and I'll be good for today. Yet while praying that someone will not come alone and F-----K-up my day. You know how it is, things going your way and someone comes and put some shit on your plate. I don't know why, I feel this way, but someone is waiting to push my door bell, and that's when shit will hit the fan. I'm sure that some of you have had one of those days. Someone wanting you to do something or go out some place, not knowing what you wish to do or go to, so you just sit back and cool it.

Now F---K me dead there's one of them at the door as we speak, trying to sell me something or those guys in the White shirts and Black pants. Now what gets to me is that I have this big poster saying" If you're selling something then you are at the wrong house. Maybe I need to add more to that poster "like keep on Walking and don't come a knocking." Maybe that will work.

Well my day is already off to a bad start, so maybe I'll go on down to Leroy's place and play some bones with the guys and have a cold Bud or two in order to pep myself up; was thinking about going to Reno to get away for a while. This just might be a good for me, it's only a 2 ½ hour drive and the weather is good. Hell, maybe I'll call my Road-Dog and see what she is up too, and see if she wants to get out of town for the weekend.

Man, that's what's nice by having a Road-Dog and not a Friend. You see friends want too much and plus you have to tell them ahead of time to do things. Right now I just want to go and kick it, not really looking for anything special; just some me time and company. Damn, that's what's nice about being retired with no strings; Man, you can go out and do those things and not having to rush back home to anyone not even for the dog. Knowing that I have earned this after Forty-three out there giving myself to the world. Twenty- Ones to help keep the country safe, and Twenty-Two years to make sure that you got your mail, no matter what the weather was like.

Now all of that was good, because I loved the military and the Post Office was my job. Well I thought I thought that I was going to spend this weekend in Reno, but the Road-Dog wants to go to the Red Woods and kick back. That'll work for me.

Man, it's Wonderful out here seeing those trees that are over one or two hundred years old and still standing tall. Well here we are; pulling into the parking lot, I see others who are out here for the weekend kicking it, and you see that sign that reads "Bed and Breakfast" knowing just what that means ain't got to rush out for anything. Just the two of you and you have told the world before you left for this trip to go to Hell; after getting set-up and got to rest, we thought that we should go out and do those things that people around our age should do or would do. And that's to go for a walk and hold hands and smile at those that pass by; knowing that we are old in age, but feeling young in heart.

Man, this is one very good feeling knowing that you aren't alone, because you see so many others around you are doing this, holding hands You pass by the young ones that are all held-tight to each other, but chocking the hell out of each other, as they walk your way. You look at them, but you only smile and keep on walking; for today is yours. The warm sunshine and that soft wind as it kiss you, as the two of you slowly walk through the Red Woods.

Hearing the birds sing their own soft song of love, these things do something to you; you feel it, but yet you are not ready to reach out and pull it into your heat, because it's not your time.

NOTES

In one of my books I made a statement about people coming into our life. I believe that I made that statement in "How Strong is Your Love" but it's funny that people do come into our lives and we never say to them "THANK YOU" or Appreciate them, for they come and they go; here today and gone tomorrow!

Sometimes we want to "Thank" those people for the things that they have done for us, yet sometimes we just can't find the words to say or express one self. To me it doesn't matter how short or how long those words might be. Only to say that YOU all have played a part in making me "Who I am today". There have been so many of you who have played a role in my life. Helping me to become "Who I am" I would like to take this time to THANK each and everyone for what you have done for me.

Not everyone of you were there to help me, some of you were out to get what you wanted for yourself, but still you were a part of my life story, and I did learn something from each and every one of you.

My readers I only ask for you to sit back and take it easy. Has a cup of coffee or a cup of tea, Hell take off your shoes; at this time I would like for you to meet those who have played a role in my life.

Mom: If it wasn't for you I would not be here today, and be the person that I am today. Yes, you had your "RULES" and these very same rules kept me out of JAIL and off of TWELEVE MILE ROAD. (The grave yard) Mom, some times when I tell your grand children, and the great grand children, how it was when I would be acting a fool and knew that I was going to get a whipping.

Mom, your words always came out saying "Boy this is going to hurt me more than it's going to hurt you. Wow! Mom, at that time I didn't understand those words, but today those very words makes me laugh when I think about them.

"Hell I was the one who was getting that ASS whipping and not you Mom.

POPS: My step-father, thank you for being there for me. You were more than a step-father, you were my FRIEND.

Grandmother: You were full of wisdom; you always knew what to say at the right time. I only wish that I had taken more time to learn your ways and obtained your Wisdom.

SHIRLEY: the very first girl that I had kissed and that kiss burn my lips, which made me to become afraid of you and not wanting to kiss any other girls. Yet, you did kick my ass when we were attending Moore School. The very first ASS whipping in my life and it came from you, a "GIRL". I never told anyone about this. I lied and said that some boy had done it, and not a girl.

BABBARA: My high school sweet heart. There was something about you that has kept you own my mind. It's been over sixty years now since gradation from Northern High School and I still think about you. I have turn to some of our classmates and even the Face Book looking for you and wondering about you and where you were?

PAT: You were someone that I cared for and a very beautiful person. I wish to thank your from opening up my "EYES" to a dumb love. One that could not have been, but most of all, you just might have saved me and my "LIFE" from becoming a part of your world and life style of Pills, the Bottle and the Drugs.

RED: What can I say? You were just sixteen years old when we first met, with fire in your hair and that warmth in your eyes. It burned deep down inside of my soul. I fell in love with you. Red throughout the years this love for you has been there. I mean for over fifty years. When I was living in the darkness you open the door and let the light shine in. You gave me hope, when I thought that hope was lost.

JONNIE: You turn me onto Jazz and the beauty of it. You also help me to understand not only Jazz but ALL types of music.

RENA: Wow! You were there for me when I was young and didn't understand that saving Money was the "KEY" to it all. The very first thing that you said to me when first join the Air Force was "Save your money for when those clouds cover the sun. I didn't understand that then, but I do now.

LUNA: the older woman who became my teacher, who taught me how to make love to a woman, and the things that I should do to her.... You showed me those "Tender Spot's" on a woman's body and showed me how to Explore those spots to bring Joy and that Wonderful feeling to you and any other woman that I might have sex with, Yet! To you I was only your "Boy-Toy to be used and to bring joy to your body and world.

LEE: The master at Loving. I learn so very much from you, not just how to give love, but how to receive it in return, and love that person for "WHO" they were.

TESS: You need to go KICK some rocks. You only wanted to use someone for your very own thing. You wanted to put them in the Three "F" club.

1. Find them
2. Fool them
3. Forget about them

NANCY: Your sorry ASS would catch the very first thing on Wheels out of town, after Sucking Them bone dry, not even thanking them for being your Sugar Daddy.

The YOUNG ONE: You said that "Age" does not matter, that it was just a number, but what was in the Heart that counts. Yet, on the other hand you were looking for someone to replace that special person that you lost. Your father.

However you were in love with me (so you say) not thinking about the kind of love that you and I would have together. It would be a "ME and Mrs. Jones thing" lovers behind closed doors only to keep the world out of OUR life. Dear, deep down in your heart you felt that you loved me, but what you didn't understand was that I wasn't in love with you.

However, I do wish to thank you for opening up that door and once again allowing me to have that feeling of Someone loving me, and to be able to return that love back to them.

TO YOUNG TO LOVE

This morning I woke up with trouble in my mind. I met someone on line and this person is so much younger than I. Yet this person feels that age is just a number, but you are twice that person age. It does become more than a problem I feel that this person is looking at this through Rose color glasses. I can't speak of her name, but she is from overseas, and some women from those overseas don't look at age, but what's in the heart and what you feel.

I have explained to this person about our age and now this person has made plans to come here to the states, and she hopes to make something of a love life that I feel is not right. I have explained to this lady how will I bring her to meet my family? Only to hear those words! Damn, why are you going with a Child? Armour, not only is she a child, but she is not a woman of color. I' neither speak of her name nor of her words, I can only speak of mine; because my words come from the heart and hers came from a feeling. I speak of this while I'm sitting here at your feet. Jennifer because it's a nice day here and there is only a few people here. It's funny that the only time that I come here on a Sunday is when I have trouble on my mind. Who else can I talk with? Who else will hear these words and know that they came from the heart.

Baby, I think back when that Rain and Pain which ate away at my heart back when those tears burn my eyes, and I couldn't see anything but only felt that pain. That I was all alone in this world without someone to love me like you. Daddy, forgive me for what I am about to say or how I say it, but I shall become you. "Let her ass go." She is looking for more than you think. Hell, you have raised my brothers and my sister. Why another child! You said that she is from across the pound (overseas) now Armour, ask yourself this? Is she looking for a husband and don't care what his age is? Now is she really looking for that Green Card?

You haven't known her that long, is this love or is this bull-shit. Sorry about that, but dad I'm being up front and being real. You see if you really did love her' I know what you would go to this woman and WASH her body clean so that you will see just what your are getting or what is there, or is another layer behind this, that is covering something up, because you were blind by what you saw up front.

Armour, I can only speak to you, but I can't speak to your heart. I am only here in your heart, or when you come to the grave yard to see me and talk with me, because you are deep in thought and you have trouble in mind. Dads tell me what did you say to her when she spoke of age? I want to hear your words, just what did you explain to her about coming here? You see I feel that I know her words and her story? Talk to me! Do you want to tell me those words or should I speak those word's that's in her head?

A. I am young and beautiful
B. He is an Old man without anyone to love him.
C. If I put this Wild Cherry on his old ass the right way, he would lose sight on the world
D. I have a home there in the states.
E. He has some money

Am I right or am I on the right track! Has she ever told you how long she will stay here, or did you ever ask her that question! I don't think so, because you only saw what was in front of you or that picture where she is letting you see what you think you might be getting? Daddy, she could say that I'll be good to you, but is she good for you? I am still waiting for those words that you spoke to her. Take your time, don't rush I'm not going any place, because I am at home here, without any worries, and I don't have to deal with all of that bull-shit, you see I'm at peace here.

So whenever you are ready, lay those words on me, besides I'm dying to hear them, by the way that's a joke I'm dying. Can't you take a joke Armour?

Now that's funny, because whenever you call me Armour, that means that your ass is on fire, and you are ready to get off into my ass. Yes I know that I have forgotten the rules of the Jungle and once again looking for love in the entire wrong places. Damn, you are not here and I don't have anyone to look out after me and keep my sorry ass out of trouble.

Baby you do come to me in my dreams, sometimes warning me that I am about to step into shit again. I'm sure that some of you might think that I'm crazy or full of shit, because I come here and sit by her grave and talk with her. Let me ask you this! How many of you have gone out to the grave yard and had a talk with your love ones?

Honey, those words that you are waiting for, goes something like this! Are you sure that this is what you want, knowing that this is only a dream for now.

Yet, knowing in the end it wasn't to be. What if we gave ourselves to each other and enjoying something that was not to be? Could WE both walk away without feeling the pain of love that was built on a lie? I want go into other things right now, but I'm sure that I will get around in telling you about it. Well baby-girl it's starting to get late and I need to get home so that I can feed Topper, plus I too need to eat something. It has been a very long day for me, so honey if you don't mind I'll be off to the house, but we shall talk again. Oh yes daddy we shall talk again, because whenever you step in shit, here you are right on time.

Damn it; now finish telling me what you said to her, because I know you. Talk to me, what else you said. Well if you must know what I said to her. I said these words "How would you feel if I wash your body down and loved you like I have never loved anyone before, by giving all of me and enjoying your pleasures and that juice of your love, only to walk away from you and out of your life never to return again? Dear you and I came into each other's life for a reason; you see you lost someone that you really loved "your father" and maybe you are looking for someone to love again. I lost a daughter, who was the world to me, and I loved her very much, is this I want from you a "daughter" to love again.

That's the words that I spoke to her, remembering that you told me when we would sit around the house and have our little talks. You would say to me daddy if you go out there and meet some lady, be up front with her, as you are with me. Jennifer when I came to you with trouble in mind, that's why I told this woman that age does matter; Yet, her thing is that it didn't matter, it was what's in the heart and the love that goes with it.

Baby, now this isn't' no bull-shit, at the age of eighty-one I feel that I was on top of my mountain and like being there I'll be the first to admit deciding to embrace age and make the most out of it, but a young woman of that age wasn't in the cards for me and aging is one of the Greatest Contradictions. Its everyone dream to live Longer, Healthier; Man life is one of Mankind's Greatest Accomplishments.

At this age in life, a young woman of that age is not for me, nor is she meant to be a part of my life. Because, hell that would only be adding another problem. Some of us have seen those old men walking around with that young one on his arms and some of us ask is that his daughter with him. Can't be his wife, a fine young thing like that! For me, I want her, the one with all of that Salt and Pepper in her hair.; because I'm not becoming younger, as I get older I benefited from the Experiences and Wisdom that life has brought me by the comfort that comes from having a better Understanding of life. I like where I am at, and look forward to the years ahead, with an older person at my age.

You see she and I have both been to the mountain top, and now it's time for us to enjoy that fruit from the mountain top. Jennifer you know the reason why I haven't been able to love another woman. I am talking about really loving her, that new woman. Yes daddy, I know the real reason why you haven't given yourself to any other woman. Dad, when I speak of not giving yourself, I'm speaking of the heart. Sure you could go out there and think that you have given yourself to someone, but dad if it's not from the heart, then you have not done a thing. You see I know you and how you think, because I have watch you sneak off into your bedroom and look at her picture when you think that no one is watching you. Dad, I'm speaking of that picture that you keep under your bed.

Yes, I know all about it. You see sometimes when you weren't home, I would go into your room and pull that picture out from under you bed and look at it. And say what a beautiful lady she is, and I understand just why you married her. Let me tell you something daddy you can't keep on holding onto the past, you have to let it go. You are not being fair to some other woman who just might want to love you. You sure haven't been fair to yourself dad. Damn, you have put road blocks in place even before allowing someone to come into your life.

What about that lady that you have been in love with for over fifty years? Now what about her Armour? Are you going to kick her out and do the very same thing to her again, just like you did to her in 1955? Turn your back on her and walk away without saying a word?

I understand how you feel, but sometimes people do some crazy ass shit; they let a good thing pass by and take a stab in the dark. Daddy I'll tell you something from the heart, I don't want to be that one and come alone and say those words "I told you so." I remember you asking her to set you free, now daddy did you set her free? Now are you the one that's still holding on? Now you tell me? I don't know, but maybe I'm looking for that love. You know what I'm talking about the one with "TRUST."

Baby first you need to LOVE in order to TRUST, but to love someone is to understand each other, to laugh together, to smile with your heart and to "TRUST" one another. It should be given "RESPECT" and it should receive that kind of love back in return. Baby, true love is the greatest thing that you can "EXPERIENCE," it can weather any storm. Loving, Trusting and respecting each other totally can bring you TRUE Love and Happiness.

It's hard to love someone new. A relationship should NEVER be taken for granted. What if I can't give this new lady these things because I'm still in love with the one that's in the grave? You see for forty-seven years I had TRUE love, because that love was Wonderful and full of Compassion and Satisfaction, baby-girl it was a GIFT from the heart. Now you see just where I'm at.

LETTERS TO MY FAMILY

LOVE! It's a Wonderful and its amazing gift to those that we truly Love and that Love is not Love until it's expressed.

Yet, sometimes we hold back that love and so many other things, because we don't want you to worry about us or feel our pain, because we are sick. I must come forward and tell you things that you have already found out about, those things that should have come from me. Somehow I locked those things behind my shield of love, that maybe someday when we have mastered the winds and the mighty seas and the outer limits of the sky; Then and only then will we have captured the Energies of Love.

Those words touch my heart, because it's the time for the "Celebration of Life." The National CANCER Survivors Day...

I say "Thank you Lord" it's almost ten years now, that I have been 'FREE" from the Devil (Stage Three Lung Cancer) that thing that has taken so many away from us. Those that we hold so close and love so very, very much. Now I must stand TALL alone side with so many of my Brothers and Sisters, Fathers, Mothers and so many more in "Recognizing the other Cancer Survivors' throughout the world.

Mom: What can I say? You were always there for me when I was a child; you put food on the table each and every day. I can still see those Friday night's meals with Fried Fish, Pork N Beans, Potato Salad, Corn Bread but most of ALL moms, that Bread Pudding which was out of sight. Mom, you kept cloths on our backs, even if they were hand-me-downs.

The Good Fellow things and those Red under wear, with the flap in the back. You kept me safe from the riots there in Detroit when I was a small boy. Knowing that you loved me. I can still re-call some of the things that you would say when I was stealing fruit from people's trees or Christmas Trees and re-selling them to others.

Mom, you would make me go out into the back yard and get my own switch for my ass beating. Those words that you would say "Boy" this is going to hurt me more than it's going to hurt you. Wow! Mom, I laugh about it now, because it's funny then hell. "It's going to hurt me more than it's going to hurt you. Damn, Mom I was the one who was getting that beat down.

I am almost eight-two years old and I can still remember those words, alone with many other words, but the ONE that I remember the most and I have even passed those on to my children, grand children and great-grand children. Those words went something like this: "Son, whenever you walk out of this HOUSE, son make sure that you have on "CLEAN UNDERWARE ON"

Mom, THANKS for the WORD and everything else that you have done for "ALL of US, but most of all moms.

"Thanks for your LOVE."

Grand Mother:

You were old, but you had more wisdom in one finger then I had in my life time. Your eyes had seen things that I would never live to see and your feet walking those Red Clay roads there in Georgia; surly if those feet could talk they too could tell me stories that one would not ever believe.

Grand mama, I never told you just how much that I loved you when I was a child. Because back then I was a young wild and crazy. I didn't have the time to hear those words of Wisdom from you and from all of the other older people. Yet, your words as I grew older kept me from stepping into Quick Sand and drowning in the Sea of Love.

Those very words that you told to me as a child, those words are my "BIBLE." They are embedded in my head, but the best part of it all Grand mama is that I have put those words on a "CHART" and placed that chart right next to my bed. It's the very first thing that I see at night when I get into the bed, and it's the very first thing that I see when I get up each and every morning. Your words of "WISDOM"

Sons "IF THAT'S NOT YOUR CUP OF TEA, DON'T PUT ANY SUGAR IN IT.' Those very words have kept me out lots of trouble, when I became a young man, because you see grandmamma, I was still running around acting Crazy and being a FOOL.

Thanks ever so very much for those words of "WISDOM" Grandmother I love you.

Francis R. Armour:

As a child you never asked for much, or asked for anything. Even today, you have not put any demands on me. Francis, as a child I wasn't there with you or for you. I wasn't there to walk with you to school nor was I there to rock you to sleep or tell you bed time stories, Baby, at night even in the darkest of night when you had those dreams, I wasn't there. I was away from you.

Even today I find myself away from you. A grown woman, the mother of two boys, my grandsons. Who I have never held them in my arms when they were small. Today I only have the pictures of them to look at, wondering will I ever see them. I can still hear those words today that you said as a young lady at an early age.

"Daddy, no matter what I do or what I become, just always Love me and never stop loving me for Who I am" Baby, you are my blood, my body, but most of all, Francis you are my Daughter. Your letters come to me that were full of love, NOT the bull-shit love, but the TRUE LOVE that comes from a Daughter to her Father.

Jennifer C. Armour:

What can I say? We found common ground and Love as a father and a daughter. You were the Sunshine of my life. You became that other daughter that I longed to have in my life. You always had my back. That day when you told me that you wanted me to give you away on your wedding day. A day that I shall never forget as long as I shall live, that's the day that those Dark Clouds came rolling into and covered up my Sunshine.

Jennifer you always had my back and showed me love and Respect until that day that you were taken away from me by a drive-by shooting on your wedding day. You lay there in my arms in the cold streets feeling your warm blood on my fingers, hearing your last words. "Daddy, hold me, hold me tight Daddy." Then you were gone from my life, but not from my heart. I remember my very last words, "My baby is gone, she's gone...

Jennifer I can't forget the guilt that I feel and the hurt that's deep down inside of me. Sometimes we ALL feel guilt and that feeling of pain and hurt that's deep down inside of us. Sometimes we ALL make mistakes, but the guilt of knowing that you have given more to one daughter and less to that other daughter is what hurts, and eat your ass up. I know it might sound crazy, but the back of my throat ached as I said those words.

Jennifer for all of the people in this world, you are the only one that really knows "Who I am? They say that things happen for a reason that you came into my life. For we have had our little talks and if people knew that when I come out to the grave we talk with each other, they will think that I was crazy because I talk to the dead. Baby you know that I can't talk with the dead, because if I could, I sure would talk with her.

Baby, for some reason that you and I can communicate with each other in the time of need (my need)

Jennifer deep down inside of your heart you really know that I am the Son of the Seven Sons. Baby you do understand that the Seventh Sons importance stems from the scarcity of the number 7. One that ultimately roots in the Seven Island of Atlantis and the Seven Seas of Humanity. That's a part of who I am.

Baby maybe this is the reason that you and I can communicate so well with each other. Jennifer my question is "Who are you"? I really do mean who are you really, and where did you come from? You have never told me much about you or your people. Well dad, my people came from the North West Coast of America, and some believe that we were of the Mongoloid Racial stock. Dad, they say that things happen for a reason and that is why you came into my life. When I was deep in trouble waters you brought warmth into my life alone with love.

Honey, you were with me when I was running around acting crazy; you are here with me now that those troubles have return back into my life. I find myself turning to you here at the foot of your grave, looking for some answers. Now please tell me who are you. You were taken from away from me, yet for some reason you have found your way back into my life and in my heart. Now baby pleases tell me who you really are? I need an answer to this question, because for sometimes this has ate at my heart wondering who really Jennifer Clark Armour is?

Well daddy, if you must know who I am? My name is FLY with the Birds! This is the name that my mother's tribe gave to me when I was a small child. They said that I was a Special child, because I was able to fly into people's life and heart, when they were at that lowest point in life and bring joy unto them.

Dad, I was raised by a Shaman (Medicine Man) the oldest in my mother's tribe. The Shaman taught me many things, because I had the POWER to communicate with the SPRITE World. Dad, this is why you and I are able to talk with each other, because there was a reason why you and I have become as of ONE in Sprite and also in Body and Soul.

Lucia Manelse Armour:

There's an old saying "You never miss your water until your WELL runs Dry." Well my well has run dry for me. November 27, 2006 was a very dark day in my life! That's the day that my well ran dry. Lucia, when I first met you, there was a mystery about you. Honey, you were Warm and with Fire in your touch, your eyes SPARKLED with Joy and said "come drink of me, for I am what you "DESIRE"

Lucia, you were comfortable with yourself and where you were in life. Our water began to flow on February 14, 1959 that's the day you became my wife. Mrs. Lucia Manelese Armour, and it lasted until November 27, 2006. Mrs. Armour, that's the day that my WELL really did run dry. "GOD dispatched his Special Angle to see you home."

Thank you, Mrs. Armour, for FORTY-SEVEN YEARS of YOUR LOVE.

LOVE is a very strong word, and yet it has a deep meaning and a feeling for those that we care for and those that our Hearts belong too. I don't know if this is true or not, nor have I seen this written in stone. But some people say that you can only love once! In the first part of "Letters to My Family" I only spoke of my Daughters and of my wife. Now I speak of the others that some of us NEVER speak of them in this manner as being part of the family.

I am speaking of "SHADEY, ANGLE, PEPER, KATHY, and LADY my DOGS. Who was a part of my family? Even today I find myself thinking of them, because these family members played a MAJOR role in the family. One of those family members was there for me when my well ran dry. This one gave me the "WILL POWER" to go on and not hit the JUG like so many of us have done after we have lost those WE LOVE AND CARE FOR.

SHADY

2/11/1935 UNTIL 1949

SHADY:

You were born on February 11, 1935. The very same day and year that I was born. Our family doctor gave you to the family for me to have. That Love for you (Shady) lasted until 1949. In April of 1955, I join the Air Force and like so many other young men, I got myself a Tattoo, not wanting to put my mothers or my girlfriend's name on my arm.

I put your name (Shady) on my arm to remember who you were and just what you meant to me.

SPOT

1970 until 1976

SPOT:

You were born in 1970 close to the end of November. Lucia (your mom) was getting on my ass about having another child. I was not ready for another child, because being in the military with a large family at times was not to cool.

We were all sitting around the house doing nothing, because it had been raining that day; at that time we were living in Florida. I was reading the newspaper in the pet section and there you were up for sale for only ten dollars. I told the wife about this thinking if I got you that would stop her from thinking about another child. Now the ass kicker of all was that I didn't have ten dollars on hand and the bank was closed. Somehow between the four of us we came up with that ten dollars for you.

We end up out there in the woods to get you, going down a dirt ass road of Red Clay to get find that house where you were. You had a small White spot on your chest, so my son Horace called you spot. Lucia saw you and there was love at first sight. Yes! There went this ideal about another baby.

If someone would have told me about what was going to take place over the next few days, weeks and years to come. Man, I would not have believed it? That you would end up sleeping in our bedroom. Lucia would not let you sleep any place else but in our bedroom.

She (Lucia) was happy with you and I was also happy that I didn't have to get up for no three a.m.. Feeding. When we lost you it really hit Lucia hard, it was like that we had lost a child.

ANGLE

5/10/1990 until 10/27/1997

ANGLE:

You were born on 5/10/1990 and lasted until 10/27/1997. Angle you were my heart and soul. You would give your life for me and other members of the family that you loved. Angle you were a Rottweiler. I had read about you and I have seen others who were like you. I didn't know what type of dog you were until I got you. Angle, you were strong and very beautiful; always walking the house at night making sure that we were safe while we slept in our beds.

I remember the very first time that you got sick; I slept with you in the front room on the floor, feeling the heat from your body letting you know that I was there for you. This lasted for three days and three nights. I was always at your side then on 10/26/1997 you became worst. I took you to the doctor, and was told to return back to the doctor for your operation on 10/27/1997. Yet, it was kind of ODD that when we return back home that night from the doctor's office. You went up stairs and stuck your head in each bedroom, but you did not enter into those rooms.

Angle you went into your own room, and the next morning you were gone, Damn I could not hold back the tears, I cried because I had lost you. Yes, you were not only a dog, but you were a part of the "Armour Family.

I didn't go to work that day or for the next two days, I call the Post Office and told them that I was sick. I didn't lie, because I really was sick, because "I had lost you." I have your remains here in the house in a Special place.

PEPPER:

1993 until 1998

PEPPER:

I have had lots of dogs in my life time, but there was something about you that struck fear into those who came over to the house to see us, and those that saw you sitting outside on the front lawn or playing with the little blind girl next door. Maybe it had to with your eyes, because one was Green and the other one was Black.

Yet you would give your life for those that you loved. Remembering that time when I had left the front door open, and I heard someone cry out calling me, Mr. Armour please come and get your dog because he is killing someone's dog. I rush out of the house to see just what was going on and why someone was calling out to me. Pepper you had this dog down and I knew that if I didn't stop you this Black dog was dead. My wife took the water hose and sprayed you down while I pull you free from this other dog that was covered in blood running from his neck.

I ask John from across the street did he see what had happen and why my dog was attacking this other dag, and trying to kill him. He said that the little blind girl (Jo-Ann) next door was playing out front and this dog for no reason attacked Jo-Ann I guess your dog heard her crying he ran out of the house and attacked this other dog. Knowing that Jo-Ann was his baby sitter (when we would go out of town) He was only protecting someone that he loved and cared about his baby-sister.

It really hurt me when I lost him, little Jo-Ann it really hurt her really badly. It had been raining and I called for him to come inside out of the rain, and when he didn't come when I call for him, I went into the back yard to check on him. I found him just laying there; I took him to the Vet. To see what was wrong with him. The Vet. Said that he had eaten something. He asks me had I set out any food for rats. No I said.

Wondering who had done such a thing to him like this; but knowing what part of Richmond that I was staying. Well anyone could have put that food in my back yard, knowing that was a guard dog and the kind of dog that he was, that struck fear into people, they wanted him out of the way for their very own reasons.

KATHY

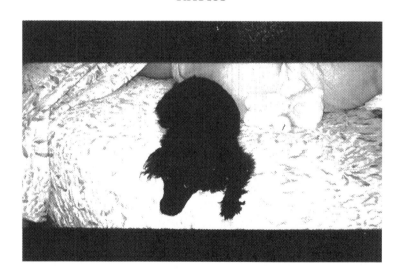

1999 UNTIL 2010

KATHY:

It's kind of funny in away as how you became a member of this family. It was that my wife was thinking about a Foster child, because she had seen this child on TV, he was a Special needs little boy, who had a steel plate in his head. My youngest son said why we don't check into this about a Foster child, because it was only the two of us. We put our name on the list about becoming his Foster family. We put our name on the list and attended the required classes and training that was setup for us and the interview and back ground check.

I had this feeling that we would get this child, not like others where the husband and wife were both working my wife was a stay home mom and not working and could spend lots of time with this child. Yet luck wasn't on our side another family got this child. When I ask about this, the answer that we received that we already had children. Yes it's true that we had children who were 29 and 30 years of age. They wanted a family to have this child who didn't have any children. Yet, the family who did get this little boy, both husband and wives were, working. So that was that, but I did receive a letter later on asking us if we would like to be a Foster Family for a little girl.

Kathy, you became that child the Love of our life. Remembering when Nicole threw you down on the floor and hurting your hip. I slept there on the floor with you; I took you outside to do what you had to do. You end up in the bedroom not sleeping on the floor, but in the bed sleeping between us. You were Special because no other dog has ever slept in our bed. You and Lady were sisters, in that you're the only dog that Lady didn't like. Then on 5/30/2010 you became sick and I had to put you down, it hurt.

That day was Memorial Day. Even today when I go out into the back yard, and I find myself standing at the spot where you lay, and each Memorial Day I place a flower on that spot.

LADY

11/17/2000 UNTIL 8/5/2014

LADY:

The apple of my wife Lucia heart. Lady you was Lucia baby, where ever Lucia went you were always there. A one person's dog, you didn't like people and you hated other dogs. We would go out for a ride on Tuesday night. Wow! This became what was known as "Dog Night" I wouldn't go out nor would I take any phone calls on that day. This might sound crazy but I told MY FAMILY and even my doctor not to call me on Tuesday Dog Day.

Lady you became a baby sister for my wife, when she became ill. You were always at her side. Never leaving Lucia (your master) even if Lucia had to go to the bathroom, you were at her side. I had this thing with you. When I would go out I would tell you to watch the house and don't let anyone in, but if you did let them in, then don't let them out. When I lost Lucia in November of 2006, you became my pal. We form a bond between you and I. Lady, you kept me from going out of my rabbit-ass-mind, when this house became cold and empty. You kept me company.

I was in Detroit, MI. on that day when I got that call from Robert, telling me that you were sick and he took you to the hospital. The doctor explains that there was nothing that could be done for her. You died in Roberts arms and he told me that it really hurt him, seeing you there in his arms, only feeling your warm body and the pain in his heart;

But I was the ONE that was hurting, because not only had I lost a dog, but I lost a member of the family. Who gave me so much LOVE and DEVOTION, but most of all YOU kept my ass from drinking right after I had lost Lucia (my wife) of Forty-Seven Years.

I'm sure that some of you are wondering why I never wrote about my family, or any other members of the family. It's not that I have or had forgotten about you for being a part of the family. It's like I wanted this book to be all about me and my family (Wife, Children and Pets) Yes even though we are family sometimes we like to keep some things only for us, because I didn't want to tell a lie. You see, I know of the family, but I don't really know the family.

Let me CLEAN that up, I knew the family, but I didn't know my family. You see I left Detroit, Michigan in 1955. I was only 20 years old going into the military. We were close, but not really close because I was a longer and lived in my own world. I believe that some members of my family or friends felt that I left Detroit because I was hurting for some reason. The REAL reason that I left Detroit was because that FACTORY life was kicking my ass and killing me. Man, I couldn't deal with Ford Motor Company; so I gave up Ford Motor Company, Detroit and my family for the military.

Just to let you all know that I haven't forgot about you.

Bertha: I remember when you would dress me and you would take me around the town and people would think that I was yours. Sis, when I got older you would do-my-do (hair) with that hot comb in the kitchen on Friday night, so that I would be ready to hit the clubs on Saturday night. Sis, not for getting that you wrote for the JET and also for the Detroit Free Press.

EUSCHAL: You and I would go out on Saturday mornings picking up junk to sell to the junk yard, making a little extra money for you and me to have for the weekend.

BOBBY: You would go down to that little church with your Bible in hand and you guys would be having a hella of a good time up in there. Bobby I also remember the times that I would drive you back up to be it Clearwater or Coldwater to that hospital where you were working.

NELSON: Thinking about the times when you were working in the Packing House. Man, you would bring home meat from the job. Also those times when we would go down to the Old Farmers Market. Man, it would be cold as hell down there; people would be standing around those 50 gallon drums of fire trying to keep warm.

Nelson, you the painter. Wow, you had it going on. Man, you could make a paint brush sing. That time when you done the front room in a two-tone color. Damn, I had never seen anything that looked that good.

ROGERS: You were the one that made sure that mom had the million dollar smile and those White teeth that stood out like a charm. Rog, you help me to get my very own first car from Dick Green Yes! My first car a brand new 1971 Sports Fury Four door, Green in color. All mines, with my name on the Bill of Sale. Rog, you also gave me Air Fare when I join the Navy to make sure that I got to the base on time.

You had other names also others knew you as Doctor Armour. The man, which could pull teeth without you feeling any pain. You kept your office in that part of town where you were needed in the poor and middle class area, not up-town like so many others have done.

DAVID: A little bit older than I. The Baseball player, the Track man at Northern High School there in Detroit. You set the BAR for ALL Armours' coming into Northern High School; because of what you had done we had to raise that bar up a little higher for the next Armour, and keep that name going.

PUDDING (ALLINE) in a way I hated your little ass! You would always run back to the house and tell mom what I was up to, and the things that I was doing. Girl, I really wanted to kick your little ass, but knowing that mom would get off into my ass for what I had done to you. Girl I had to find a way to get back at your ass, because you didn't know how to keep that BIG MOUTH of yours closed.

Then ONE day I got your little ass. I put some COLROX in my drinking water, because you have always wanted whatever I was drinking or eating. Pudding, if I didn't share things with you, your ass would run off to mom with some crazy ass story about what I had done something and get me into trouble. Girl, I gave that water to your little ass. Damn, just watching you drink it, saying to myself "GOT YOUR LITTLE ASS"

It's funny I never told anyone about this until now, when we were all sitting around the table telling stories. Pudding it was funny at that time. Girl, just to see your face now, 30 years later that you learn how that COLROX got into that water and who put it in there.

To you my brothers and sisters that were before me, those that I didn't even know or learn about you until sometime later on in life. It wasn't until I was trying to get a new Society Card, because I had lost my card, and I had to apply for a copy of my birth records. That's when I found out that there thirteen of us, only to find out that there were really ten of us living; Damn, the ass kicker of it all is that I didn't even know the names of those that were missing.

Hell, to the truth I didn't even know this until I was trying to get that new Society Security Card. Well this is where David (my older brother) comes back into the picture, once again, even through David has some health problems, and he is still the one who could tell you about the family and the history of the family. Man, I shit you not, you could ask David about something that took place back in 1945 and it's now 2016, man David could tell you about that event like it just took place two days ago. Damn, going to miss David the "Family history book."

I say to you my Sisters and Brothers, I am very sorry that I have not spoken of you in this book or in any of my other books. One of the reasons that I didn't speak of you in those other books was because back then that was the time of "Who I was."

CLOSE THAT DOOR

Right now I'm on my way back to Detroit, not only to see my family but to see her too. Where it all got started from back in 1955. Now the question is this the new beginning or the time to close the door forever? Anyway she and I aren't on the same bus ride. I speak of this because I see it in her heart and through her eyes. We speak of things but there is something missing, maybe it's because we both are still on that other train where we still love that person that's in the grave. Has she gotten over him? I don't really know about this. Yet for me my past wife is still in my thoughts or is it that I only believe I marrying once and that's it!

Now, is there any other woman that I could love as much as I have loved my wife? Am I being fair to myself! By holding on to the grave and not allowing anyone else to come into my life? To really love me and bring joy into my life? Will this trip to Detroit give me that answer that I'm looking for? Or will this word be the word to set me free to love again? Or will I still be that guy that's looking for love in all of the wrong places?

Will I find that love in the place that I don't want it to be? Will that turn out to be a part time love? Can I close that door for good and set myself free from the grave, and move on to a fresh love that will bring me that joy and happiness that I so long for.

We all think about that lost love at times, and ask can we reopen that door and how will it be the second time around. Sometimes we play games, by asking oneself should I or shouldn't I? Yet knowing that LOVE is a powerful thing, it makes us do some crazy ass things, like trying to open a door with the wrong key. Yet at times I ask myself is this what I'm doing? That I have the key which fits into another door, but I'm still trying to make this new key fit an old lock which is only open in the head and not in the heart.

My real question that keeps on running through my head is that I have been on this road without love for so long, that I don't want it anymore! Am I okay where I stand, or is it that I want it, but I don't want it?

Some people say that the second time around can be a bitch and lead your ass down the wrong road. Man, I look at my life right now, it's all good, maybe I don't have Happiness with someone being in my life, but I do have joy in my heart. There are other things that keeps us from being on the very same bus and that's distance it's 2,900 miles between us. Can I give up what I have and move back to a dying city of Detroit? What's there? Where is there to go too? Can I give up what I love and move to a place that I don't even know an unsure what the outcome will be!

You see that the last time that I walked out of that door, I didn't close it. I was looking for something and that was "Who I am", because I was wondering through the wilderness looking for something. I found a woman that I loved and a very Wonderful MATE at that. I speak of a MATE and not of a wife, because that MATE will be here with you through Thick and Thin, but the wife is only there because you ask her to become your very own friend. Through it all I ask myself now that I have lost my MATE, can I find that joy again? That joy that has brought life into an old tree, which was standing there with open arms waiting for that one special person.

The one to come alone and climb that tree and hold tight as the wind blows, and the storm comes trying to rip that special person from you. Both of you hold tight knowing that you can't give up what is truly yours. Well we know that life has its own way to make one think about the past. Hell like they say, the past is the past, and one can't go back and relive it all over again. This morning it's a wonderful blessing either sunny or stormy, it stands for hope... Giving us another start on what we call "LIFE" sometimes we find one self in am situation of doing what we should do or what we think that we should be doing.

I sit here asking myself, "Armour" should I go out and enjoy myself or what? You see I just got myself a 2016 Dodge Ram 1500 and I want to take the Wizard out for a run. That's the name that I have given to her; but to really tell the truth, I ask myself where I am today and what do I want?

Well you know that life has its own way to make one think about the past, many times I have ask myself that question. How would it have been if I had married this lady? Would I have found joy, or would it turn out to be that I was just married and my joy was still out there waiting for me to reach out and pick it up and say to the world that "I GOT YOU."

Yet I have held back on something's from this lady never telling her that I was once sick with Stage Three Lung Cancer. The word "CANCER" alone has had a very deep effect on one's mind and life style. Some of us just gave up saying that this is it, and others like me stood fast and said that "I can beat this thing" I will fight it; at times I ask myself could she have dealt with it. Knowing that I have kept this from her and now "MISTRUST" sets in, which can be a bitch. Making one to think what else has this man held back from me?

Are there any other children out there that I don't know about? Those that are hidden, that we don't say is ours? Those phone calls that you run off to the bathroom to hear, saying oh! That was just Aunt May. Yet I do believe in that Old-Bull-shit, let sleeping dogs lay, and keep that shit from the world.

Yet I feel that I owe it to this lady to explain to her about my cancer and also why I did walk out of her life in 1955 and never telling her why I did so? This too has eaten away at my soul. Yet I can' tell her why I did so, because it would not bring true love into our life.

I want LOVE and she wants that same old world that she is living in, which will never set her FREE; because of her mind set and her and I getting together will only cause some problems in the world that she is living in.

Knowing and understanding the "BIG PICTURE" I must close that door and throw away that key forever, knowing that I love her, but I am not in love with her.

I WISH THAT

Sometimes I wish that I could go back and relive parts on my past years, because they were some of my joyful days. Even my childhood was good there in Detroit. The move to the military was a new life for me. In fact even today I still feel that the military saved my life I ran off to the military because that factory life was an ass kicker and I couldn't deal with it. Alone with some of the crazy things that I was doing when I was much younger. Now that I am older, I still find myself with trouble mind.

Asking myself what must I do or whom should I talk to. Knowing that I must go to her, because she is the only one that really understands me and knows just what's in my heart. Well look who's here with his hands in his pockets, like you have lost something. Tell me Daddy who piss on your shoes or is it the same old thing? A married woman that you have gotten mix up with again? Well miss know it all, it's none of those things, no one has pissed on my shoes and it's not about a married woman this time. I see, and then there can only be one thing or reason that can make you look like this, and come out here to see me.

It's her again? Am I right? That young one! Did she bring some smoke to your ass and tears to your eyes again, or did she make you cry? Damn, you are still hung up on this woman! Now tell me, what about that other woman, the one who is around your age, that you are trying to get that summer and winter home with. Just one question Armour, is this lady (the young one) from overseas? I thought so, well I'm not trying to be Dr. Do-Little, but let me ask you this? Do you find yourself looking at women from overseas more than you are looking at women who are from the states, those who are born here and who are not Asian?

That's your problem Armour, it's in your head and in your heart, if she is not from overseas you have a problem because of what you have seen and dealt with for over the last Forty-Seven Years. Dad, please be up front with me, because you aren't really telling me the whole story, but most of all you aren't speaking from your heart.

Come on, it's me, you can bull-shit some people, but one thing that I do know for sure, that you can't hide the truth from me. I know you dad. What's this really all about? You are right I can't hide the truth from you. Baby, what's eating away at my soul is something that you have seen with your own two eyes and felt the pain of seeing those things that I am speaking of and just what happens to you when you become old.

Baby, you see I have been down this road before with the grandmother of your step-mother I have seen how the people from overseas treat the old people. How my wife took care of her grandmother who lived to be 105 and also how all the others were there for her. Even I was there, because that old lady was there for me, when others turn their backs on me because I was an outsider and a Black one at that. I watch the love that was given to this old lady and I still see that kind of love here in the states from the Asian community for the old people.

Baby, I'm starting to get up there in age, and I wonder at times that who will be there for me? Will I end up like my half-sister in one of those homes? Only to pass away all alone. I watch my second family, who are Mexican how they were there for their mom and dad when they were well and also when sickness was there and in the end when death came a calling. The love and support that was given to both of them. Will this woman show me that kind of support and love? I worry about this, but knowing all alone if two of you were here I wouldn't have to worry because the two of you would be here for me.

Yes, I am speaking of her, the very one that I wasn't there for. Jennifer, even though she is not here with me, her Love, Support comes to me in her letters. Baby there has been many days and nights that I have been ashamed of the way that I have treated my other daughter...Jennifer you have seen this when you have caught me looking at her picture with those tears in my eyes. Never saying a word to me about this, knowing that there was some pain in my heart.

Baby, is this why this young woman has become so very important in my life? Not just for a lover but to take the place of you and Francis? Maybe you think that she is just out for my money? Well I have thought of that a long time ago, even if I did ever re-marry to someone else. You see about five years ago I made out my "WILL" and if your ass was not in that "WILL", then your ass was shit-out-of-luck, even if that person just became my new wife.

Baby, just to set the record straight this lady has her very own money. Sometimes I ask myself am I the one after her because she is the one that has money, and wants to pay off my truck Jennifer, you understand me, because of what I have seen and felt, this lady love and care for me, here for me and not asking for anything, but always giving to me and trying to please this old man.

Yes! I saw what this other lady did for her mother and her late husband, but will there be enough of that love and care be there for a third time? Now this is something that I must ask myself or will it be the case now I got you and all that you have; so I must put you into that home, because I too am sick and I can no longer take care of you. I know baby that this is a hell of away to think about things like this, but I have seen so much of this so call LOVE that one thinks about.

Those homes are full of old people that their love ones have give up on them, and many cases money has taken the place of love. I'm being for real about all that I say to you baby, because who's here for me? Who's here to love me? But most of all who is here now that you were taken away from me by that drive-by. You know that day? It's still here in the back of my mind. Oh! How beautiful you were standing there in that White Dress that belongs to your grandmother. She had saved that dress just for you over the years. That look that was in her eyes, just seeing you in it.

Standing there with tears in her eyes, Oh! How happy she was seeing her only granddaughter grown into woman hood, and in a matter of time that dark cloud came rolling into your life and you were gone from us. Now daddy, we have somewhat of a problem that's coming up in just a few weeks? You will be off to Detroit; what are you going to tell her about that other lady who has come into your life. The one that believes that age doesn't matter and it's what's 'in the heart that counts.

Armour, what if this lady comes right out and say let's get married right now! What then? I know how you feel about getting married? How about her? What are you going to tell her! That you need a little more time to think about it! I know just what I would tell you if I was her!

Damn, Armour, it's been ten years now, and you need a little more time; what in the HELL are you waiting for? Are you waiting for HELL to freeze over, shit we aren't getting any younger?

Well daddy that's your problem and all I can say is to stop and think before you open your mouth; because I know how you are at times, when you think that people are rushing you into doing something when you aren't ready for it, or you are unsure about what you want. Well your ass becomes Hot enough to F----K and no one wants to be around your ass at that time, not even the dogs.

Armour, you know that's a bitch when the dogs run away from your sorry ass. Sorry to talk like this, but I did pick up this from you, and I did learn that you don't do things unless someone gets into your ass about it; before you get up and do things. By the way how long will you be there in Detroit this time? Will it be two months this time or what? Will you be there just long enough to tap on the old girl, and rush your ass back home to that young cherry that's waiting for your return?

Daddy, I do hope that you remember what grandmother said? If that's not your cup of TEA, don't put no sugar in it; but I guess that does not apply to you, because I see that you now buy your sugar in the Fifty pound bags. Well I'll leave you for now, because I have lots to do before I leave for Detroit, so what can I say, but it's been nice talking to you. Yes daddy it's been nice talking with you also.

Dad, do come back and tell me just how it went and daddy make sure that you bring a lunch, because next time your ass will be here for a while; plus I am dying to hear about it, that's a joke. "I'm dying" you can take a joke, can't you! Take care and I will talk with you later daddy, and I do love you.

Sorry, that I can't be there, but you know just where to find me when you come back home, besides I'm not going any place (funny) I see that you are still your old self.

In a few weeks I'll be on my way to the city of Detroit. Wondering what the place will look like this time? Last year they were doing some work down town, It's funny that they are working on the down town area and not on the run down parts of the city. Those homes that were set a fire and the run down areas are still there, but I guess down town are more important than the Inner part of the city. Like all things, down town is where the money is.

Got to keep the down town area looking good, well one thing for sure, Detroit is not by its self, there are other places which is just as bad, but some of those places have a reason for that (run down) because when you F---K with mother, the "STORM" will come, and then you will pay the price. Hell anyway it will be nice to return back there, because it's always nice to see the family again (in some cases) plus there is a family reunion going on there in the city and also there is one going on in Georgia, that one is on my mother's side of the family. Thinking about going there, when I leave Detroit, but don't know anyone from that side of the family.

Yet, it would be nice to learn something about that side of the family, after all I don't have anything to rush back home for. There's no one there waiting with open arms to rush back too, plus there will be no one sitting at the front waiting for me to walk through the front door and jump up into my chest and say hello and welcome home, with a kiss or a bark. Damn, this is what I miss most of all; it still hurts that Lady (my dog) is gone from my life. It's been two years now, but I do miss her. Sometimes I tell myself, Armour go out and get yourself another dog, but can't do it.

Even when I see others out enjoying the day with their pets, that pain return back to me, missing my Dog Days that we had with each other. Knowing that I don't want to deal with that over again. I think that I'll let that go for now and keep on doing what I am doing now. Don't have to run back home to let her out, that means I can stay out at night just a little bit longer; but I still miss her so very much. Plus another dog want fit into my life right now. I'm just trying to get my life back together.

Got to put you down for now, but will catch up to you later. You know how it is when you are trying to get ready for a trip. I really don't know about you, but I like to make sure that all is in order before I leave going out of town.

Glancing out the window that over look my back yard, I was memorized by the steady stream of rain pouring down over the dry grass that's in my back yard. When the rain finally stopped the Sun broke through and its warmth began evaporating the moisture that was in the air and that pond of water slowly went dry. I felt that it was that time I'm off for my trip to

Detroit. I decided to take the scenic route. I normally saw rolling hills, vibrant colorful fields; cows and horses grazing by the roadside, but today all that I could see was what was left of that mist.

I felt like I was driving into the Golden rays of the warm sunshine. Wow! That drive echoed my life at that time. The Sun illuminated the Scenery, and once again those surroundings mirrored how I felt about my life at that time. It's like you have faced times of uncertainty when the road ahead is not clear. Yet, we move on, not wanting to stop; but that's life, because sometimes we can become too comfortable with the daily life, and think that everything is fine. Only to run into a road block which throws us off of our game?

It's so nice out here on the open road, because this time I am seeking some answers which just might make my life to take another turn? I can only ask myself will this be a good thing or will it turn out that love has been BLIND? We all wish that things could turn out our way, but at times it want work out for us, but I have over two thousand more miles to think about this and the questions that I must ask this lady about our life? Will it become as of one? Sometimes I wonder what my life would be with this lady.

Now once again I find myself sitting on the fence like I have done before when my wife was on one side, and that married woman was on the other side of the fence, that's when I wrote my first book "How Strong is Your Love." Now history once again has repeated it's self again. Now it's that older woman on one side and that younger one on the other side.

Knowing that it will be a hard road with the older one, because at times I feel that I love her, but it boils down to that I'm not in love with her. With the younger one who says that she loves me. I do remember those words that my daughter has told me before, "Dad, let her young ass go." Am I trying to hold on to her because I am getting up there in age only wanting to have someone to care for me and look after me?

Yes! I have this older woman who's miles away from me, who don't really know me, she only knows of me. Yet somehow I feel that she too is looking for someone to care for her; because over the last few months she and I have drawn more closely. The phone calls and reaching out to and for each other in ways that we have never done before. Yet, looking at the BIG picture there is something that's missing. Is it that wanting to be loved and care for each other has taken the place of love for each other? We all know that at times just having someone in our life has become the most important thing in the world to us, and love has become SECOND to us. We all worry about getting old and what will happen to us? Maybe I am thinking about this, because my sister, who was in that home with no one to care about her. Just only those who were ripping her off for her things.

Will I too become like her, because when that time comes there will be no one there for me? Then again I ask myself what about that younger one! Will she give up on me, because I have become old and at times all I can do is just roll over and look at it? Knowing that it's there, but you can't do anything about it. After all she to is only human and being human we all have our needs. Well I should put a lid on that shit and enjoy myself while I'm here in Detroit, and deal with those cards when the hand is dealt to me.

With a CD going and the music is good, the miles just roll away on this warm sunny day. No rain clouds in sight, only you and the open road, and your music and the Black top which is putting its heat off on top of you as you drive on top of it, going home to see family and to that one woman that you feel that you are in love with.

Somehow this open road does something to me, last year when I made this very same trip it made me feel free, to get out and see the world and enjoy life, because it's so very short. Sitting in one of the rest areas with a cold coke in one hand and a hot dog in the other one, seeing all those others out here, who's just like me, some making this trip because school is out with the kids.

Well I want bore you about how wonderful it is out here, because many of you have done this very thing that I am doing and I am telling you something that you already aware of, because life is short and should contain as much Peace, Relaxation, Fun and Interesting Exploration as POSSIBLE.

I am going to get as much of this as possible, so get off of your butts and come join me on this trip. Here in the city now and things look just like they did last year when I was here. Maybe they have made some improvements in other places but here on the West side of Detroit, to me it's the same. Now here at my girlfriends place, there is something wrong? I can feel it in the air, not a welcome like it was last year. More of Honey I need you feeling. Maybe it's me, because I was looking for so much more from her and out of her.

I shouldn't make any judgments right now, give it more time to see what turns out between us, but once you get that feeling it's there; but it's crazy I find myself thinking more about the other one, then I do of her. (my girl friend) yet, I find myself searching for words when I speak to the other lady, somehow I just can't find the words to tell this other lady that I do love her.

It appears that history has once again come alone and hit me in the ass one more time, because once more I have two women in my life. One a younger person and the other one close to my age. Hell knowing all alone that one of these women has to go from my life. Then again it just might turn out to be that they both might go! One because she is young and the other one is that she doesn't want to commit to a long turn deal. I feel that marriage is not on the table for this one. As they say time will tell, but this time before I leave Detroit. I shall have my answer, as to will I have a girl friend or will I turn to my road-dog?

As they say time don't wait for anyone, and this time in life I don't have time for any bullshit. I feel that I have given this woman time to make up her mind, as to what she wants to do. When I speak of time, I am talking about over six years, now that she has lost her husband. I feel that within those years you should know just what you want to do.? Stay as you are or move on. I am ready to move on in life. It' like my daughter has said Daddy, don't keep on FISHING in the SAME old waters, if you don't catch anything. Maybe she is right, because all I have been getting is those same old LITTLE bites.

Well I guess when I leave Detroit this time I should have my answer, will hope still be alive! Yet deep down inside I feel that she is not ready to move on with her life. There are still something's that she needs to work out. For me I have this question that I must really ask of myself, and that's! Am I in love with this woman! But yet I don't think that I love her or is it the other way around, It's that I love her, but I'm not in love with her? I am sure that this sounds F----K-up?

There are so many things that I need an answer for? How are we as of ONE? How is our Sex life? It's been a while that she and I have been in the bed with each other! Is that fire still there! We both are up there in age, for me almost 82 and for her it's 78, is there still any fire in our souls or will we be just two people there for each other, but the sex is gone; because age has come along where sex is on the back seat like for so many of us after we reach that age or get to that age!

There are other things besides sex, do we feel anything for each other, or is it that we just want to have someone in our life, just because we are old. Well let's get away from that, because this is something that she and I will have to work out and work on. A long distant love can be find, but at times it can be a bitch. I want you, but you aren't here and you need me and I am 2934 miles away. Shit! I have gone down this F----K up road before when I was in the military. I was in one place and away from home. Man that shit at times almost made me go out of my-rabbit-ass- mind.

I look at love and it's not a thing that can be explained, and it's a blind thing that can be Harsh and Cruel when not SHARED by TWO people. Sometimes this is how I see and feel about love with this lady. That I care for, because it can't be forced into or made to happen. Is this what I'm trying to do with this lady, force my love on her? Knowing that in the very end it want happen; because we both did not share it with each other.

Well like they say LIFE can be a bitch when you are a fool in love. I need to tell you a story! Some years ago when I was out there running around acting wild and crazy; I found myself in a Storm and I was "CRYING" out for some help, and this lady a stranger heard my cry, she didn't judge me, for what I had done or the things that I was into. This lady put out her hand and pulled me out of that storm, and set my feet on dry land.

Now I would like to tell you another story! It's about a lady, she too was in a storm and she was crying for help, I heard her cry and came to her aid. Her storm was not like mine. I understood her because my storm was like being in jail? You see I had lost a wife, a son and a daughter who was the joy of my life. My storm was that I didn't allow anyone to love me.

Yet over time me and this lady has become very close to each other, yet we came into each other's life for a reason. Was it to become Father and Daughter? Or was it for us to become LOVERS, and not really shearing each other with the whole world; because of what they might say about us! Are you father and daughter or are you lovers? We both want to be close to each other, but a new kind of love has come into the picture, you now find yourselves wanting to become lovers. Who is this lady? She is the other woman that's in my life, the younger one that my daughter is always getting into my ass about, because maybe it has come down to two things!

The first one is that I find myself so close to this lady that I am worried about who will be there for me. The second thing is it that this Wild Cherry has got me so blind that I don't know if I should shit or get off of the pot. All I can say, what it is, is what it is. Sometimes we do find ourselves reading the hand writing that's on the wall. That the younger one is for real and the older one is saying what I think she wants me to hear and I believe what she says to me.

At times I ask myself Armour, can I wait another three years for this lady to make up her mind or should I take love where I find it? I am starting to look at things the way that they are? I have ask this lady many of times to take a trip and come out and stay with me and not to worry because you would have that round trip ticket in your hand before you left home. It's crazy as hell because that ticket is still with the AAA travel service on hold.

Does it come down to the fact that there are other things that are more important than us getting with each other? I don't know but I am ready to move on with my life and say to hell with it. What's that old saying that "a bird in the hand is better than a bird in the bush?

I have a bird in the hand now, but the question what will happen when I get old and that bird grows up? Like I have said I have made my bed, and I have a choice to sleep in it with someone, or don't allow anyone to sleep in it with me. It's nice outside today and I have just finished washing my things, but it's not like it is when I am back home in California. I put my things out on the line after the wash and let the sun do its thing. Well in a few more weeks I'll be on my way back home and Detroit will be something of the past, only thinking about what a waits me when I return back to California. Will she be there or off on one of her trips and I will be missing out on my home coming.

Hell, I will worry about that when I return back home, if she is gone, there is nothing I can do, but do my thing and wait for her to return back home. Knowing that this time, I will not be fishing in a pond where there is no fish biting, which only keeps you sitting there wishing that you will catch something before the sun goes down. (Like I was doing here in Detroit) Too old for that shit any more. It's like they say, when you want it, you want it now.

Well in two more days it will be Friday, and off to the race track. I don't go every day like I would do if I was at home. Here in Detroit I only go on Friday nights. One dollar Hot Dogs, and two dollar Beers, and those FLAT ass cold drinks. I need to put you down for a while, but will catch up with you later, after I find a cool spot to cool off in and get my mind working right.

Before I leave you trying to find that cool place, I just like to ask you a question, but I need for you to put yourself in my place and in my life! For those of you who are reading this book and for those of you that has been with me when I was out there acting a fool and running around acting crazy, you do remember those times that I all most step in quick sand and gotten my ass eaten up, because I had forgot the rules of the jungle.

"Am I wanting too much"? Or are my needs more than my wants? I ask this of you because there comes a time when we ALL will need someone and their input. That's why I need your answer to that question? You have heard my cry about getting "OLD" and the things that I want. I'm sure that some of you "are me" thinking about those things about old age and also about who to love and who do you want to love you in return? We all have needs and wants' in life, but yet some of us do NOTHING about it, only saying "WHAT EVER" Now you do understand just why I ask this question from you. "Are my needs more then my wants"?

Now that you have become "me" and you are in my place. What do you think? Am I only talking about myself or am I talking about you and telling your story. Yet sometimes others can tell our story better than we can tell those things about ourselves. This is a question that has been eating away at my soul. I think back at those times that when my daughter Francis told me, Daddy come live with me and let me take care of you. I understood just what she was saying, but more so I could read between the lines. It goes something like this" Daddy you are getting old, let me take care of you.

Is this where that younger lady comes into my life? To take the place of my daughters! The one that's here with me now and the one that I have lost. Maybe I'm wrong in the way that I am thinking, but I just can't help myself.

Looking at that "Big" picture that has open up in front of me allowing me to see those things that I have not seen in all of these years, cause I was blind, because I thought that I had found love and that I was in love. Maybe it's true like my daughter have told me time after time, that I was still in love with her? The one that's in the grave and all others can't and will not take her place, and also that word that I have spoken so many times and that's ribbed into my heart.

That I will only marry just one time and one time only; maybe the problem just might not be all hers. It's my problem. Why I and this woman will not be as I have dream and wish for over the years that her and I would become as one! Now this has nothing to do because of this other woman, Shit ten years is a long time to think about what you want to do? Hell, all in all, right now life is good and I shall do my very best to enjoy it, and stop and smell the Rose bushes as I past them by, knowing that I shall only past this way in life only one time. I do not know just what tomorrow might bring, as that old saying in the Navy: "Here today and gone tomorrow, for I have given Love and I have received love in return!

Well its Friday here in the city and 5:30 pm will be here soon and I must be off to the Race Track. That's my Friday night thing while I'm here in Detroit to enjoy myself, because soon I must put you down and return back to California... Right now I must stop and put this story under the looking glass to see that all is well, but most of all that I have been TRUE to you in what I have put down on paper, but most of all that I have been TRUE to myself, without any bull-shit in trying to paint a picture of who I am not

Sometimes we like to add some extra sugar to our coffee when it's not needed, only to find out we didn't even need it at all. What's that old saying? You can't bull-shit, the bull shitter! You do understand what I mean, and just where I'm coming from. I can only say that the things that I have written in this story of "who I am" are true, for the way that I have lived my life up until now. Without any bullshit.

You know it's crazy as hell, at times being human some of us like to add a little more sugar to our coffee, in order to make it sweater than it really is; for if I thought that this is what I have done in this book, then I am very sorry, that I have waste your time in reading this book, but more so that I have wasted my very own time in lying to myself about my life, because I wanted to paint a picture of someone who wasn't me, a good old boy, or someone who could walk on water. Yet even as I write this story of my life I feel that I have left something out of it! Something that I feel that you should have known about me, besides being young wild and crazy back in the day.

Now I ask myself, what did I leave out, and just what I have not written about or kept from you! So that you'll get to know me and "Who I am." The only thing that I have left out or not told you about is this other woman. You see when I first met the young one; let's just call her that for now. Even through her and I have become close to each other, I still can't speak of her true name. Man, this just might sound crazy as hell, but you see when I first met her, she as well as I, we both were in a storm. Yet my storm wasn't like hers, because she had just lost her father and her mother is one that I shall never speak of, My storm was that I wouldn't allow anyone to get close to me or love me for whom I was.

At first I thought that this lady was trying to get into my life for what she could get for herself and after my money! I did loan her some money, you know how that goes! I swear I'll pay you back bull-shit. Now after the third time, I felt like I was a fish out of the water. The thing that really got to me was that she wanted to spend some money to my bank, because she had some money coming from her father's "WILL" and wanted me to save it for her, because there was some problems in the family (with step-children) about who should be getting that money and other things. Her words were that her bank needed that information before they could transfer money into my account. I knew that this was not so.

Man, this shit kept coming up time after time, and I told her that her bank was full of shit, and if they wanted to send me that money they had to do it my way, I went out and open an account by putting $25.00 in there and sent her that account number. Now if I was going to be a fish out of water, all her ass was going to get was just $ 25.00 dollars... Now she kept coming on with that bull-shit, but I didn't come in out of the rain and asking myself was this the worm to catch this fish and clean his old ass out.

I kept telling her to send that money to my bank, and stop that entire crazy ass story about the information that her bank needed from me. I did receive word from her, that her bank had sent some money into my account and she wanted me to send her some money. I did check with my bank and there was some money in there and I sent her what she had asked for. To make a long story short, that this lady in deed does have some money in her bank account, just like she said that she had. Sometimes with things going on like they are, we feel that someone is trying to rip us off, and take what we have,; Special in my case an older man and she is much younger than I, that I was an easy target, and that young Wild Cherry was the key to it all.

In the end I was wrong about this lady; all she had wanted from me was to love her. Later I ask myself what kind of love that this lady wanted. The love of a father? Or was it to love her as a lover? Now this has been going on for quite a while between her and me. Just last week I received word from her asking me if she could put some more money into my account. I said to her sure, and how much will you be putting into the account? She said Armour; I will be putting a large sum of money into your account saying to myself, yeah when I see it, and I'll believe that shit. Man, I'm like this when someone puts that kind of money into your bank account there is more to that?

I want to check my bank account, but can't do until I return back home in September! Now the thing is am I a lover with some money or a daddy who just got himself a daughter with money? Only time will tell, Right now I don't care about her saying that she has money, all I want right now is to make love to her, but doing so it's hard for me to tell her that "I love her."

That's one of those words that I hear people speak of when they say that "Life is a bitch." Hate to do it, but it's 5:30 pm, and I must be off to the Race Track and do my thing and that will keep me from going out of my rabbit-ass mind thinking that if this lady did put that kind of money into my bank account why? What does she really want from me? Hell I don't have a pot to piss in or a window to throw it out of. Is this a set-up for the long run?

Now let me try and paint a picture of her? She is 5'7 about 32 or a mouth full up top; nice waist, and some meat on the rear end, not all that beef, but enough that you know that there's something to hold onto. Long Black Hair, and soft Brown Eyes, the kind that would suck you right into them and a smile that would make you wonder what else does she has that will make you want to Stamp Air Mail on her ass and send her home to mother. Legs that are soft and smother than a baby ass.

There's more to say, but I shall keep all of that under wraps for now. Man like they say "Never let anyone know what and how much fruit that you have on your tree, because sure as hell someone will try and get into your back yard and pick that fruit; Shit, if it's good, their ass will try and eat the whole thing. Hey, sometimes when I have nothing else to do but to sit up there in the bed room, I find myself reading my Diary. Yes, I have one of them. I don't feel that it's not wrong for a man to have one of those; after all it's so very nice to be able to sit down and recall or read about those things or events that were spoken too you that came from that special person, who lay next to you and you could feel that love as it flows from that person lips.

Like one time when I was laying there in bed, she read to me from her Diary, those words came to me: "Oh, my care for you is from the ground up to the sky. It's over, under and up above, down below and to the side." There's no use in pretending, no use in saving face. My love is never ending and you are my saving grace," or that other time when she spoke those words in my bed room, it was just like being in heaven.

These are only a few of the words that I have received from this lady. While laying there in the bed, it makes you feel so very good; those words are all you need to feel the love from that person. You roll over and find sleep, a deep sleep that's full of joy.

Things like that can make ones bedroom so full of joy, just knowing that the person who's lying next to you have spoken those words. Thinking about that time in January, knowing that it was going to be a cold night. I put on an extra log in the fire place as her and I lay there in the floor, with some soft muic on and sipping on a cold glass of wine; for no reason this lady rolled over and took my hand and laid it on her breast, saying to me "Armour" loving someone takes courage; fearing it could end at any moment and yet having faith it will last forever.

Man, I never thought that a front room could be more than a place to be sitting around and checking out the TV. I feel that it's a heavenly place, which is, if you make it that place of Joy and Love. Man, you see we are never too old to find ways to bring joy into our life and in our world. It's there for us only if we reach out for it and bring it into our life. I only wish that I could speed up time and rush August the 27th here. That day I shall be on my way back to California into her waiting arms. Knowing that Joy is there for me. Yet not wanting to rush out to see her. I am talking about my daughter Jennifer.

Knowing that Jennifer will have lots of things to say concerning my stay there in Detroit, and other words like: (Jennifer speaking) Well daddy I see that you are back in time for her birthday! How old will she be on this day? Fifty or fifty-three years old? Wow! Now let's see you are what 81, so that means that you are 31 or 28 years older than she! Well dad it's your thing and if that's what you want, then enjoy it, but remember that I am that other woman that's in your life, and I also love you too. Well let's not rush things, for I shall enjoy the time that I do have here with my family and also with her.

I speak of her, only knowing that in the end that there is nothing there for each of us, only friendship and respect. I say this for those things that I have seen, and the way that she acts and speak about things. There comes a time that one must close a door in your life. Man, it's the second time for me that I shall close a door in my life and open up a new one. This just might bring me that Joy that I have been missing out on and going without for over the last ten years, because I would not allow "Love to come into my life and into my world.

Only time will tell that story and give me that answer of what's it's like to have someone to Love you for who you are and not for what you have. Oh! Baby, once before I have been down that CRAZY road of love, only to have my ASS burned, because I had forgotten the rules of the JUNGLE, looking for love in all of the wrong places.

My question to myself is! Have I learned my lesson or am I setting myself up one more time to step into quick sand, because I am looking for love in all of the wrong places again? While I write this note to be tucked away in my book, hearing them wreck another home down the street from my brothers home. Thinking that in one time or another there might have been so much love and joy in that home and now it's all gone, never to return.

I look at life and love it's just like that old house, because life is so full of warmth and love. It's there for us to reach out to enjoy it; because there are so many beautiful things in life. Yet for some of us, we are like that old house, just standing there and not enjoying what's inside of it or the love that was once there. Is this me that old house? That's standing there or is this why I keep looking for love in all of the wrong places? Maybe I am still looking for Joy, Warmth, but most of ALL wanting someone in my life to LOVE me and bring Happiness and Joy into this Old House. Knowing that one day I too will be gone just as that Old House that once stood there on this street of life, where Joy, Happiness and Love was once found there.

I think that I shall walk down there and take a picture of that old house to remind me of LIFE and the Joy of LIFE before it's all gone and only a empty LOT that remains standing there just as life was once there for all of US to enjoy it, and in the very end it's ALL GONE.

I look at this as if it was I! but the only thing is that I might not understand and follow the rules of the jungle, because I am always looking for Love in all of the wrong places; but you can bet your sweet ASS on this, I shall keep on trying to find and bring some joy into this Old Ass House. I only wish that I could put these pictures in this story and you shall see just what I am talking about. Hey, just walk around town today and take a picture of an old house. Come back in a few weeks and take a look at that very same house after it has been torn down. Again come back to the very same house in about a week, all you might see is a lot that's clean; The Old House is not there anymore.

Now picture YOURSELF as that house! You were built, You stood tall, You became OLD, and you are torn down and you are gone from this earth in the very end, That's how I look at life and myself, so if I must keep on stepping in QUICK SAND to find and bring me some joy into this old house, I shall keep on doing it or until this old house is gone and all remains is the empty lot, that was once me.

We all have our own ways of looking at life, and how we view it, but if we aren't For Real about love and what we want out of life, well man, we are just Shit-Out-of –Luck and we will only be that EMPTY LOT not knowing that house, that once stood there which was so full of Love, Joy, Warmth and Happiness.

No! I have not gone out of my rabbit-ass-mind, maybe it's because of age comes wisdom. When you stand there at the cross roads only wishing that doing your life time, that you had allowed someone to love you and hold you tight and say these very words. "Baby I love you." Oh! How sweet those words do sound to the ears and do bring some joy to the soul. Hell I am at the point in life, I just want to be loved and be able to love someone in return. Shit, without loving someone it's like a tree without roots. Your are just standing there and it's only a matter of time before the tree falls, only making that sound that can be heard around the woods.

I'm sure that you have your views on Love and Life just as I do, but maybe in a different way, but in the very end it's all the very same. In that we all want love, but in order to receive love, we must be able to love someone in return. Maybe I should put you down for a while, and go out and take some pictures so that I can remember how it is, and maybe next year when I return it will look better and I will see that Detroit is on the rebound from what it was and what it is today. I feel that you have other things to do besides hearing me talking about Homes and Life. Yet, that is something that we all must face! The Old house and Empty Lot.

Maybe not in the way that I have explained it, but we all have our very own way in how we paint a picture of LIFE? Yet for some us, we don't want to paint that picture or look at life, we just want to roll on and not care about life or even tomorrow; if this is your picture "I say right on. It's your life." In a few days I shall be returning back to California, and I ask myself, Armour, what have you done here in Detroit, and what have you found out? I did find out that a good relationship requires two constants: (A). Constant Communication (B). Constant Sacrifice.

One without the OTHER, you are fighting a HELL of a war. I look at this older woman there is something missing in our relationship, and it's the part on SACRIFICE? I feel that she don't wish to be free from all of that bull-shit that she is dealing with, in allowing others to hold her back in what could be a start to a new and better life for her. (That's what I think)

I will not down her, because like so many of us, we are set in our ways and even though we see the hand writing on the wall, things prevent us from reading those words. We are in a trap, because I too have been at the cross road and understood that if you don't help yourself, then no one else will help you. It's like they say "You have to SHIT or get off of the POT". Man at times I felt like I was driving into nothing and that drive echoed my life at that time, and I knew that I had to get off of that pot and get my shit into one bag. Now, is this the real reason that I came back to Detroit for? To get all of my shit into one bag between me and this lady?

Only asking myself "Armour" will this lady be there for me? Not just there, but really there for me? I have found some answers, but I need her input on things. Let me explain what I mean by this? For years I have ask this lady that her and I should get a summer and a winter home. So when I return back to Detroit each year in the summer time I would stay with her. Man! All I ask of her was to come out to my place there in California in the winter time. When it's cold there in Detroit. Damn, it's only her, no kids in the house. She is retired. Yet she can't make up her mind to do so. Shit eight years is a long time for anyone to find out if they want a trip or not

Maybe some of you are asking this question? Armour, has all of this come about now that you have met this younger lady? By the way Armour you did say that you were 30 years older than she? (The young one) I know I'm old enough to be her father, that's not the point. It's that I feel that there is something for me and NOT that shit "it's all about you, and what you can do for me." Now age is not a factor. It's what I feel and have learned in all of these years. Wanting something? I have learn what you want just might not be Good for you. And don't be that "man that's standing there in quick sand waiting for the morning tide to come in and drown your sorry ass while you are sinking in shit.

Is this what I wish that I had an answer for! All of this crazy shit that one has to deal with in life. I'm sure that there are others out there just like me are sitting on the POT and have taken that shit, but for some reason we don't move from that pot. Knowing all alone that shit does stink. Is that me, wanting my Cake and Ice Cream, knowing that this Ice Cream just might melt, before I can get a lick of it?

Sitting here having a cup of coffee, with only four more days to go and I shall be on my way back home; Only to say that this was the very best time that I had when I came back home to Detroit. Maybe it' because some of the family was there for my going away dinner. Some of them weren't there because they were working. Still it was fun being with those that was there.

The BBQ Ribs, Chicken, Potato Salad, and all of the other things that makes an outing in the back yard great. Those stories that comes up about who did this and who did that, and how mom would get off into your ass when you were acting a fool. Man, all of that was good; She was there also, because she and the family still remain close, just like in the good old days and times that we had on East Euclid. Nicks store there on John R. Jeans Drug Store up there on Woodard Ave. and now that's all gone, just as the history of East Euclid, how it was back in the day,

I wish that I didn't have to write this letter, but it's one of those things that I must do, because my dreams wasn't what I thought that they were going to be. So I must close this door, the one that had been open for so many years; through the Good times and those Bad times. A love affair that was there, but not to be. How do I explain this? For you to understand just what I am trying to say! I must once again turn back the clock of time when I stabbed myself, without even knowing that I had done so. It was on April 25, 1955! I stabbed my girl friend (in a way of speaking) because on that day I join the U.S. Air Force and walked out of her life without telling her why I had joined the military.

I saw that pain in her eyes as she stood there in the Train Station along with my mother and pops. Who had taken off of work that day? Reds pain became my pain and for many of years this pain, has become a part of me and my life, and for years it has been with me... Yet, for over fifty years I have never told this lady why I gave her up for the military, Why do I speak of this today, because I'm about ready to close another door in my life. A door that has been open for so many years, that I have found out that I shall not be able to walk through that door.

For many years, I was living in a dream world of love, wanting something that was only a dream. You see I was in love with this woman, but the truth of the matter is that I didn't love her? Have you ever loved someone, only to find out that you really didn't love that person? Maybe that our world was only a dream. (I know that's cold, but it had to be said) This lady and I can only be friends, even if she and I would ever find ourselves in bed with each other, it would only be two people having sex, only because we were feeling a need for it.

Maybe some of you are wondering or asking yourself or saying Armour after all of these years, why are you walking away from her now? Does this have to do with that younger one? To be up front after waiting for ten long years, it's a very long time to find out that you and her are not on the same track. Hearing the way that this lady talks about things, one under stands that there is nothing in the cards for the two of you, but only friend ship between you two.

Sure, I know that we live miles apart from each other, and our feelings towards life and the things that we both want out of life aren't the same. My feeling is don't force yourself into something that one day you might wake up and kick yourself in the ass, because you had found out that this was only a False love. Now about this other lady, it's not what one might think. It's only that our relationship is more like a Road-Dog thing? Giving to each other and not asking for nothing in return, but only respect, and not to judge each other because of what we both want out of life.

Well it's that time that I must be on the road, and once more so to all of you thank you for everything and that going away dinner was out of sight. You know you guys should do more of this, don't wait until I come back to the city, and have this type of outing. Hell, you all are here in Detroit, why not come together don't wait until it's too late, because all of the fun and stories will not be the same. Donna, again thanks for everything I am very sorry that I had to cut our Friday nights short, but like they say, things happen for a reason.

"Hell, we have next year to pick up on our Friday nights at the Race Track.

Well I am home now, and it's so nice to be in my very own bed, where all of the lumps are all in the right places for a good night sleep. Its morning now and I have some place to be and someone that I must talk with and say hello, because if I don't show up and talk with this lady. Man, I would be up shits creek.

Well, well, look who is back in town (my daughter Jennifer speaking) with that shit eaten look on your face. Damn, daddy that looks only tells me one thing and that the old girl is still alive and that old wild cherry did a job on your ass. Daddy I do hope that you did remember those words that I told you before you left for Detroit? Now you do remember them don't you? I said no matter how hard that you try you can't wear that "TANG OUT". I see that you did bring a chair and some water with you, and that only means that you will be here for a whole; so lay it on me! How was your trip? Did you leave a smile on the old girl face?

Ain't going to talk about that, because you might start asking me some crazy ass questions like, did she make me cry or has she got hair on her legs? Baby that's the reason that I aint going to talk about it. Well if you don't want to talk about it, then what did the young one say when you told her that you were back in town? Did she say "baby come on over here and get yourself some of this Cherry Pie? Damn, you are full of questions, did someone leave the water on again and your ass got all wet.

First of all I did not call her and let her know that I was back in town. I came here to see you and talk with you first. Oh shit! That old ASS Cherry really got to you, and the old girl let your ass know that there was still fire in the hole. Thank God for that (funny) Man, at times it's best to keep things to yourself, because somewhere you just might end up saying" I Wish That ?????

Baby, there is one question that I must ask myself? If I am that old man who has found that Pearl, but just don't know how to tell this woman the truth? That I can make love to her, but I don't love her from the heart. Jennifer, I can't let this pain pull me back down into the pits of hell and eat me a live, like it has done before, because the truth hurts. Knowing that you want to tell her the truth, but something just want let those words come from my lips.

Now a hand is being dealt to me, and I don't know which way to turn or what road should I take; because once before I took the wrong road and went out into those fields and I almost became the joker of the deck. Baby is I that guy who finds him wishing that he could rub the hell out of the bottle and wishing that the genie will come out and will she tell me about love and what I must do?

I yearned to be with her, but realized that I need to do a serious self-examination and determine if I was emotionally prepared to really open this door and tell this lady that I could love her, but I need for her to teach me how to love her. Baby, you are my Angle. What do you think that I must do?

Well first daddy, you have to ask yourself how much do you really care for this new lady that's in your life! Second of all daddy, you really need to get off of your ass and go sit down and talk too this lady. Dad, you are asking the wrong person about your love for her and your love life.

WHAT YOU WILL LEARN

Sometimes when I'm sitting around the house I find myself thinking about the old days. I remember hearing some people say as you get older you forget things? Well I would say yes to that, and then on the other hand there are things that one never forgets even if you are over the hill. I shall always remember about my childhood days. The "Street Lights"! Yes those street lights? Those lights were my clock, knowing that I had to be in the house when they came on; if not you were late getting into the house.

You knew what a waits for your ass when you got home. As you read this book, you will learn that I use to run the Rice fields of Korea, the back streets of Japan, ran the roof tops of Hong Kong. Oh yes! Hung out with the camp-fire-girls in the parks at nights. I ran with the Flower children back in the day in San Francisco, California. Drank, popped a Pill and had a Fat Boy or two in my day. Then on the other hand some of the ladies that I use to run with, those who wanted what I had and not for whom I was. There were some good ones; all in all, they too help me to become who I am.

Hell even when I was out there acting wild and crazy and looking for love in all of the wrong places, only because I had once again forgot about the rules of the jungle. I speak of this for I am not alone there are others out there just like me or the way that I was, and they too just might be sitting at the water's edge asking that very same question that I have been asking myself for a very long time and that question is?

"WHO I AM"

Am I still that same old person or am I a new person? Yes and No? I am still looking for love, but this time I have my eyes wide open. Yet, remembering just two things? One: Walk softly and carry a big stick. Two: If that's not your cup of tea don't put any sugar in it. Yet my life has been very good. I was married to a very wonderful woman, for forty-seven- years. The Severn Son. A Vietnam Vet. With over twenty years in the military. Even I was given a second chance in life to get my act together.

You see while serving in Vietnam in 1966, I came into contact with "Agent Orange" from 1966 until 2006 Agent Orange was slowly eating away in side of my body for Forty years. Then in 2006 I found out at that time of my life, that I had Stage Three Lung Cancer.

I am good now, but with a few health problems, even through that there were many trials in my life, "GOD" gave me a Blessing. So I am here today trying to explain or find out "WHO I AM"

IN CLOSING

To you that have brought my other two books. The first one "How Strong is Your Love." You were there when I defined the rules of Society by being in LOVE with two women. One my wife and the other one a married woman. You heard my voice throughout those pages of that book and you felt my Rain of Pain, which ate at my soul for twenty-four years; and even when I spoke about the BEUTAL truth about loving another man's wife.

You walked with me and held my hand when my "WELL" ran dry; Forty-Seven years of marriage gone. It's still inside of me. That LOVE for her. If not for you, I would have stayed in my bedroom and drown in my own tears.

In my second book "Coming Home" you were also there with me, as I wondered through the Wilderness of Love, trying to find my way home to the ONE that got away. You were also there when I lost my way and also step in quick sand. Yes! You stood with me when my Sunshine was wiped out of my life, on my daughter's wedding day. As she lay there dying in my arms and her warm blood tricked off of my fingers and the SUN danced on her blood as it made its way to the gutters of the streets of San Francisco on that warm day.

You also held my hand on that very same day that I sat there in the court room facing that man who took my daughter's life and took her away from me, alone with my unborn grandchild. What more can I say to you, but only to thank you for being there with me, but most of all for hearing my voice and my cry as you wondered through those pages of "How Strong is My Love, Coming Home and now these pages of Who I am"

I'm sure that you alone with my family and some of my friends are wondering why I named this book "Who I am." Well to tell the truth about it! I didn't really know who I was? Thinking back when I wrote my very first book, I left something out some things in that book, things that I felt need not have been in there.

Some people had ask me Armour, why didn't you write about a Black child born in Detroit during the dark days and what you went through as that Black child? Hell, back in those days, Black kids and White kids went through the very same things. Your ass was poor. I could have written about a young child growing up there in Detroit, which I grew up without a father and the whole nine yards, but somewhere down the line I would have end up telling you a lie, and more lies on top of that.

You see I lost my father when I was about seven or eight years old. My mom was a single mother with ten others to look out after. You see what I fail to tell you in that I had a very wonderful man come into my life. "POPS" my stepfather. Who was a very tall strong Black man, who took me under his wings, if I was his very own flesh and blood! Pops, never laid a hand to me or a belt on me. That was moms' job; she was the CIA, FBI, ATF, Matt, Wyatt and Pat Garrett all into one. She was the Head of the house hold, and I was raised by the VILLAGE.

I'm sure that some of you have heard those words "That it takes a Village to raise a child." It's true, because in those days we had that village around us 24/7, grandmother, Aunt Bee, the old lady across the street, and Aunt Fay (who really wasn't your aunt, but all the kids called her that) who lived three blocks away from you. Those old people were also members of YOUR village, because they also looked out for and after you. For those of you that don't quite understand just what I'm talking about, and then talk with some of the old people that came from the South and those that just might be still around today.

Man, they will tell you about that VILLAGE and just what it meant to ALL of us, and the very, very deep LOVE that came with it.

Year (2016) that Village is GONE. We talk about it, yet we sit on our ass and do nothing about it. I could go on and on saying things that I'm sure will piss someone off: Like where the father's are? That's the very first thing that we speak of, poor old sorry ass dad! Man, what about the mothers? They too play a deep role in this picture. Yet some of that mother's that we never speak of, some of them just keep on having a baby after another.

Maybe I'm from the old school, but I still believe in the Village. I hear that old bull-shit on the TV or from other people if his/her had been there then he/she wouldn't have turned out like that! Now my question is? Where is grandmother, grandfather, Aunt Bee and all of the others? Shit when I was coming up, man I didn't have the "Bull by the tail" that was because my back yard was so FULL of people from the village. Hell I didn't need anyone else. I can only speak for myself and of my Village.

For some reason that if I did PISS someone off by saying what I did, so be it, but the real truth of the matter is that the Truth will set your ass free. I'm not Dr. Phil, I am just me, an eighty-one year old man who's trying to understand "Who I am"! I have tried to turn back the hands of time in order to answer that question. Yes my brothers and sisters there are millions out there who are just like me, looking in the Trash cans, behind closed doors, doing the very same thing as I. looking for that answer that you have heard that "CRY" when people ask? "Who's your Daddy? Some of us laugh about this, but its real people. "Who's your daddy and who are you?

I'm not trying to be funny or blow smoke up anyone's ass about what I have just said. This isn't any bull-shit. If you think that this is bull-shit? Then open up your computer and type in those words that you see on TV, when one is looking for that answer, where did I come from and who was my grandfather, and who was my great grandfather. Some of you know just where I am coming from, because you too have been out there trying to find out "Who you were? Just like the millions out there who are just like me and looking for that answer. Where did I come from, but most of all "Who am I"

I look back on my life and had to believe not to be afraid to do things, but some of my friends told me that I'm crazy because I wrote about my life and just what I felt. If we could just close our eyes and look back to those things that we wanted to do, but FEAR played a role in our life. I'm trying to understand myself, but I just don't know who I am. I need nothing else in my life then to answer that one question that has me wondering through the Past and Present part of my life

Damn, if I could just close my eyes and see just what I want to see, then only then will I know "Who I am." I remember grandmother telling me that

"WE" are all of two people? Is this the side that I'm looking for? Then you tell me, what side am I looking for? There's a part of me that's dying every day, but yet there is a New side being born Every Day, because I have learn how to LAUGH and have FUN in life.

History has been established and those stolen moments will never come to me AGAIN, because those dreams have created PASSION in my life. Through all of the BAD times and the GOOD times, plus wondering through the WILLDERNESS of life. I did stop and Smell the Rose Bush, and I finely come to the cross road of LIFE.

Well my friends we are at the end of the road. I wish to thank those of you that rode this train with me. Yet before I turn this page, I feel that some of you are still asking me 'Armour" why did you pick this name for your book. "Who I am or Armour should it have been "Who Am I? Like I have said before it's all up to US how we want or wish to say it.

Maybe my reason for saying "Who I am", is that I had to turn back the clock of time once more. You see at first I was called Colored, then Negro, and Black and now I am an Afro/American. I put all of this into a Brown Bag and I began to shake and shake that bag and then I poured everything out of it and what came out of the bag was a surprise to me? It all came out to be "Who I am. Horace D. Armour, Sr with an Irish last name.

There is just one more thing that I would like to say before I put this pen down, and never to lift it up again. When I was young and running around and acting a fool and didn't take the time out and read the writing on the WALL, but I did stop and receive the word from my grandmother and also from my mother. I would like to pass those words on to you:

(a) Grandmother told me "Boy if that's not your Cup of Tea don't put any sugar in it; and Son NEVER sell your soul just to have someone in your bed.

(b) Mama, say "Boy whenever you leave out of this House, always put on CLEAN UNDERWEAR.

I'm 81 years old and I might have forgotten lots of things in my life, but you can bet your Sweet Ass these are the TWO RULES that I live by.

Just some food for thought.

PERSONS OF INTERST

There have been so many people in my life and on this road in trying to find out "Who I am," and some of the people were just Wonderful and then there were those people who was just there for the ride and played "HELL" in my life and YOU were a pain in the ASS;

1. Mary: Thank God that I woke up.
2. Barbara: My high school love.
3. Ann: Wanted something that I could not give to her.
4. Tess: Need to go and kick some rocks;
5. Nancy: Will catch the first thing on wheels out of town.
6. Carol: The mother of them all.
7. Sandra: Need to hit the rain locker (shower)
8. The Devil in the Blue Dress: She had hair on her legs
9. Mary-Ann: Trying to keep her dress up and panties down.
10. Slick: Looking for that window, to throw his piss out of.
11. Little Rich girl: Sleeping in doorways.
12. Paul: Didn't want to follow the rules.
13. Church Boy: Got four years to think about it.
14. Iva: Her husband the Meat Packer.
15. Red: The one that got away.
16. Harris: Made me look into the looking Glass.
17. Johnny: Turn me onto Jazz.

18. Pops: Thanks for NOT only being my Step-father, but for just being my friend.
19. Mom: You kept me safe from the Riots there in Detroit.
20. Grandmother: Your words kept me from astray and drowning in Quick Sand.
21. Lady: My Dog, you gave me Support when my Well ran dry. Waiting at the door for me.
22. Lucia: My wife you gave me love, even when I was acting a fool.
23. Horace: (me) was looking for that answer
24. Jennifer: My Sunshine
25. The Young One.

Yet there were so many others that I can't even remember who they were or even their names. To ALL of you, I say THANK YOU for being there for and with me.

THIS IS MY STORY, WHAT'S YOURS

We all have a story to tell, for some of us. we don't know how to put it in words, then again there are those who wish that their story was not told; for FEAR that people or Society will judge them, so they keep that story hidden from the world behind that steel door. Never thinking that their story is someone else's story, or that their story might set someone FREE from pain.

I'm not sure just where my story might fit into some one's life, but I'm sure that my story just might be someone else story! For they like me have met at the cross road of life and just stood there not knowing which way to turn. In their march they too have walk down the dark roads of Society and Wondered the Wilderness of Love looking for that Special person, just as I have done, and even forgot the RULES of the jungle in search of that one very Special person just for them self's

This is my story, of a man who has Wondered the roads of life In search of only one thing, and that was for "Who I am' Knowing who he was and not knowing Who I am, is what drove me in seeking that answer. I am not alone for there are millions of US making Family Trees" in order to find out where we came from and who our daddy is. Without knowing this you are just like me. In a way of speaking looking for "Who you are". I too have a family tree, but the main thing that I have written about in this book is to understands and to find out just "Who I am"

Society speaks of me as just being Horace D, Armour, Sr, with that NINE numbers attach to me for I.D. I feel that I'm more than that nine numbers which is attached to me, that society I.D. me by. So maybe this is one of the reasons that I sat down and wrote this book, because I feel I am more than that nine numbers attached to my body and soul, which everyone is always asking for, just to see who I am.

I look back to my very first book that I wrote "How Strong is Your Love" I stated that the story of my life might be interesting to some and not to others, which is so very true. Yet, I have always thought that the purpose of a relationship was to have someone with whom to share or lives with. We all at one time or another have gone down that road in life.

I'm sure for those of you that have or are reading this book; you just might be saying "Who am I? or did this guy tell my story, because I didn't have the words to express myself, then again you might be saying that he wrote this book for me, because I am him, and he is me telling my story of "Who I am", just as I have lived it and would have put it down in this book just as I might have done it if I had written this story.

Some of you have wondered the Wilderness of Love just as I and even step into quick sand, because you were looking for love in all of the wrong places, then just like me you forgot the rules of the jungle. Hey, through it all I have had people to come into my life and never said to them Thank You or Appreciate them for what they have done for me.

Donna, when things were bad, and I was living in the darkness, you open the door and let the light shine in. You gave me Hope when I thought that Hope was lost forever. Maybe some of you are also feeling this right now and you also feel that you have walked in my own shoes and you understand 'Who I am", I really do mean "Who I am" because like they say You are me and I am You. Could this be why I said that "This is my story, and what's yours?

Is this you! Or were you that person that was standing on the road side crying out to those that pass you by, only wanting them to say "That I understand you" for I too have been in your shoes and I have felt your Rain of Pain.

THANK YOU

To ALL of you that have brought my two books, the First one: "How Strong is Your Love. You were there when I defined the rules of Society by being in Love with two women. One my wife and the other one who was a married woman. You heard my voice throughout those pages of that book and you felt my Rain of Pain, which ate at my soul for twenty-four hours a day, for over fifty years. In that book I even spoke about the Real truth about loving another man's wife. The very one that I had walked out of her life and join the military and never telling her why I did so.

You were also there when I lost my way, all most stepping in quick sand and being eaten by the lioness that waited for me out there; because I was looking for love in all of the wrong places. Yes! My readers you held my hand through out those Dark Days when I lost my sister, my mother, my brother, my son: but most of all you were there when my "WELL" ran dry, after forty-seven years of being married to my wonderful wife Lucia Manelse Armour.

You Hug me when my Sunshine was wiped out on my daughter's wedding day, as she lay there dying in my arms, and her warm blood tricked off my fingers and the sun glister on her blood as it made its way to the street gutters of San Francisco, California on that very hot day, after being shot by-a-drive by.

There was a gaping wound and her blood ran from there. You hear her very last words as she gurgled out those words, "Daddy" hold me, and I love you. There was neither time for a doctor or any time for anything; before I could say a word, her eyes rolled back in her head and she exhaled a strained breath.

My baby was gone, she was dead. Her White Wedding dress and the ground around her glistened with blood. Her very own blood I cried out "My baby is gone, my baby is gone. Emergency services arrived; two Paramedics' came rushing in to take over. I froze! The image of her lying there, I kept my eyes averted so no one could see my tears.

It was too late for her. Who had wanted to do a thing like this? Take away my Sunshine from me and leave a hole in my heart, with that one question "Why, Why her.

In my Second book: "Coming Home." You were there with me as I wondered through the Wilderness of love, trying to find my way home. To the One that got away, the one that I could not forget. And the very one that I had walk out of her life and end up in the arms of another woman, who became my wife and the mother of my children. This other woman was the one that I had been in love with for many years. The one love that has lived inside of my heart, even when I was a married man. Her, is who I am coming home to now that special woman,

What can I say or how do I thank you for being there with me and for me, like that time when I spoke of what cause me to have that Rain and Pain, when I lost that very wonderful friend in my life. My step-father "Pops." Man you see Pops was more than a step-father. He was always there for me, I could count on him to teach me what was right and when I was wrong. I felt you sitting at my side when I went out to spend time with Jennifer my daughter. Who was gunned down on her wedding day! You have heard our talks and understood that she was the only person that I could turn too and open up my heart and spill my guts to her.

Knowing that Jennifer would not judge me for the things that I had done, the mistakes, because after all I am only human. What more can I say, but only to thank you for being there with me, but most of all for hearing my voice and cry as you wondered through those pages of "How Strong is Your Love and Coming Home and now these pages of Who I am." You held my hand on that day the very same day that I sat there in the court room, facing that man who took my daughter away from me alone with her unborn child on her wedding day.

When the judges faced him and ask him if he had anything to say? I sat there on the edge of my seat, wanting him to speak those words why? He just stood there, without a care in the world and spoke these words. "Hell" if I could not have her, then know one ELSE could have her, so I just "Popped her." I could not believe his words. "I just popped her."

Shit, I wanted to jump up and say "All hell no" but you held me tight by the arm, holding me back; but just thinking about his answer, Damn, there are others like him out there speaking those very same crazy as words as you read this letter.

I need to back up some, because I used the word "STEP-FATHER." I need to "DELETE" that word step-father and just say 'POPS". You see I never knew who my real father was. He passed away when I was very young. I can only recall that mom had said that he was a truck driver; I do have a picture of him on the wall in the front room along with my grandfather

Now, Pops was the man in my life. The only man that I knew.

I was in the Navy when Pops was called home on July 15, 1961; he was only fifty-nine years old. A tall man, who spoke with a soft voice. I came home to see him off and pay my respect to him, a man who touches my heart. I cried upon seeing him lying there never to speak my name again.

You know my story about me crying? I cried on that day of July 15, 1961 and I never cried again until Thanksgiving weekend 2006. Forty-five years later before I allowed myself to cry or feel any pain, and that's' when I stopped my 'Rain of Pain."

You my readers are helping me to find that ONE answer that I have been searching for over the last eighty-one years, which was "Who I am or should it have been who am I". Did I say this right? But it's really does not matter which way I spoke of this, because with your help I might have found that answer which I have been looking for from 1935 up until now. Over eighty years of wondering.

"WHO I AM'

Right now, I live alone, but I wish to stop that, but it has to be with the right person. Someone who understands me and my have my back and be with me know matter what I do. Not lip service but be for real in her ways, and not leaving everything up to me. I mean when it comes to doing things or making decisions, because I feel that she is a part of me and if something should happen to me, she would be shit out of luck, if she don't know what's going on and how to do things that must be done.

I'm on this journey to be with her night after night, just the two of us. Holding hands or doing whatever. I look at life in a new way now. I think back at the time when I was in the Navy, we had this old saying "Here today and gone tomorrow." If one really looks at life, one never knows that statement just might be true, for life is short, so one must enjoy life to the very best of things.

Like I say, I'm on this journey to find what life is ALL about. What I mean is, you have heard that old saying "Been there and done that"? That's me and now I'm tired, but not too tired to enjoy life.

"You see that's what "coming Home" is ALL about."

Well my friends it's about that time that I must let you go and do your own thing. It has been Wonderful having you helping me to discover "Who I am" Yet maybe some of you may have also found those answers about yourself. Who you were. Now you can add that very last word to you family tree. "Who I am."

My reads you have heard my Cry and you have walked in my shoes throughout the Wilderness of my life. You have seen that Old House as it once stood there, and now that LOT is clean. Is this your lot, where that old house once stood with Joy and Love and Happiness which was once found in those walls?

Those walls that YOU didn't want to share with those around you? What about those that you did Love? You didn't do it, because of FEAR of what others might say about YOU.

Now you are standing there at the Cross Road of life, not knowing which way to turn too. Just one question?

"Was this your story that I wrote about?

THE AUTHOR

HORACE ARMOUR, SR

ABOUT THE AUTHOR

This is Armours third Novel, in his first Novel "How Strong is Your Love, he writes about the BRUTAL TRUTH and challenging the unwritten rules on LOVE and SOCIETY views and the inner struggle of LOVING two women.

Now in "Coming Home", again he writes of Wondering in the Wilderness of Love trying to come home to the ONE that got away. The one that he could not forget. Yet she is the very same woman that he has been in love with for many years.

Now in "Who I am" Armour opens up the door on his life allowing outsiders to come in and HELP him look under the Magnifier and find that one answer that he has been looking for over the last eighty years, and that answer which he was seeking is "Who I am."

Armour, a Cancer survivor and a Vietnam Veteran with over Twenty years in the Military service. Originally from Detroit, Michigan, He now lives in Fairfield, California alone with his son and Topper his Amazon Parrot. Upon his retirement from the military service in 1976, twenty-one years after graduation from Northern High School there in Detroit. Armour returns back to school at San Francisco State Univ. studying in the field of Psychology.

WHO I AM

The only thing that I can say right now, is that I'm not WHO I used to be, because you see THANKS to you, those of you that had come into my life and help me to become a better person, and understand that Life is GOOD and that LOVE is such a Wonderful thing.

Because of YOU I have found that ONE answer that I have been looking for over the last Eighty-One years, and that is:

"WHO I AM"

In Armour's lifetime, he has been in difference to the rules of Society. He avoided he pit falls of quick sand because he forgot the rules of the Jungle. Yet he has wondered the Wilderness of Love.

This book tells a story about life. Not just the story of my life in general. Like so many others that have gone down the very same road as I; just like millions more who will follow the path of life, in their very own special way.

Armour, being human, knowing that he has made mistakes, yet he still keep trying to correct his mistakes, all alone, he knows that Life is good and Sweet! Through it all, Armour was seeking just one answer?

I am sure that we all have set down and thought about the very same thing who I Am? Now I sit here, wondering the very same thing all over again. Yet! I look back to the Four Stags of my life, where it all started from, up until now, that very first question was, did I say this right! "Who I am" or should it had been, "Who Am I?

Which way is correct? It is all up to us, how we wish to talk about one's self! So I say "Who I am."

Printed in the United States
By Bookmasters